Structural–Strategic Marriage and Family Therapy

Structural-Strategic Marriage and Family Therapy

A TRAINING HANDBOOK

John Friesen, Ph.D.
THE UNIVERSITY OF BRITISH COLUMBIA

GARDNER PRESS, INC.
New York   London

Gardner Press, Inc.
19 Union Square West
New York 10003

All foreign orders except Canada and South America to:
    Afterhurst Limited
    Chancery House
    319 City Road
    London N1, United Kingdom

Library of Congress Cataloging in Publication Data

Friesen, John.
  Structural-strategic marriage and family therapy.

  Bibliography: p.
  1. Structural-strategic family psychotherapy.
2. Structural-strategic marital psychotherapy. I. Title.
RC488.5.F75 1985   616.89′156   85-16100
ISBN 0-89876-106-9 (pbk.)

PRINTED IN THE UNITED STATES OF AMERICA
BOOK DESIGN BY RAYMOND SOLOMON

CONTENTS

PREFACE

The past ten years have brought about a rediscovery of the importance of the family. In part this may be attributable to society's growing interest in the healthy development of children and a recognition of the significance of the family in their socialization. This growing awareness of the importance of the family has brought about an ever-increasing demand for the services of people trained in handling the wide-ranging problems associated with family life. Consequently a large amount of training material has recently become available to prepare people to work with families.

This handbook presents a promising model for working with families. An effort has been made to produce a clear and succinct overview of Structural and Strategic understandings, concepts, and techniques of marriage and family therapy. In addition Structural and Strategic therapies have been combined to form an integrated system of clinical practice.

An assumption of this model is that the Structural and Strategic approaches may be combined in clinical practice without seriously violating the theoretical underpinnings of either approach. Where theoretical incompatibilities exist between the two approaches, it is assumed that the clinician will have the capacity to hold the two opposing ideas in the mind at the same time. Sometimes theoretical purity and logical consistency must be postponed or sacrificed for effective practice.

It is further assumed that Structural and Strategic therapies are in many ways complementary. Structural therapy has developed a theory of family, whereas Strategic therapy has a relatively well-developed theory of therapeutic change. Both a theory of family and a theory of change are essential in a comprehensive theory of family therapy. By combining Structural and Strategic understandings, concepts, and techniques, progress toward the development of such a theory is made.

Many people have contributed to the development of this handbook. Most notably I am grateful to the many researchers, writers, and theorists whose works I have referenced in the text. In any field of human inquiry, growth in understanding comes from the accumulated wisdom of many people. In this handbook I have selected, organized, and presented some of that understanding that appeared relevant and appropriate in an introductory work.

I wish also to acknowledge the contributions of my students who have been instrumental in stimulating, challenging, and refining many of my perspectives in family therapy.

I would like to pay special tribute to my research assistants, Wes Buch, Paul Kaufman, and Ron Toews, who provided invaluable aid in researching, summarizing, and writing some of the material.

Carol Matusicky critiqued and provided useful feedback on an early version of the handbook. Her comments were most helpful. The encouragement of Connie Hawley, the former executive secretary of the British Columbia Council for the Family, was also much appreciated.

John Friesen
Vancouver

INTRODUCTION TO THE TRAINING MANUAL

Trainers and educators typically have large files containing numerous loose papers and training materials they have picked up at conventions, workshops, and universities. This manual is more than a collection of papers. It is a systematically designed handbook to assist trainers of marital and family therapists. Theory from a Structural–Strategic theoretical perspective, training exercises, information about family dynamics, and practical applications in the form of therapy techniques and interventions have been brought together in an organized yet flexible manner. Every effort was made to select materials for this manual that had practical application to marital and family therapy training and practice.

Although the materials in this manual are directed primarily toward the practitioner, the papers and discussions could provide useful background reading for the scholar as well. It is expected that trainers interested in research would become involved in in-depth study of related journals and research documents that go beyond this manual.

Most of the material presented is based on contemporary research, theory, and practice. Some of the content is original, and some was obtained from primary and secondary sources, such as journals, research reports, and books. Serious effort has been made fully to acknowledge such sources of ideas and concepts.

This manual reflects some of the contemporary thought and practice in marital and family therapy. As such the content is uneven—some is theoretical, some is practical, and some is referenced. The major purpose is to provide material for the training of marital and family therapists. Trainers and trainees alike, it is hoped, will find this manual stimulating and useful.

CHAPTER 1

TRAINING THEORY

1.1 THEORY IN MARRIAGE AND FAMILY THERAPY

> It is clearly desirable . . . for the scientist to know consciously and be able to state his own presuppositions. It is also convenient and necessary for scientific judgment to know the presuppositions of colleagues working in the same field.
>
> *Gregory Bateson (1979, p. 25)*

There is a rich diversity of schools, approaches, and techniques currently available in the field of family therapy, all of which are proposed with equal seriousness and claims of success. The reason for this variety is that family therapists have different theories about the nature of families, their dysfunction, and how best to intervene when they are in distress.

Everyone holds to certain theories; we cannot not have *a* theory. Our theories may not be very explicit, comprehensive, or systematic, but they nevertheless represent a conceptual guide that can direct our thinking and action (Liddle, 1982). Furthermore there is reason to suggest that we hold to certain theories from the time of early infancy, although our theories at this age are very rudimentary. Robert Beavers (1977, p. 8) explains:

We no longer assume that any human past the age of six months can observe the world without a priori assumptions, either conscious or unconscious. In fact, there is increasing evidence that even the newborn has biological structures which profoundly in-

fluence his perceptions. Such assumptions, for example, as causality and concepts of time and space appear to be intrinsic.

Function of Theory

A theory is, in essence, a mental model or map that represents the way we perceive reality, and by which we are guided. Although our theories are like maps, we must be careful not to confuse our maps with the terrain; our theories are not carbon copies of reality.

Theories are constructed and shaped by many interacting factors, such as our cognitive and perceptual capacities, goals, values, expectations, beliefs, pre-theories, culture, and language. Our theories function as both perceptual filters and guides. As perceptual filters, our theories edit, organize, interpret, and transform incoming sensory data, so that we come to construe reality in different ways than do those who hold other theories. In therapy, then, individuals may perceive human problems and functioning differently because the theories they hold may be different.

Our theories not only screen the incoming data of reality, but they also limit what we can observe of reality; or, in the words of Einstein, ''It is the theory that determines what we can observe.'' Our theories, according to Howard Liddle (1982, p. 244), ''tell us what to regard as important or not important, what is to be pursued or avoided, what is logical or illogical—even what is possible or impossible.'' Our theories, then, function as perceptual guides, direct our attention to specific parts of reality, and thus determine what we shall perceive of reality. Liddle (1982, p. 244) concludes that different theories ''allow their proponents to see virtually different worlds, attend to entirely different behavioral phenomena, and consequently speak different conceptual languages.''

Again we are reminded that our theories must not be naively equated with reality. They are but partial constructs of reality. In this sense we can paraphrase an old proverb and say that ''reality is in the eye of the beholder.'' We see a part, not the whole, of reality. In fact our theories, by their very organizing, structuring, and limiting nature, may screen out the view of reality available through the lenses of other theoretical viewpoints. Our commitment to any one theory is made at the expense of being able to perceive other data.

In the illustrations (Figures 1.1.1 and 1.1.2), we perceive either a young woman or an old one in the first and a goblet or two faces in the second. Notice that it is a perceptual impossibility to see both alternatives at once in each figure. Similarly, when we commit ourselves to a certain family theory, an alternate one becomes unavailable, yet is still present. Our par-

ticular view is assumed at the temporary expense of the other.

Family Theory

Thomas Kuhn (1970) suggests that in the field of family therapy, or in any other discipline, there are various paradigms, or theoretical frameworks. The one adopted in this manual is the family systems (Structural–Strategic) paradigm. Kuhn (1970, p. 150) suggests that the diverse groups in family work who represent these various paradigms

. . . see different things when they look from the same point in the same direction . . . Both are looking at the world (family), and what they look at has not changed. But in some areas they see different things, and they see them in different relations one to the other. That is why a law or principle that cannot even be demonstrated to one group of scientists may occasionally seem intuitively obvious to another.

Clearly, then, our family theories have limitations, and this should lead us to hold on to them humbly. Yet the role of theory in marriage and family therapy is neither to be minimized nor exaggerated. When theory is minimized,

Figure 1.1.1. A young woman—or an old one

Figure 1.1.2. A vase—or two profiles

therapists cannot adequately evaluate their work, whereas when theory is exaggerated, therapists tend to consider their personal theories as being true or objective realities. Neither possibility is adequate. Instead a family theory may be seen as a device to simplify for our convenience and intellectual comprehension the complex nature of reality as a whole; it is merely a tool to facilitate understanding and action.

We can now see that theory plays an important role in determining what a family therapist perceives about the nature of families and their dysfunction, in terms of both how they interpret and what they see in working with families, and in terms of screening and highlighting aspects of what is actually happening in the family. Further it is the therapist's paradigm that suggests the best methods and strategies of intervention. Theory influences practice. Since our theory of the family influences virtually everything we do in family work, we would be wise to make explicit, and carefully monitor our theoretical assumptions.

Requirements of a Good Theory

A basic requirement is that the theory be clear, that is, easily understood and communicated. Furthermore the hypotheses and assumptions must be internally consistent and logical, not contradictory. The concepts, assumptions, and hypotheses must be logically linked and thoughtfully connected.

Second, a good theory must have wide application rather than application only to isolated cases. The usefulness of any theory depends on its comprehensiveness. It must have the capacity to explain many events in a variety of situations.

Third, a good theory must be heuristic in nature. It must lead to generating testable hypotheses and be amenable to scientific inquiry.

Fourth, a good theory relates means to desired outcomes. The techniques follow logically from the goals, which in turn are clearly related to concepts and assumptions.

Finally, a good theory is more than an elegant statement; it is something that may be used and has value. It is a tool by which predictions can be made. To the practitioner it serves as a guide to behavior and predicts consequences if certain actions are undertaken.

Theory Checkup

What we need is a "theory checkup" (Liddle, 1982) to assess periodically where we stand on issues basic to all family therapists. This theory checkup would enable us to chart the evolution of our personal family paradigm as we grow and change in response to new observations and experiences in family work. Such a checkup might include responses to the following questions:

1. *Definition*. What is your view of the very definition and nature of human beings in general, and family therapy in particular? Some theories, for example, see people and families as resistant to change and dedicated to preserving the status quo, while others see them as naturally changing and adapting.

2. *Goals*. What should your goals or objectives of family therapy be? Who should determine them? How precisely should they be defined, or should they be overtly defined at all? Some family theories put a premium on the growth of family members during therapy, and are not interested in specific behavioral goals; others, however, focus on discovering a symptom or problem to be solved, and then contracting to change it.

3. *Therapist behavior*. What is your role and function as a family therapist? What are your expected behaviors? A related issue is your view of the nature of change and the mechanisms that are responsible for change. Some family theories require the therapist to be an active, personally involved agent for change; others require him or her to be less conspicuous. Again, some theories emphasize the therapist–family relationship as the primary mechanism of change, whereas others give at-

tention to changing the nature of the power structure, roles, and communication.

4. *Optimal/dysfunctional behavior*. What is a dysfunctional family? What is your idea of an optimally functioning family? These are important questions, since you will want to know what to help families move toward, as well as away from. What is the basic unit of the problem—one, two, three, or more people? What is the role of the family history in determining why problems exist now?

5. *Evaluation*. How important is it to evaluate your work? How should this be done? What methods of assessment would be best? How important to you is the role of continuing education in the maintenance or upgrading of conceptual and therapeutic effectiveness?

REFERENCES

Bateson, G. *Mind and nature*. New York: Dutton, 1979.

Beavers, W. R. *Psychotherapy and growth*. New York: Brunner/Mazel, 1977.

Kuhn, T. S. *The structure of scientific revolutions* (2nd ed.). Chicago: University of Chicago Press, 1970.

Liddle, H. A. On the problems of eclecticism: A call for epistemologic clarification and human-scale theories. *Family Process*, 1982, *21*, 243–250.

1.2 FAMILY THERAPY THEORIES IN PERSPECTIVE

Present-day family therapy has been developed by persons who were schooled in one of the models of individual therapy (Broderick & Schrader, 1981). Therefore, to gain an understanding of family therapy, it is helpful to view briefly the range of individual approaches to therapy. The second part of this section presents the major theoretical frameworks presently used in family therapy. Also, the individual and fam-

ily approaches to therapy are compared and contrasted and the individual approaches to therapy summarized in chart form.

Individual Approaches

In the following table, the major individual approaches to therapy are described according to their basic tenets, the therapy goals, techniques used, the relationship of the therapist and client, and the major contributions of the particular approach to the field.

Family Approaches

The systems theory of Bertalanffy (1968) provides a framework for viewing seemingly unrelated parts and understanding how they are interrelated to parts of a larger system. This theoretical framework views all social systems as organized and operating from a hierarchy of levels; groups (e.g., families), organizations (e.g., cities, schools), and societies (e.g., nations). There is an interaction between both the various systems and their individual subsystems.

An individual may come for therapy presenting issues relating to the self concept. The way in which people view themselves is affected by their relationship with various members of their family or the position that they hold in their occupation. To understand the person fully, it is helpful to look beyond the individual, and at the context within which the individual moves (Goldenberg & Goldenberg, 1981).

Within the systems perspective, it is not always necessary to include all family members or representatives from other influencing systems, but it is important to maintain a systems' view of the issues.

Systems theorists consider the following concepts important as they approach a family issue: family communication styles, family dynamics, family myths, role assignments, the way in which family members unite with or against one another (coalitions), which persons are seen by others as being "the problem" (scapegoating), who holds the influence (power) in the family, and the ease with which relationships between persons can change.

Although all family theorists perceive the family as a social system, there are differences among theorists about the nature and origin of family dysfunction as well as differences regarding the use of strategies for intervention. There are at least four subsections into which family theorists may be divided (Goldenberg & Goldenberg, 1981). These are presented in the following.

Family Psychodynamic Theory

Nathan Ackerman (1958) is considered a father of the family therapy movement and has brought together many of the concepts used in individual psychotherapy with the dynamics of family life. The focus of family psychodynamic theory is on the inner lives and conflicts of family members, and the way that these conflicts come together to create behaviors that are problematic to individual or family functioning.

Murray Bowen (1978) also saw individual emotional disturbance as developing out of relationships to others. A unique contribution of Bowen was to pursue an understanding of the degree to which a family member develops a sense of self that is not joined to what he called the "undifferentiated family ego mass." This is the degree to which one can be in a family setting, but not take the difficulties of the family as one's own. The greater the lack of differentiation, the poorer is the sense of self and the greater the vulnerability to family stress. A person who is well differentiated does not negotiate away his or her opinions, thoughts, or values to please others.

Ackerman (1958) was interested in the role definition of family members and the expectations that family members had of others within the family system. He attempted to move persons toward readily changeable and adaptable role definitions, where roles were complementary and could lead to family harmony.

Family Communication Theory

Jackson (1968), Haley (1963), and Satir (1967) can be categorized as family communication theorists. Satir focuses on teaching honest and clear communication patterns. Getting in touch with feelings, listening to each other, clarifying meaning, and providing feedback regarding the communication process and content are of prime importance from Satir's perspective.

Haley examines power and control in the family from the perspective of the messages between sender and receiver. Symptoms are seen as strategies that are used to control other persons when all other strategies have failed. The person exhibiting symptoms claims that the symptoms (e.g., depression) are involuntary. Haley treats the individual problems as symptoms of family organization that are functioning improperly.

Jackson was one of the initial theorists to define family interaction as regular patterns or rules that are used in a repetitive manner by family members. He emphasized the importance of family homeostasis; that is, the family effort to preserve a familiar way of family life, and to restore this way of life whenever it is threatened. For example, children may act out during a parental conflict when they are afraid of the outcome of the conflict. The parental conflict ceases when the parents focus on the acting-out children. The children respond to the parents' attention and become cooperative. Thereupon the parental conflict returns.

Structural Family Theory

Structuralists assume that family members relate according to certain rules. These rules, which may be explicit or implicit within the family, provide the family operations with structure. Minuchin (1974) tried to bring about changes by modifying the structure. The focus of Structural therapy is on the manner in which persons communicate rather than on the content of the communications.

Of prime interest to the Structural therapist is the overall nature of the system (open or

Summary and Comparison of Individual Therapy Approaches

Therapy Approach	Basic Tenets	Therapy Goals
Psychoanalytic (Freud)	A theory of personality; a philosophical system, and the first psychological theory presented	To bring the unconscious to the conscious by delving into the past and working through repressed conflicts
Existential (May, Frankl, Maslow)	To develop human potential more fully	To develop the potential of the individual through self-awareness and growth; to foster freedom of choice and responsibility for action in client
Client-Centered (Rogers)	A nondirective approach; the client has responsibility for the resolution of difficulties	To help clients get in touch with their true feelings; to increase self-acceptance
Gestalt (Perls)	Experiential process designed to create self-awareness in the client	To assist clients in moving from external sources to internal sources of control; to assist clients to become centered and more self-aware
Transactional Analysis (Berne and Harris)	Focus on thought, behavior, and interpersonal transactions; emphasis on the present	To assist clients in choosing the manner in which they relate to others; to create greater self-awareness
Behavioral (Bandura, Wolpe, Lazarus)	Learning theory is applied to specific problems; experimentation is a major part of theory; trial-and-error learning is encouraged	To change behavior, client chooses attainable and measurable goals
Rational–Emotive (Ellis)	Problems are rooted in irrational thinking and in the systems of belief of the individual	To reduce the effects of self-defeating outlook on life; to change the client's perspective
Reality (Glasser)	Focus is on present behavior; utilizes client's strengths; sees therapy as short term	To provide guidance to responsible behavior; to develop a success orientation and plan to produce behavior change

Summary and Comparison of Individual Therapy Approaches

Techniques Used	Therapeutic Relationship	Major Uses and Contributions
Dream analysis, free association, transference analysis, testing and diagnosis, development of case histories	Therapist is anonymous, insight is gained by talking; past behavior is interpreted to give meaning to the present	Understanding of the unconscious and defense mechanisms; the importance of early life experiences
Based on understanding and relationship with little emphasis on technique	Very important; therapist closely related to the client with the focus on the therapeutic relationship; both client and therapist may change during therapy	A holistic approach to the individual; can be used in group settings with persons of various ages
Emphasis is on attitudes of the therapist—emphasizes listening and communication; skills such as reflection of feelings and clarification	The relationship is the primary feature of the therapy process; warmth genuineness, and respect are modeled for the client, who learns them and applies them to life situations	The client takes an active role and responsibility for direction of therapy; therapist is not viewed as the expert
Many are used, including role playing, confrontation, reliving of past experiences, and dream therapy	Therapist sets framework for clients who make their own interpretations of experiences	Emphasis is on action, expression, and experiencing
Confrontation, questioning, contracting, and possibly diagnosis	A relationship of peers; contract for change is developed; dependence on therapist is discouraged	Can be applied to marriage, group, or individual therapy; focus on individual ego states
Much data are gathered about what, how, when; tests of various kinds are used; desensitization, aversion therapy, operant techniques are employed	Teacher–learner relationship is utilized as various techniques are learned and applied	Can be applied in a wide range of situations from individual therapy to institutional use; the emphasis is on measurable change of behavior
Action oriented; critique of philosophy of life through reading, teaching, personal study; therapist confronts, interprets, questions	Teacher–learner; personal closeness not important; client has active role in changing behavior	Thinking is viewed as a source of personal problems; provides active ways to change thinking
Contracts are used with therapy, which is terminated when contract is complete; can be supportive and directive; little emphasis on diagnosis	Build therapeutic relationship that facilitates client's facing reality; value judgments are made of present behavior, and commitment for follow-through of therapeutic plan is established	Originally designed for young people in detention centers; can be used in individual, group, or marital therapy

closed); the nature of the hierarchial structures, alliances, and subsystems; the manner in which roles are established (age, power, sex); the alliances and subsystems within the family, and the change of member functions. Recognizing patterns of family transactions gives family members freedom to try new patterns of behaving.

Family Behavior Theory

Family behavior, as well as individual behavior is learned, strengthened, and supported over a period of time. All behavior, whether functional or dysfunctional, is acquired and maintained in identical ways. The goal of the behavioral therapist is to change the behavior patterns of dysfunctional interactions between persons. The sources of the behaviors are less important than the current issues that maintain the dysfunctional behaviors. The focus of therapy is to identify the behavior which needs change and the circumstances that support the behavior. New learning is strengthened and old dysfunctional patterns are eliminated. Common behavioral techniques such as modeling, positive and negative reinforcement, and contracting are applicable to marital and family therapy.

A Comparative Summary

The family therapy perspective sees the dominant forces in character development as stemming from interactions between family members. Family interaction is governed by rules that have been established over several generations. The members of a family are continually exposed to the same behavior and interaction patterns. These patterns are the basis for personality formation.

Individual therapy approaches, on the other hand, describe personality development as an internalized process based on the outcome of relationships between people. For example, family therapy views the mother–child relationship as highly influenced by the relationship that

the mother has with her husband. Individual therapy tends to focus on the mother–child interaction only.

Individual approaches to therapy tend to describe the development of symptoms as a result of internal conflict; the environment has only limited impact. The environment is seen as an external influence that affects the internal conflict. In family therapy, in contrast, symptoms are related to the conflict but the conflict is viewed as primarily interactional. In a healthy family, for example, the interaction and family organization is such that the individuation of family members is supported. Thus one way of producing change in dysfunctional families is to change the pattern of family interaction. These issues are discussed at length in the following sections.

References

Ackerman, N. *The psychodynamics of family life.* New York: Basic Books, 1958.

Bertalanffy, L. von. *General systems theory: Foundations, development, applications.* New York: Brazillier, 1968.

Bowen, N. *Family therapy in clinical practice.* New York: Jason Aronson, 1978.

Broderick, B., & Schrader, S. S. The history of professional marriage and family therapy. In A. Gurman & D. Kniskern (Eds.), *Handbook of family therapy.* New York: Brunner/Mazel, 1981.

Corey, G. *Theory and practice of counseling and psychotherapy.* Monterey, Calif.: Brooks/Cole, 1982.

Goldenberg, I., & Goldenberg, H. Family systems and the school counselor. *The School Counselor, 1981, 28,* 165–177.

Haley, J. *Strategies of psychotherapy.* New York: Grune & Stratton, 1963.

Jackson, D. (Ed.). *Communication, family, and marriage.* Palo Alto, Calif.: Science and Behavior Books, 1968.

Madanes, C. *Strategic family therapy.* San Francisco: Jossey-Bass, 1981.

Minuchin, S. *Families and family therapy.* Cambridge, Mass.: Harvard University Press, 1974.

Robinson, L. R. Basic concepts in family treatment: A differential comparison with individual treatment. *American Journal of Psychiatry,* 1975, *132,* 1045–1048.

Satir, V. *Conjoint family therapy*. Palo Alto, Calif.:
Science and Behavior Books, 1967.

1.3 STRUCTURAL–STRATEGIC FAMILY THERAPY: A PARADIGM

In this handbook the two predominant perspectives on family therapy—Structural and Strategic—are interwoven. The viewpoint held here is that because the two approaches have similar theoretical understandings, an integration is possible even though there are theoretical difficulties that involve disparate treatment goals and procedure. For example, the Strategic approach focuses upon the interaction patterns within the family while the Structural approach involves an analysis of the organizational patterns, hierarchies, and sequences within the family. Despite these differences the two approaches are, in many ways, complementary at the operational level.

Following Stanton (1982), the underlying thesis in this handbook is that it is possible to construct a paradigm that allows utilization of both techniques in marriage and family therapy. We identify the strengths, similarities, and differences of each approach, and present a set of rules that may guide the practitioner in the use of Structural and Strategic techniques in marriage and family therapy.

Stages in the Therapy Process

The Structural–Strategic family therapy paradigm proposed here has four stages:
1. Developing a context and conditions for change.
2. Confronting patterns and expanding alternatives.

3. Consolidating change.
4. Termination and conducting an evaluation of the therapy process.

These four stages should not be perceived as rigid steps to be followed unquestionably, but as flexible guidelines when working with couples or families. The length of each stage will vary with the needs of each couple or family.

The stages are particularly useful in providing a framework for guiding the timing of interventions. An intervention made at the beginning of therapy may be completely ineffective, whereas the same intervention may be very effective after several sessions. It is important in the choice of interventions not only to be concerned with the client needs, but also with the correct timing of the intervention. In the following section, each stage is described in greater detail.

Stage 1. Developing a Context and Conditions for Change

The purpose of this stage of therapy is to create the therapeutic conditions that will enable the individuals to change and grow. This stage has the following aspects:

1. The therapist establishes rapport with family members and gains their respect.
2. The presenting problem(s) are identified.
3. The family is assessed from a Structural–Strategic theoretical perspective.
4. Hypotheses are developed underlying the family dynamics, sequences of interaction, and why the symptom is maintained.
5. The therapist introduces a framework of interventions that may challenge or block existing dynamics.
6. A contract for change is agreed upon by therapist and family members.

Having created a contract for change, it is now possible to proceed to stage 2 of the therapy.

Stage 2. Confronting Patterns and Expanding Alternatives

This stage is in some ways a continuation of the earlier relationship building and assessment stage, but focuses more strongly on interventions. It may begin after two/three sessions into the therapy process or at the point at which the therapist has established a trusting relationship with the family members. It should be clear that the boundaries of the four stages overlap and the therapist may move back and forth from one stage to the other.

Confronting Patterns

Having established a relationship with family members, the therapist is now ready to confront dysfunctional structures, patterns, and sequences. The confrontation may be direct and straightforward in families with a strong motivation to change, or indirect, or even paradoxical, in families that are resistant to change or have a strong network of interprotectiveness and fear the consequences of change. Great care needs to be exercised in using paradoxical-type interventions. Therapists not well experienced in working with families should be encouraged to understand fully the principles of paradoxical intervention before attempting to use them. If inappropriately used, paradoxical techniques are counterproductive and potentially destructive.

A variety of interventions may be used to block dysfunctional structures, patterns, and sequences. Structural interventions may include such activities as enactment, focusing, reframing, intensity creation, boundary building, unbalancing, and other techniques laid out in detail in other sections of this handbook. Strategic interventions may include reframing, positive connotation, directives, metaphors, and paradox.

Evidence for the completion of stage 2 may include such new behaviors as the elimination of or reduction in the severity of the symptom, increased differentiation of family members, change in the family structure and organization, and a change in the nature of the family patterns and sequences. Having produced change in

stage 2 of the therapy process, it is now possible to move to stage 3.

Stage 3. Consolidating Change

It is usually not enough for the family to achieve the desired changes temporarily; these changes must be nurtured, tested, and celebrated, and the family must believe it can maintain them. Omer (1982), quoting Milton Erickson, addresses this matter and suggests that, in many societies, significant life changes are accompanied by rites of passage. An important component of these rites is raising boundaries between the old situation and the new one; that is, celebrating that the old is replaced by the new. Consolidating change involves blocking the family's return to old patterns and structures in an attempt to maintain the gains made in the therapy process.

The goals of stage 3 are to help the family members (1) celebrate growth and the development of the new behaviors, (2) create warm and close networks of relationship outside of the family, (3) develop greater awareness of dysfunctional patterns of interaction and their alternative functional patterns, (4) reinforce new images and metaphors of reality, and (5) generate greater awareness that the locus of change resides within the family rather than with the therapist.

Stage 4. Evaluation and Termination

The final stage of the Structural–Strategic therapy model involves evaluation and termination of the sessions. Although evaluation occurs continuously during the therapy process, the final evaluation is designed to identify the outcomes of therapy. Various therapy outcomes can be examined, such as (1) change in family relationships, (2) symptom control, (3) change in family structure, (4) improved social networking, and (5) change in the family members' views of reality and life goals.

After the evaluation has been completed, termination of the sessions occurs. Whereas the family members have been prepared for termination in earlier sessions by such strategies as increasingly congratulating them on their willingness to assume greater responsibility for the change process, the last few sessions lay the groundwork for termination.

There are several important considerations that should guide the termination process, including: (1) the family members will increasingly use the sessions to report and receive feedback on the problems they have identified rather than look to the therapist for direct assistance; (2) the time intervals are increased from weekly sessions to biweekly or monthly sessions; and (3) the family members are encouraged to return for a few sessions at important transition points. In this way the therapist is available to family members over the life cycle.

In the preceding discussion, we identified four stages that can be used to guide the process of Structural–Strategic therapy. We now review the common viewpoints held by both the Structural and the Strategic theorists.

Common Viewpoints Arising from Both Orientations

As Stanton (1981) (1982) has proposed, a number of common threads can be identified in Structural and Strategic therapies. Generally speaking both schools adhere to the following concepts and therapy methods.

Common Views Regarding the Couple or Family

1. Change occurs within a context that influences and is influenced by the component parts.

2. The family life cycle and developmental stages are significant considerations in the assessment and therapy process. When tasks in a particular stage are not adequately completed, problems may be created at future stages of development.

3. Symptoms are both system-maintained and system-maintaining.

4. Sequences, interactions, and patterns represent important dynamics within the couple or family.

5. Destructive ongoing cycles of interaction prevent the family or couple from achieving its basic purposes.

Role of Therapist

1. The therapist is an active agent who joins the family in a personal relationship in order to make structural and interactional changes in the family.

2. The therapist must become a real member of the family, and be accepted and trusted as an emphatic, approachable helper.

3. The therapist needs some distance from the family to ensure objectivity and autonomy.

4. The therapist needs to provide a supportive but challenging therapeutic relationship.

5. The therapist must be capable of intense relating, rapid assessing, and active intervening. This requires the ability to develop a flexible, creative, unpredictable, and engaging therapeutic style.

6. The therapist requires a repertoire of techniques and a knowledge of timing. He or she needs to know how to adjust intensity, and to regulate pressure and involvement.

7. The therapist must learn to use self as the most important instrument of intervention.

8. Resistance is resolved through the relationship, including use of personal charisma, knowledge, influence, and strength.

Therapy Process in Structural and Strategic Therapy

1. Therapy is viewed pragmatically.

2. The focus is the present rather than the past.

3. Repetitive and destructive behavioral sequences are focused on, and efforts are made to have them blocked.

4. Symptoms often represent dysfunctional family dynamics, and are an important focus during intervention.

5. The emphasis is upon process rather than content.

6. The therapist facilitates the process and takes considerable responsibility for change.

7. Assessment involves the process of observing, hypothesizing, intervening, and making sense out of the feedback.

8. Contracts are negotiated jointly by the therapist and client and are based upon the presenting problem and the goals of change.

9. Reframing or relabeling is emphasized rather than insight.

10. Tasks or homework assignments are employed to initiate or consolidate change.

11. Therapy is generally brief and usually does not exceed six months.

Each of the foregoing statements is enlarged upon in various sections of this handbook. The major purpose of this succinct analysis is to give the reader a brief overview of the major dimensions of the Structural–Strategic paradigm.

In the following section, an overview of the Structural approach to family therapy is presented. This approach is most clearly identified with Salvador Minuchin (1974) and others (Aponte & Van Deusen, 1981).

Basic Structural Therapy Concepts

Structural theory is relatively simple, and is more concerned with the organization and structure of the family than it is with a theory of change. The following concepts are illustrative of the Structural approach.

1. Dysfunctional patterns of behavior result from problems in three major Structural dimensions, namely, boundaries, alignment, and power.

2. Boundary dysfunctions involve the extremes of enmeshment and disengagement.

3. Enmeshed boundaries between people are too diffuse, allowing little autonomy between individuals and fostering emotional overinvolvement.

4. Alignments include both concepts of alliances or healthy links between members and dysfunctional coalitions in which two members form a partnership against a third, often crossing generational boundaries.

5. Power problems signify a lack of appropriate influence in the family arising from the absence of an appropriate hierarchy system.

6. Change involves restructuring the system to enable it to handle the tasks at any stage of the life cycle.

Structural Interventions

1. The therapist takes charge of the sessions to facilitate the family's development and competence.

2. The basic goal of the therapy sessions is to promote a more adequate family organization.

3. Interventions are designed to restructure the family by loosening the boundaries in a rigid family, differentiating members in an enmeshed family, and increasing involvement in a disconnected family.

4. The therapeutic plan is developed in response to the family members' expectations and to what is considered "normal" development in a stage with due regard to cultural and socioeconomic factors.

5. New family patterns are enacted within the session.

6. Numerous techniques such as enactment, focusing, reframing, altering the intensity of impact, and unbalancing are used to facilitate change.

Strategic Therapy

In contrast to Structural therapy, which has a well-defined theory of family, Strategic therapy has developed a sophisticated theory of change. This theory not only conceptualizes the nature of change, but also emphasizes what to do and how to do it to help resolve persistent problems. Many of the interventions appear strange in and of themselves, but when they are related to some rationale, they become understandable and logical.

Some of the leading exponents of Strategic therapy are as follows: Don Jackson, John Weakland, Paul Watzlawick, Richard Fisch, Arthur Bodin, and Carlos Sluzki from the Mental Research Institute (MRI); Gerald Zuk, Milton Erickson, and Jay Haley; Mara Palazzoli-Selvini, Luigi Boscolo, Gianfranco Cecchin, and Giuliana Prata from the Milan group; and Lynn Hoffman, Peggy Papp, and Olga Silverstein. Although all Strategic therapists have much in common, they have their own styles, similarities, and differences. In the following section, an overview of the major concepts within the Strategic framework is presented.

Strategic Concepts

1. Symptoms are the result of unsuccessful attempts to balance or alleviate stress within the family.

2. A symptom is viewed as a homeostatic mechanism regulating marital or family transactions.

3. A symptom is an act of communication.

4. All families develop patterns of behaving as well as patterns for responding to stressful anxiety-producing situations.

Strategic Interventions

1. Change comes when the therapist intervenes in the interactional processes.

2. The therapist works to substitute new behavior patterns or sequences for the vicious, positive feedback cycles.

3. The therapist utilizes tasks and directives. The emphasis on directives is central to the approach.

4. Positive connotation of the family, its

symptom(s), and its homeostatic tendencies are readily employed.

5. The problem must be put in solvable form. It should be something that can be objectively agreed upon; that is, counted, observed, or measured so that one can assess whether it has actually been influenced.

6. Strong emphasis is placed on extra-session change and altering the processes occurring outside of the session.

7. Power struggles are usually avoided and the Strategic use of one-down and one-up positions is emphasized, thus turning the family's investment to positive use.

8. Paradoxical interventions are common and may be directed toward the whole family or individuals. This may involve:

    a. Prescribing the symptom.

    b. Restraining or discouraging.

The Interface of Structural and Strategic Interventions

It is the thesis of this handbook that Structural and Strategic interventions may be used interchangeably or concurrently in marriage and family therapy. It is, however, important to be sensitive to the dynamics of the individual, couple, or family in deciding which intervention to employ. Furthermore the timing of the interventions is particularly important since an intervention may be inappropriate at the beginning of therapy whereas it may be quite effective at a later session.

The following general rules for delivering interventions are suggested. These rules are consistent with the 4 stage model of intervention described earlier.

Rule 1

The first rule is to begin with approaches that are relatively unthreatening, structural, and relationship building. Such techniques as joining, accommodating, restructuring, testing boundaries, empathy, reflection, summarizing, and other client-centered approaches are particularly useful at the beginning of the therapy process.

The use of relationship building and Structural approaches is also very effective in facilitating an assessment of the family. These approaches are more straightforward and, therefore, more helpful in the assessment of the family and the development of hypotheses.

Rule 2

When the Structural approaches are not producing the desired effects, Strategic interventions may be employed. Strategic interventions have been developed from work with highly resistant clients and are often metaphorical and paradoxical. These techniques are more fully discussed in the following sections of this handbook.

Rule 3

When the system has become unbalanced and progress toward change has occurred, revert once again to the use of Structural approaches. The Structural approach may form the final phase of the therapy process or become part of the consolidation stage. The final phase of therapy may be recognized when the "identified patient" no longer is the central focus of therapy, and the family members appear much more differentiated, with well-defined boundaries, and able to communicate effectively. At such a time in the therapy process, Structural techniques again become useful in consolidating the gains made by the family members.

References

Aponte, H. J., & Van Deusen, J. M. Structural family therapy. In A. L. Gurman & P. D. Kniskern (Eds.), *Handbook of family therapy*. New York: Brunner/Mazel, 1981.

Haley, J. *Uncommon therapy*. San Francisco: Jossey-Bass, 1976.

Keeney, B. P. Ecosystemic epistemology: An alternate paradigm for diagnosis. *Family Process*, 1979, *18*, 117–129.

Madanes, C. *Strategic family therapy*. San Francisco: Jossey-Bass, 1982.

Minuchin, S. *Family and family therapy*. Cambridge, Mass.: Harvard University Press, 1974.

Omer, H. The macrodynamics of Ericksonian therapy. *Journal of Strategic and Systemic Therapies*, 1982, *5*, 34–44.

Palazzoli-Selvini, M., Boscolo, L., Cecchin, G., & Prata, G. *Paradox and counter-paradox: A new model in the therapy of the family in schizophrenic transaction*. New York: Jason Aronson, 1978.

Stanton, M. D. Marital therapy from a structural/strategic viewpoint. In G. P. Sholevar (Ed.), *The handbook of marriage and marital therapy*. Jamaica, N.Y.: S.P. Medical and Scientific Books (division of Spectrum Publications), 1982.

Stanton, M. D. Strategic approaches to family therapy. In A. S. Gurman & D. P. Kniskern (Eds.), *Handbook of family therapy*. New York: Brunner/Mazel, 1981.

Stanton, M.D. An integrated structural/strategic approach to family therapy. *Journal of marital and family therapy*, 1981, Oct. 427–439.

Watzlawick, P., Beavin, J. H., & Jackson, D. D. *Pragmatics of human communication*. New York: W. W. Norton, 1967.

Watzlawick, P., Weakland, J., & Fisch, R. *Change: Principles of problem formation and problem resolution*. New York: W. W. Norton, 1974.

1.4 LEARNING TO THINK SYSTEMICALLY

There is a tendency for living systems to join up, establish linkages, live inside each other, return to earlier arrangements, get along whenever possible.

Lewis Thomas

What Is a System?

A system may be described as a holon which is derived from the Greek word *holos*, which means whole. Every individual, the family, the extended family, and the community are both a part and a whole. As a whole a holon exerts competitive energy for autonomy and self-preservation. As a part a holon contains integrative energy. A whole contains the part, and each part contains the program that operates the whole. Part and whole are integrated with each other in a current and ongoing process of communication and interrelationship (Minuchin & Fishman, 1981).

The Holons

Individual

The individual holon is defined as a person in context. It includes the personal and historical determinants of self as well as the current input of the social context. The individual is connected to social realities outside of himself or herself that give meaning to existence and reinforce behavior.

There is a circular, continuous process of interaction between systems and their components that tend to maintain a fixed state or pattern. Nevertheless individuals and their context have the capacity for flexibility and change. Change in systems is sometimes called transformation.

Spouse

The spouse holon is formed when two individuals, a man and a woman, join with the purpose of forming a family. They bring with them a set of values and expectations, conscious and unconscious, by which they have been programmed in their families of origin. Differing values between spouses must be reconciled over time to make a life in common possible. It is necessary for each spouse to give up part of his or her values and expectations in order to obtain belonging. In this process a new system is born.

Parental

The parental holon can vary in composition. It may include grandparents, or even other extended family such as aunts. Or it may be only one parent or a parental child delegated to discipline the other siblings.

The responsibility of the parental holon is to rear the child, a responsibility that includes protection, socialization, and education of the child. The problem of control and discipline is always present and is often resolved by trial and error. The nature of parental discipline will vary depending on the developmental stage of the family. Families may get stuck at a particular stage of development and may require expert assistance to resolve the problem adequately.

Sibling

Siblings are the child's first peer group. As such, siblings are very influential in the child's life. The sibling holon forms a structure containing hierarchies, alliances, and power alignments, and develops transactional patterns for negotiating, cooperating, and competing. The patterns the child learns will be transported into other systems with which it establishes membership. For example, a child who learns to criticize and blame in the sibling holon will tend to do this as an adult in a new relationship with a spouse.

Symptomatic Behavior in a Holon

Symptomatic behavior, such as alcoholism or classroom misbehavior, is not isolated and treated separately within a system's perspective, but is defined as an event in a circular sequence of social interaction. It is viewed as serving a function within the sequence. Therefore, the focus of therapy is on the function that it serves rather than on the symptomatic behavior itself. All behavior is defined as a response or a communication to the responses or communications of others.

Symptoms, although they may be caused by traumatic events of the past, are reframed in terms of the present and perceived as being system "maintained" in the present by an interactional process or program. This program may be changed through therapy. A major responsibility of the therapist is to study the way in which each person in the family programs and is programmed by others through power plays, hierarchies, and sequences. As a result of effective interventions, the therapist interrupts the escalating cycle of interaction and extricates the individuals from the power struggle.

Marital System

In a dysfunctional marital system, the spouses are assumed to exhibit certain coercive behavior to each other, such as blaming and placating. This perspective is in contrast to intrapsychic approaches, which assume that spouses have static states such as ego deficiencies, acute sensitivity to rejection, or deep dependency. From a systems' viewpoint, dependency is both a response and a communication.

The following is an example of dependent spousal behavior. The husband may act increasingly dependent as the wife becomes overly involved with a newborn child. The wife responds to the husband's signals of needing attention by relating more to him and helping him with his problems. However, the husband responds only minimally to her in order to maintain her support and attention. The wife feels more and more frustrated and defeated, begins to exhibit hostile behavior toward her husband, and moves again more firmly toward her child. At this point the husband acts even more dependent and helpless to get her back, and the cycle repeats itself.

In Figure 1.4.1 the helplessness and dependency of the husband serve the function of keeping the wife involved with him whereas the hostility of the wife serves to make the husband more responsible. Thus the symptomatic behavior is interconnected, and forms a sequence or pattern of events; it is also purposeful and goal oriented, as is evident in the example.

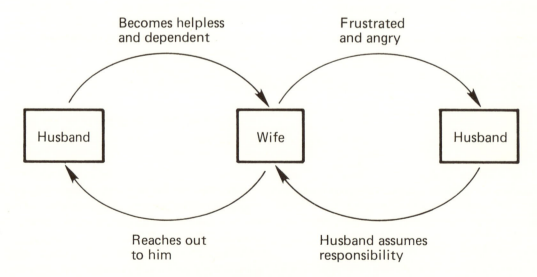

Figure 1.4.1
Interactional Feedback System

Nonjudgmental Concepts

A systemic perspective views all members of a system as contributing equally to the disruption or strengthening of the family. A therapist who espouses a systems viewpoint begins with the assumption that both husbands and wives are equally involved in defining the sequence of events that may be experienced as supportive or coercive. Resistance to therapy is defined as residing in the system, that is, in the system trying to maintain itself, rather than in the spouses, as in traditional theories of therapy.

Role of the Past

A systems therapist recognizes that each spouse carries certain attitudes and behaviors over from the family of origin, but focuses on the unique way these attitudes and tendencies combine and interact to form the present program. This program becomes the *quid pro quo* and determines the rules by which the couple interacts. These rules are seldom explicit and overt, but are indigenous to the system. As the program changes, the spouses act, feel, think, and experience their world differently. In other words, their relationship becomes ''transformed'' into a different configuration with new communication and behavior patterns, hierarchies, rules, and power structure.

References

Minuchin, S., & Fishman, H. *Family therapy techniques*. Cambridge, Mass.: Harvard University Press, 1981.

Sullaway, M., & Christensen, A. Assessment of dysfunctional interaction patterns in couples. *Journal of Marriage and Family*, 1983, *45*, 653–659.

1.5 FAMILY THERAPY TRAINING

The field of family therapy is expanding rapidly, and with this expansion has come a corresponding increase in the demand for training (Liddle, 1982). This section discusses four basic areas pertinent to family therapy training within a Structural–Strategic framework:

1. Family theory and training
2. Personnel
3. Methodology
4. Evaluation

Family Theory and Training

It is appropriate that the theory of family therapy should govern how training should proceed. For example, if a trainer holds to the theory that insight into family dynamics causes change, then he or she trains student therapists by giving them insight into themselves and their family dynamics; on the other hand, if a trainer believes that positive reinforcement causes change, then he or she trains therapists with positive reinforcement procedures (Haley, 1976). Structural–Strategic family theory adopted in this manual likewise has proposals for training, specifically in the areas of personnel, methodology, and evaluation.

Personnel

Life experience is important in the selection of trainees. Haley (1976) suggests that since Strategic therapy stresses problems in the real world, it is best to choose trainees with experience in that world. He advises (p. 180) that ''mature students who have been married and have children will be easier to train than young people just starting out on courtship.'' Minuchen and Fishman (1981, p. 10), who advocate a Structural perspective, go even further:

Too many young therapists go into healing without the life experience necessary to understand the problems with which they are intervening. Ideally, they should exclude from their case load families who are in a developmental stage that they have not yet experienced themselves. If that is impossible, they should acknowledge their ignorance and ask the families to educate them in these matters.

Formal training can be a help or a hindrance to family work, depending on the type of training received. For example, those who have had training in psychodynamic therapy may have difficulty thinking in terms of more than one person (Haley, 1976). Another consideration is whether family therapy comes naturally to some people, as if they were born therapists, or whether it is all a matter of training (Liddle, 1982). Probably there is an interaction between talent and training. That is, we cannot become family therapists as a result of talent or training alone. Rather a trainess ideally will possess personal qualities important in marital and family therapy, such as creativity, spontaneity, and intelligence, and will also be trained in therapeutic strategies.

Methodology

Haley (1976) suggests several implications for training family therapists. First, just as the therapist is responsible for initiating change in the family through planned interventions, the trainer is responsible for initiating improvement in the trainee's therapy style and skills through planned training strategies.

Second, just as problem solving is emphasized in therapy, so problem-solving skills and strategies are emphasized in training. It is assumed that trainees grow with success in their work; therefore, the focus in training is on helping trainees solve the problems they encounter in therapy.

Third, just as action by the therapist is viewed as influential in changing the family, so also action by the trainer (guidance, suggestions, and even direct intervention in live therapy interviews) is viewed as influential in the improvement of the trainee's therapy. Furthermore this emphasis on change and improvement of the student therapist through *doing* therapy points to the related issue of inductive/deductive teaching methods. In the early days of family therapy, the traditional deductive training process was avoided in favor of inductive training, that is, learning by doing. Haley (1976, p. 181) explains:

Therapy is a personal encounter and a therapist can only learn how to do it by doing it. All other training activity is peripheral if not irrelevant. Ideally, he learns to do therapy by doing it while guided by a supervisor at the moment therapy is happening.

Minuchen and Fishman (1981, p. 9), however, say that "twenty years of teaching have shown us that there has to be a middle ground" between deductive and inductive training. While it is true that an understanding of theory can emerge from actually doing family and marital therapy, it is also true that the teaching of new skills can so disorganize the beginning therapist that he or she misses the overarching theoretical concepts and goals.

It is clear, then, that *both* inductive and deductive training are needed. Aponte and Van Deusen (1981, p. 338) explain:

There is a place in training for literature and lectures to communicate concepts and informational data. Nevertheless, this mode of teaching is not the most practical for the practitioner who must develop not just ways of thinking, but skills for doing. Reading and lecturing do not precede practical training. They are given concurrently with and as a part of the experiential exercises.

Another concern in family therapy is that the trainee must learn how to implement action through directive skills. Student therapists who have been trained in a nondirective style of therapy are likely to feel anxious about being directive, and may give directives badly as well as reluctantly. Haley (1976, p. 184) suggests that training in giving directives must include:

. . . teaching students to motivate someone to do what he is told, how to give the directives, how to clarify whether they have been understood, how to anticipate reluctance to follow them, and how to check to see if they have been followed. . . . The students should learn to give straightforward directives as well as subtle, indirect, and metaphoric ones.

Just as the family therapist insists on directly observing problematic behavior in the therapy session instead of relying only on the family's report of such behavior, so the trainer will insist on directly observing the trainee's interaction with a client family, instead of relying on the trainee's report of the therapy session. An important part of training, therefore, involves supervised therapy sessions using a one-way mirror or videotape.

Haley (1976, p. 177) suggests that the supervisor does not believe the therapist "can accurately report what happened, just as a family member cannot accurately report what happens in his family."

We have seen that family and marital therapy (1) makes the therapist responsible for initiating change in the family, (2) focuses on family dynamics and problem solving, (3) is action oriented, and (4) uses direct observation for data gathering. Therefore, in training the trainer is responsible for (1) initiating change and improvement in the student's therapy effectiveness, (2) teaching problem-solving techniques and restructuring skills, (3) directly focusing on what the trainee actually does in live therapy sessions using a one-way mirror or videotape, and (4) collecting data about the student's interaction with a family via direct observation. In keeping with this training orientation, the following outline is suggested.

Training Orientation

1. Both deductive and inductive methods of training are begun from the outset. A deductive approach will include lectures, group discussions, films, and reading assignments about marital and family therapy. Inductive training may proceed in the following two phases (Minuchen & Fishman, 1981).

2. Trainers model marital and family therapy in live family interviews, which are observed by a small group of student therapists. While they observe the session via a one-way mirror or videotape, another trainer provides a running commentary on the dynamics of the sessions, including a description of the various techniques and interventions used. In addition, the group of trainees also observes tapes of other therapists doing therapy in different family situations. Trainees are encouraged to practice the skills and techniques of marital and family therapy in role-playing situations, and to receive feedback from the trainer and group members.

3. Student therapists receive live and videotape supervision of their own therapy sessions with a client family. The trainer-supervisor and student group observe another trainee as he or she works with a family. Minuchen and Fishman (1981) suggest several levels of trainer intervention, all of which may occur during the trainee's therapy session: (a) a telephone call is received, in which the trainer offers one succinct idea pertinent to the therapy session; (b) the student therapist briefly leaves the room for consultation with the trainer; and (c) the trainer enters the therapy room to consult with the student therapist on the spot. There are several advantages to live supervision: (a) trainees can begin therapy before they feel ready, due to the trainer's supervision and support (Minuchen & Fishman, 1981); (b) the trainer not only protects the client family from a beginner's inadequacies, but offers on-the-spot guidance for the trainee (Haley, 1976); (c) the trainee also benefits from the encouragement and constructive criticism of the other members of his or her student group who have observed the session along with the trainer.

Evaluation

Haley (1976) suggests that after a few months of training, student therapists should conduct follow-up interviews with their client families to determine whether their therapy has produced change. Haley (1976, p. 185) explains:

The purpose is not to produce therapists who can do outcome research but to produce therapists who think about the outcome they want as it will appear months or years from now. Focusing on outcome forces the therapist to orient toward change, to formulate problems that can be changed, and to think about how the people he is assisting now will manage without him in the future. It also helps a therapist think experimentally. If his outcome is not good, he can change his procedures to do better.

References

Aponte, H. J., & Van Deusen, J. M. Structural family therapy. In Alan S. Gurman & David P. Kniskern (Eds.), *Handbook of family therapy*. New York: Brunner/Mazel, 1981.

Haley, J. *Problem-solving therapy*. New York: Harper Colophon Books, 1976.

Liddle, H. A. Family therapy training: Current issues, future trends. *International Journal of Family Therapy*, 1982, *4*, 2.

Minuchen, S., & Fishman, H. C. *Family therapy techniques*. Cambridge, Mass.: Harvard University Press, 1981.

CHAPTER 2

FAMILY DEVELOPMENT

2.1 THE NATURE OF FAMILY HEALTH AND DYSFUNCTION

In this section the focus is on the key concepts of family health. The material presented is a summary of the work of various writers such as Beavers (1977), Aponte and Van Deusen (1981), Luthman and Kirschenbaum (1974), Minuchin (1974), and Stanton (1981). These authors bring uniqueness to their understanding of healthy families, and at the same time share much in common in their conceptualization of family health.

Community

Beavers (1977) describes a number of characteristics that are seen in healthy families. One such characteristic is community. Community is an integral part of human growth and development. The experience of community is prominent in the nuclear family, and does not necessarily give way to isolation as an individual matures and leaves the parental home.

Implicit in the concept of community is the idea of a common goal or purpose. Without a common goal, the family does not have a central focal point and becomes fragmented.

Boundaries

Each of the persons in a healthy family also has a clear understanding of who participates and how they participate in various activities both inside and outside the family (Minuchin, 1974). A family requires boundaries that create distinctions between parents and children. The most effective boundaries between parents and children are those that are well defined and accurately identify the activities that are appropriate for persons in either group. Appropriateness of information to be shared between parents and children is also clearly understood. Within healthy families there is a clear boundary between individuals. Persons are aware of differing viewpoints between a parent and child or between parents. Individuality of choice is respected. Differences of perspective between family members may produce intimacy when those differences exist in a context of caring and common pursuits.

An extreme degree of individuality and separation (disengaged) produces little or no interaction between family members (see Figure 2.1.1). Such family members are independently involved in their own lives and have little concern for each other. Although they exhibit little emotional contact within the family, they may nevertheless have a high amount of contact with sources other than family, such as individual friends, interests, and recreation.

In dysfunctional families there can be a complete blending of family members so that all

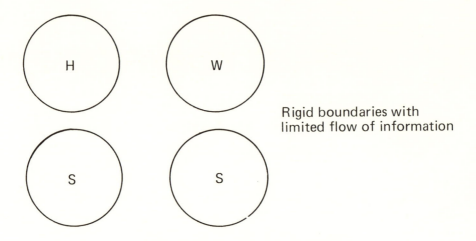

Rigid boundaries with limited flow of information

Figure 2.1.1. Disengaged family

independence is lost (enmeshed). In enmeshed families all decision making is on a joint basis and most activities are shared by all family members. Each member is overinvolved in another individual's life (see Figure 2.1.2).

Families can be separated (disengaged) or pulled together (enmeshed) on three levels: parents versus children; husband versus wife; and families versus the community around them.

Persons from outside the family, such as teachers, play a significant role in the life of a healthy family. Parents and their children need to determine what information is kept within the family and what is shared with outsiders. Dys-

functional families have boundaries that are blurred—family members are uncertain about what information is kept secret and what is to be shared.

Boundaries need to be sufficiently strong so that they are maintained during times of family stress to keep stability in the family interactions. Conversely boundaries need to be sufficiently flexible to change as the individuals in the family mature. Clear and sufficiently flexible boundaries are those that allow family members to pursue their own interests and incorporate their interests into family life (see Figure 2.1.3).

Satisfaction that is experienced in outside

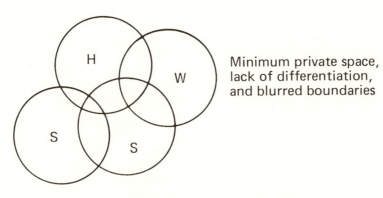

Minimum private space, lack of differentiation, and blurred boundaries

Figure 2.1.2. Enmeshed family

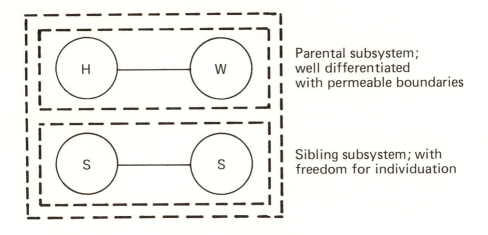

Figure 2.1.3. Healthy family

Parental subsystem;
well differentiated
with permeable boundaries

Sibling subsystem; with
freedom for individuation

activities is carried back to the family and shared, contributing to an interesting and diversified family outlook.

Roles

Roles are expectations of behavior within a given setting. The roles that persons play within a family can be determined by what has been learned in the family of origin, within the marital relationship, from the culture generally, and through personal experiences. In healthy families there is a clear definition of parental and child roles (role clarity). This is maintained primarily by declaring generational boundaries and defining who holds the power.

The role of the child is not confused with the role of parent; therefore, the responsibilities of both child and parent are clearly defined and appropriately distributed. Children are not expected to act as parents and the parents (either one or both of them) do not abdicate their responsibility to the children. The clear definition of child and parental roles is rooted in a strong parental relationship. The parents do not ''parent'' each other, but jointly maintain the family structure.

Role distribution between marital partners may or may not fit traditional patterns. In satisfying marriages some specific tasks tend to be fulfilled by one person (complementary), rather than to be rigidly shared (symmetrical). Healthy families tend to assign specific tasks with the objective of meeting family goals, and then having individuals work to meet those goals. The tasks are clear within each family (though they will differ across various families and traditional cultural distinctives). Task or role allocation is not a constant source of friction between marital partners; though they share a similar amount of influence within the family, they do not necessarily fulfill the same roles. Role fulfillment is based upon meeting the family goals that have been established by the marital couple. As the family matures and the family goals change, role distribution is sufficiently flexible so that it can change to meet the needs of the family.

Power

The degree to which each family member influences the outcome of activities is referred to as power. Parents are the architects of the family; they establish and maintain influence. In healthy families parents have sufficient resources and skills to maintain the family atmosphere on a level where there is seldom a clash of power between parents and children. Parents also share power with their children, with the older tending to have more power than the younger. One source of intimacy in the family is the mutual sharing of power and directing it toward the meeting of family goals.

Families that are dysfunctional often exhibit inappropriate distribution of power. A child may form a coalition with one parent against the remainder of the family leading to a continual battle between the parents. The partner who has lost power attempts to regain it, while the child is continually challenged by the other siblings to share the power. This arrangement also separates the husband from the wife and the more influential child. In addition the more influential child is separated from the other children and the parent of lesser influence (see Figure 2.1.4).

Another common source of power imbalance can be the single-parent family where the parent forms a coalition with the eldest child, who thus fills the vacant parental role (see Figure 2.1.5).

Rules

A concept closely related to that of power is family rules. Rules are patterns of interaction or behavior of which everyone in the family is aware. Family members who have the most influence will have the greatest impact on family rules.

Rules may be spoken, or unspoken; they may be readily changed (flexible) or unchageable (rigid). In healthy families rules tend to be explicit, sufficiently flexible to allow for change as the family matures, and relatively few in number.

Communication

The patterns of communication within the family are descriptive of the patterns of behavior between family members. Messages are given specific meaning on the basis of the context in which they are given. The meanings of specific statements change as the context changes. A parent who says to a child, ''I need you to help me,'' can be asking for assistance in a nominal household task or can be exhibiting an unhealthy dependence on the child.

In dysfunctional families the context is often unclear and there is uncertainty about the meaning of the messages sent. A message that carries opposite meanings at two levels is a double-level message—for example, one says ''I don't want to talk about this issue now,'' while con-

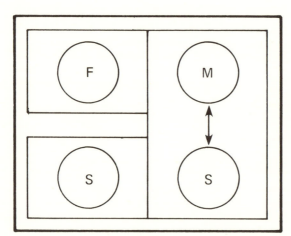

Mother and son form a coalition in order to increase mother's power.

Figure 2.1.4. Mother and son form a coalition

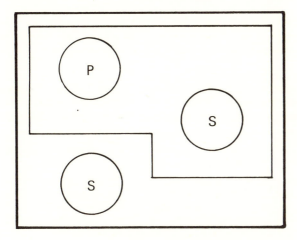

Single parent and son form a coalition. The eldest son fulfills vacant parent role.

Figure 2.1.5. Parent and son form a coalition

tinuing discussion on some aspect of the topic. When a double message occurs, it is impossible to fulfill its intention because either response is in opposition to what was stated. Healthy families tend to have clear, direct communication where the various levels of the message (content, tone of voice) carry the same meaning. The general tone of the communication tends to contain warmth and spontaneity, rather than a staccato production of feelingless words.

No Single Thread

Perhaps the single, most comprehensive study on family health was that carried out by Lewis et al. (1976). The study was conducted over a six-year period using the healthiest and most effective families the researchers could find. The research emphasis was on functioning, not pathology, and on systems and interaction rather than on an artificial isolation of individuals for study.

After absorbing, sifting, and evaluating the data from healthy families, the researchers divided the sample into two groups, which were termed ''optimal'' and ''adequate.'' Although the two groups differed significantly, there was a continuum, and an arbitrary cutting point was chosen to separate the optimal from the adequate group. Both quantitative and qualitative differences between the two groups were determined by use of clinical, self-report, and microanalytic techniques.

From these analyses eight variables emerged that the authors considered to be most important in differentiating optimal from adequate families. These are:

1. A systems orientation
2. Boundary issues
3. Contextual clarity
4. Power issues
5. Encouragement of autonomy
6. Task efficiency
7. Transcendent values

Each of these concepts is enlarged upon in the following discussion. They are discussed more fully by the researchers in the book, *No Single Thread: Psychological Health in Family Systems.*

A Systems Orientation

Healthy families had an open systems view of life, that is, they knew that people do not prosper in a vacuum, that they need each other

Summary of Healthy and Dysfunctional Families

Characteristics	Healthy Family	Dysfunctional Family
Family goals or purpose	There is a sense of community to which all members make unique contributions.	Individual objectives are placed ahead of interests of the family; uniqueness is unacceptable. Goals are rigidly pursued and all members must work in the same way to attain them.
Boundaries	Members are aware of their individual identities and also have the pleasure of sharing in the lives of other family members; boundaries can change readily to meet family needs.	Boundaries are unclear to family members and to outside observers. They may be rigid and not permit movement during the family life cycle.
Roles	Roles are fulfilled in a complementary manner. There is satisfaction in role fulfillment. Roles may be changed.	Roles are undefined. Members try rigidly to fulfill all roles in a symmetrical manner. Children and parents may reverse roles.
Power	Parents hold the most power with the children contributing to decisions. Parents are skillful and resourceful in handling challenges.	There are constant parent–child clashes. Children manipulate to gain influence. Parents are in conflict with each other, or there are parent–child coalitions again the remainder of the family.
Rules	Flexible and negotiable limits are set by the parents. The rules are given and accepted with a sense of caring for each other.	Rules are rigid or chaotic, implicit, and constantly changing.
Communication	Congruent messages are sent. Messages are direct, clear, and open. When there are differences of opinion, the content of a message focuses on the issue, not on the person.	Double messages are constantly being sent. Persons do not respond to the messages being sent; messages contain hidden agendas that are not understood. Emotional content may be missing from most messages, or messages may be primarily emotional.

for input, stimulation, feedback, and relationship. Human needs are best satisfied in an interpersonal context. As a child develops and matures, he or she leaves the family to enter another system, such as college, career, or marriage. He or she must develop interpersonal skills to adapt to the next system. Healthy families accepted the inevitable changes that occur with growth and development and defined maturity as the evolution of new relationships. People were viewed as social beings who grow up, leave home, and necessarily establish new relationships.

The rules of optimal families were compatible with those found in the larger society. People with very different values find it harder to leave home, and are more vulnerable in their passage into the larger system. Compatibility of rules increases the chances of healthy functioning and ease of movement through the family life stages.

Healthy families recognized that causes and effects are interchangeable. Dysfunctional families looked for simple causes for their difficulty, such as fate or destiny, or a bad seed within the household, or human perversity, rather than assuming personal responsibility. Optimally healthy families recognized that hostility in one person promotes deception in others, and that deception promotes hostility.

The third difference was that healthy families saw human behavior as resulting from many causes whereas dysfunctional families were trapped by linear ruts, inflexible cognitive sets, and stereotyped relationship patterns.

Finally, healthy families possessed an awareness of the finiteness of time, and of the fact that humans are limited in power, and that self-esteem lies in achieving competence.

Dysfunctional families attempted to gain absolute control over their children. Healthy families knew that negotiation is essential for success in the human enterprise and that individual choice must be respected.

Boundary Issues

Optimal family members were actively involved in the community. These contacts were shared with the family and brought excitement and interest to family discussions. Some families emphasized intellectual and cultural activities; others, athletic interests; and still others, political and social interests.

This openness to the viewpoints of others contributed to the open-system functioning of optimal families. Openness to the world increased their ability to alter their views of reality and themselves and eliminated the need to live in two worlds—the mythic and the unacknowledged ''real'' world.

The optimal families had clear boundaries between members. Mother, father, and children had specific viewpoints that were respected by the others. Negotiation within the family was prevalent; it consisted of accepting those differences and working toward shared goals. The family was highly differentiated and power was shared within the family so that even the very young children's views were valued and sought during the deliberations.

This respect for the individual made it possible to achieve high levels of intimacy within optimal families. Members of the family shared opinions freely without fear of rebuke. In deciding on family plans, compromise was usually unnecessary as the individual goals of family members could be expressed within the group plans.

Contextual Clarity

Optimal families had interactional patterns that were clear and hidden messages were seldom evident. Body language was congruant with verbal messages.

Optimal family members had a clear definition of generational boundaries, and although power was shared, there was no question as to who was parent and who was child. There was a clear definition of roles for both parents and children. No parent felt the need to give up his or her adult power, and no child was obliged to assume premature responsibility. This clear definition of relationship made it possible to develop closeness and warmth within the family system.

Contextual clarity began with a strong parental coalition, in both functional and affectional terms. Both partners had relatively equal power, and pleasure was obtained in open, congruent and above-board interaction.

Power Issues

In optimal families there was a clear hierarchy of power with leadership in the hands of the parents, who formed an egalitarian relationship. The children were less overtly powerful, but their contributions influenced decisions. Power struggles seldom occurred and family tasks were undertaken with good-humored effectiveness.

Optimal families demonstrated complementary parental roles. This complementarity allowed for equal distribution of power without competitiveness and rivalry.

Mid-range families tended to insist on referee-oriented symmetrical roles and felt that both partners should work outside the home and share the housework and child care equally. None of the healthy families studied had such symmetry. Long-term and short-term complementarity and role differentiation seemed necessary to allow pleasant interaction.

Optimal families sometimes deliberately expressed authoritarian control to enforce rules. This allowed the family, when under undue pressure, to revert to a more control-oriented style if necessary. Since these families were seldom under great stress, they did not need to resort to these methods of control very often.

Encouragement of Autonomy

Optimal families possessed the following qualities:

1. Ability of family members to take responsibility for individual thoughts, feelings, and behavior.
2. Openness to communication from others.
3. Respect for the unique and subjective views of others.
4. Minimum reliance on an omniscient referee.

Family members expressed their views clearly. There was little blaming and personal attack, and no internal scapegoating. Members of the family could fail without feeling a loss of face. They could be open, candid, and vulnerable. Honesty was expected, with resulting family trust. One was not punished for telling the truth as he or she knew it, and thus lying was unnecessary.

Affective Issues

Optimal families had a warm and optimistic feeling tone and an impressive emotional intensity. Family members were interested in each other, and their transactions were filled with affirmations. Caring, warmth, and hope for the future characterized their interactions. There was a general openness to feelings. Anger was expressed and acknowledged, and, whenever possible, adjustments were made. Nonhostile humor was frequent and served a powerful purpose in evoking light laughter.

Optimal families scored high on empathy. Members had the capacity not only to predict each other's quality or state of thought or feeling, but also to share in another's subjective experience without loss of the individual self-boundaries.

Negotiation and Task Performance

The optimal families showed great capacity to accept directions, organize themselves to respond to tasks, develop input from other members, negotiate differences, and provide an effective response to problem solving. The family functioned smoothly. Ideas from everyone were integrated and plans of action developed with input from all family members.

Transcendent Values

Optimal families viewed life through a conceptual and relationship system broader than themselves or the family. This helped them to make sense of events and of the world, to accept the losses of loved ones, and to recognize the finiteness of human life.

Optimal families fostered transcendent meaning systems that allowed them to center themselves in the universe and to give meaning to their lives. Such centering was found in conventional religions or in individuals with values and goals incorporated in a transcendent system of beliefs and values.

In the continuing debate on healthy and dysfunctional families, Constantine (1984) has developed a useful perspective on open families. A comparative summary is provided on page 32.

References

Aponte, H. J., & Van Deusen, J. M. Structural family therapy. In A. S. Gurman & D. Kniskern (Eds.), *Handbook of family therapy*. New York: Brunner/Mazel, 1981.

Beavers, W. R. *Psychotherapy and growth: A family systems perspective*. New York: Brunner/Mazel, 1977.

Constantine, L. L. Dysfunction and failure in open family systems. *Journal of Marital and Family Therapy*, 1984, *10*, 1–17.

Lewis, J. M., Beavers, W. R., Gossett, J. T., & Phillips, V. A. *No single thread: Psychological health in family systems*. New York: Brunner/Mazel, 1976.

Luthman, S., & Kirschenbaum, N. *The dynamic family*. Palo Alto, Calif.: Science and Behavior Books, 1974.

Minuchin, S. *Families and family therapy*. Cambridge, Mass.: Harvard University Press, 1974.

Skynner, A. C. An open-systems, group analytic approach to family therapy. In A. Gurman & D. Kniskern (Eds.), *Handbook of family therapy*. New York: Brunner/Mazel, 1981.

Stanton, M. Marital therapy from a structural/strategic viewpoint. In G. P. Sholevan (Ed.), *The handbook of marriage and marital therapy*. New York: S.P. Medical and Scientific Books, 1981.

Watzlawick, P., Beavin, J., & Jackson, D. D. *Pragmatics of human communication*. New York: W. W. Norton, 1967.

2.2 FAMILY LIFE CYCLE

One useful way to conceptualize the family system is in terms of the developmental stages that occur over time. Each family that remains intact (husband and wife are married with children remaining in the home at least until their late teens) passes through similar developmental processes. Critical transition points (such as marriage, birth of the first child, retirement) occur in all families and bring predictable stresses to all family members.

We are aware that not all families remain intact, that not all families have children, and that some couples get married much later in life than others. Even though all families do not follow the identical developmental patterns in precisely the same time frame, a developmental framework is helpful in understanding family dynamics.

Various conceptual frameworks have been designed to describe a family developmental life cycle (Duval, 1977, Scherz, 1971; Rhodes, 1977; Solomon, 1973). An adaptation of these frameworks is presented in the following.

Stage 1: Premarital—the courtship period

Stage 2: Early marriage—marriage with no children

Stage 3: Childbearing years—birth of first child to 6 years of age

Stage 4: Children in school—first child from 6 to 18 years of age

Stage 5: Reduction in family size—first to last child leaves home

Stage 6: Empty nest—last child leaves home to parental retirement

Stage 7: Advanced age—retirement to death of both spouses

Within each stage there are common psychological tasks that need to be completed for the family to continue to develop in a healthy manner. When tasks in a particular stage of development are not adequately completed, a crisis may occur in the family and a dysfunction may arise at some future stage in the life cycle (Rapoport, 1965). For example, a beginning

A Comparative Summary of Healthy and Dysfunctional
Open Families

Dimensions	Healthy	Dysfunctional
Problem solving	Environment viewed as manageable, and trustworthy. Open to input from contexts. Sensitive to external cues. Logical search for solutions. Objective evaluation of data, freely exchanged. Delay closure until maximum of evidence is analyzed. Consensus on solutions sought. Effective starting on projects and committed to completion	Inability to surmount difficulties. Overly sensitive to cues; take in excessive, inappropriate, or irrelevant cues. Persist in logical research in overly emotional context. Inundation with information that defies objective analysis. Procrastination, and excess evidence sought. Projects tend to be unfinished and overwhelming, seldom are abandoned.
Sexuality, marital relationships	Validation and acceptance of sexuality over life cycle.	Permissive sexually with tendency to overeroticism, sexual deviance, or perverse sexual behavior.
Parent–child relationships	Nurturant, affectionate, effective involvement. Democratic, egalitarian with negotiated limits. Responsible, with freedom and suitable demands.	Enmeshed boundaries. Parental abdication with boundaries ill defined. Overeroticized and potentially incestuous. Child is independent too early and has excessive responsibility.
Process, communication	Flexibly connected, authentic, emotion sharing, free expression. Tolerance for ambiguity but investment in closure. Open expression of differences, "having it out." Willing expression of thoughts and feelings.	Chaotically connected, large emotional mood swings, emotional "burlesque." Conflict habituated. Excessive pursuit of solution with unrelenting ambiguity and ambivalence. Intrusive, invasion of personal privacy.
Roles	Flexible, individuals freely take initiative. Definitions adaptable.	Excessively fluid; individuals shift responsibility and blame. Definitions are ambiguous, and individuals aggressive, and/or sexually acting out. Symptoms of stress, and exhaustion from the process are present.

Adapted from Constantine, L. L. Dysfunction and failure in open family systems. *Journal of Marital and Family Therapy*, 1984, *10*, 1–17.

family without children may not complete the first-stage task of role assignment and this will continue as a point of conflict. When the first child is added to the family, there are increased duties in the home and the task of role assignment becomes a greater stress. Dysfunction may become evident (e.g., depression by the wife regarding her inability to maintain employment, household duties, and give primary care). To move toward health, the role-definition task that was not completed in the stage of early marriage will need to be pursued. Furthermore the process by which role definitions are determined may need to be examined (e.g., conflict-resolution skills, communication).

Premarriage

In the first stage, premarriage, the major issue is the choice of and commitment to one person. Many of the activities at this stage are related to parental and peer pressure, and the choice of a marital partner. The degree to which the individual has become independent from parents and holds values similar to those of the parents will influence the level of difficulty at this stage.

The ability to establish relational qualities such as trust and intimacy along with personal qualities of self-acceptance and identity are major factors in the formation of a long-term, healthy relationship. The discovery of common recreational interests, basic values, expectations, and long-term goals in life are also issues that influence the establishment of a healthy premarital relationship.

Early Marriage

In the second stage, early marriage, the basic task is the development of a marital relationship based on a realistic perception of the partner rather than on a romantic notion or idealization. In the difficult task of moving from an over-emphasis on romantic notions to realistic perceptions, couples may, for example, react by temporarily withdrawing, and terminating the relationship, or by remaining in the relationship and creating rigid patterns of interaction, or by confronting each other and working at "coming together" (Rhodes, 1977).

Tasks that are important at this stage are developing sexual compatibility, balancing autonomy with interdependence, and accommodating to an affordable standard of living. During this period the couple needs to invest itself in the roles of husband and wife, to alter the relationships with friends that interfere with the marital activities, and to modify earlier patterns to fit the marital relationship (Rapoport, 1965).

Childbearing Years

The third stage, the childbearing years, begins with the birth of the first child and continues until the child is 6 years old. The key issue involves the development of nurturing patterns within the family. Until the arrival of the first child, the marital partners may have been dependent on each other; and had the capacity to care for and support each other. Upon arrival of the first child, the parenting tasks are so demanding, and the physical energies so depleted, that there is considerable stress on the marriage (Rhodes, 1977). Failure to find resources may result in the family focusing in on itself.

Changing tasks to which the couple must adapt are related to the new parental roles, a reduction in income if the wife ceases outside employment, greater dependency of the children, and ensuing life-style changes. During this time a spouse may become overinvolved with a child, resulting in further stress on the marital relationship.

Children in School

In the fourth stage, in which the children are in school and the eldest child is between 6 years old and old enough to leave home, family energies that have been directed toward dependent children can be directed to activities outside of the immediate family. Until this point the children have required almost constant parental observation and care. The focus of time spent with children has tended to be intrafamilial. When children begin to attend school, the range of family interests can broaden and new friends, ideas, adult contacts, and independent learning experiences may be encountered. Parent influence may be challenged and counterdependency developed in the children. Conflicts may be generated by parents whose identity is bound up in their children, particularly on the part of the primary care giver (Rhodes, 1977).

When parents are overprotective of their children, for example, not allowing any peer relationships to develop in the community, or viewing all outside influences as bad, rigid and inflexible boundaries are created and energy is used to maintain the status quo. Children are not allowed to feel comfortable unless they move within the confines of the family.

The marital relationship also faces changes at this point. Couples may categorize themselves as ''good'' or ''bad'' on the basis of their ''success'' in parenting, and thus affect the way in which they value themselves and their relationship. Financial needs of the family are great at this point. Parental unity is challenged by teenagers who grow in independence during this stage and explore the borders of family rules on issues ranging from sexuality to occupational choice.

Reduction in Family Size

The fifth stage, the reduction in family size resulting from the eldest child leaving home and lasting until all the children have left, is often very difficult in a marriage relationship. The major task during this stage is to support the children as they leave. Families that have rigid rules may react in one of two ways: cause children to leave at an early age, or impose and enforce restrictions so that children are fearful and unprepared to leave home. Families in which children leave early are often marked by open conflict and tension, while those children who stay unusually long may be part of a marital triangle (for example, a son is close to mother, and plays referee in marital conflict) (Rhodes, 1977).

The quality of the marital relationship is a major variable that will indicate the ability of the family to function at this time. This is the first time for any family that the marital relationship will function without primary gratification from children.

Empty Nest

The sixth stage begins with the last child leaving home and ends with parental retirement. This stage:

. . . is the first of two postparental phases. The significance of the tasks is felt when you consider that about 50 percent of a couple's married life cycle is represented by these last two phases. On the other hand, marital dysfunction is so unsettling that there is a high percentage of divorce which terminate the life cycle of the family during these two stages. (Rhodes, 1977, p. 309)

The couple now has freedom to concentrate on the marital relationship and pursue special enjoyments together. The couple may choose to focus on one another, or may elect to put energies into developing new relationships across generations.

The children no longer play a role in conflict resolution, and stress is placed on the couple to be dependent on each other in decision making and conflict resolution. Triangling and other supports provided by the children are no longer available.

Financially the couple is usually at its highest level of earning with the possibility of both partners being employed. The husband is often at the height of his career and has high status.

Advanced Age

Advanced age, the seventh and final stage, which begins with retirement and ends with the death of both spouses, can often be a time of loneliness and sadness; for example, when one partner dies, the other spouse may become increasingly dependent on others, and have to cope with a loss of income. Social networks that have been previously established, such as friends, family, church, and community, are called upon to provide support. There is often a sense of ''uselessness'' when few opportunities for contributing to the community are available. As health fails, the focus of the family is turned inward in an effort to maintain physical well being.

A developmental model for viewing the healthy family has been presented. The key feature is the notion of orderly progression through life stages. What is achieved at one stage is foundational to success in the following stages. Unchecked dysfunction at the early stages is magnified as it develops through the life cycle.

References

Duval, E. M. *Marriage and family development* (5th ed.). New York: Lipincott, 1977.

Goldenberg, I., & Goldenberg, H. *Family therapy: An overview*. Monterrey, Calif.: Wadsworth, 1980.

Rapoport, R. Normal crises, family structure and mental health. In H. J. Parad (Ed.), *Crisis Intervention*. New York: FSAA, 1965.

Rhodes, S. L. A developmental approach to the life cycle of the family. *Social Casework*, 1977, *58*, 301–311.

Scherz, F. Maturational crises and parent–child interaction. *Social Casework*, 1971, *52*, 362–369.

Solomon, M. A. A developmental, conceptual premise for family therapy. *Family Process*, 1973, *12*, 179–196.

2.3 FAMILIES WITH PSYCHOSOMATIC ILLNESS

Beth and David seem to enjoy a happy and harmonious family life. They appear to be married well in spite of David's current unemployment problems. Recently, however, they have become increasingly concerned about their 10-year-old son, Mickey, who has been suffering from asthma attacks. The family therapist wonders whether Mickey's attacks might be psychosomatic symptoms of dysfunction in the family system.

Structural–Strategic theory suggests that certain family relationships are closely related to the development and maintenance of psychosomatic syndromes in children, and that the illness, in turn, contributes to the maintenance of family homeostasis (Garfinkel & Garner, 1982). Minuchen et al. (1978) have described a series of characteristics seen in families with a child who has psychomatic illness. These are presented in the following discussion.

Family Environment

In families with psychosomatic illness, family togetherness and sharing are often given an exaggerated importance, resulting in a lack of individual privacy. There are weak boundaries between individuals. Family members intrude on each other's thoughts and feelings. Individual autonomy and self-realization are sacrificed to achieve family loyalty, closeness, and protection (Garfinkel & Garner, 1982).

Family Overprotectiveness

The psychosomatic family is also often characterized by overprotectiveness. There is an excessive concern for each other's welfare. Children may become self-conscious and very sensitive to family expectations due to parental preoccupation with their behavior. The children in effect become "parent watchers."

An inappropriate and intrusive familial interest in children's psychological and physical functioning retards their development of autonomy, competence, and involvement outside of the family home. Children find it difficult to protest since parental control is expressed as innocent parental concern. In fact disagreement and initiative are viewed as acts of betrayal. Family members, therefore, express their wishes indirectly and unselfishly in keeping with the family spirit of self-sacrifice.

Family Rigidity

The psychosomatic family may be characterized by rigidity, that is, there is a serious commitment to the maintenance of the family status quo (homeostasis). Times of normal growth and change, such as adolescence and early adulthood, and their corresponding demands for increased age-appropriate autonomy, are tense, and even traumatic. Extrafamilial stress such as unemployment or a career change may require adjustments that the family is unable to make, thereby precipitating illness (Garfinkel & Garner, 1982).

Unresolved Family Conflict

The psychosomatic family is further characterized by a lack of ability to resolve conflict. Harmony is highly prized in spite of a low family threshold for conflict. Such a family needs to learn conflict-resolution skills (Garfinkel & Garner, 1982).

The Child Factors

The child's involvement in parental conflict is a key factor in the development and main-

tenance of psychosomatic symptoms. At least two patterns of child involvement in parental conflict have been identified (Minuchen et al., 1978).

First there is triangulation in which a child is openly encouraged to side with one parent against the other. Alternatively the child switches sides from one parent to another, depending on the circumstances, or the child enters a more stable coalition with one parent against the other.

Second there is detouring, in which the parents submerge their conflict in a joint effort either to blame or protect their sick child, who functions as an "avoidance circuit" (Garfinkel & Garner, 1982). Moreover the characteristics and patterns described must not be construed as the single pathogenic factor in families with psychosomatic illness, but as one variable in interaction with other variables within the individual to produce a specific psychosomatic disorder.

Finally, it is important to stress that these characteristics and patterns may be only describing the nature of families with psychosomatic illness, and, in fact, may prove to be unrelated to the cause(s) of such illness in a family member (Garfinkel & Garner, 1982). Probably the causes of psychosomatic illness are multidimensional. The family is one strand in the mosaic of determinants.

References

Garfinkel, P., & Garner, D. *Anorexia nervosa: A multidimensional perspective.* New York: Brunner/Mazel, 1982.
Minuchen, S., Rosman, B., & Baker, L. *Psychosomatic families.* Cambridge, Mass.: Harvard University Press, 1978.

2.4 ANOREXIA AND THE FAMILY

The study and treatment of anorexia nervosa have proceeded along several interwoven dimensions. The psychoanalytic school has focused primarily on the psychodynamics of the individual, with some attention given to the dyadic relationship problems such as the mother–daughter relationship in early childhood. Other researchers have concerned themselves particularly with the current interactions in the mother–daughter dyad or the disturbed father–daughter relationship. Still others have focused on the conflict within the marital dyad.

In the past 20–30 years, family therapy concepts have been used to explain anorexia nervosa. For example, Minuchin et al. (1978) developed a nonspecific model for psychosomatic disorders from a Structural family therapy perspective. According to this model, anorexic families are enmeshed, have a poor boundary structure between individuals and between generations, have an inability to resolve conflict, and are overprotective and overly concerned about each other's welfare.

Clinical studies of anorexic families suggest that these families emphasize the themes of closeness, avoidance of conflict at all costs, unrealistic expectations, no separate emotional existence, and an inability to tolerate sexuality.

In some families the anorexic acts as a buffer between parents. This is especially the case during illness, when the parents focus all their anxiety on the anorexic; thus the anorexic becomes the burden bearer for the family. In other cases a female anorexic is in a competitive relationship with her mother. She 'mothers' her siblings, and her father, and freely shares domestic duties, such as cooking for the family. By sharing the mothering role, the anorexic establishes close contact with her and on occasions acts as her mother's comforter, replacing the absent father.

Whatever future studies reveal about the role of the anorexic in the family, it is clear that at the onset of illness, he or she becomes a very central and powerful influence in the family. The anorexic takes advantage of this power and often manipulates the family to serve his or her viewpoints by simply varying the food intake.

On the surface, families of anorexics do not appear overly disturbed. They seem well adjusted without much divorce occurring between the parents. During therapy, however, the disillusionment with each other often appears. The competition between the spouses in regard to making the greatest sacrifice may surface. The mothers are often achievement oriented. Career mothers are often frustrated by the many demands of work and home. They appear submissive to their husbands without truly respecting them. The fathers are often successful in their career but feel a lack of fulfillment in their life.

In the following section, a number of therapy interventions are proposed. Many of these suggested interventions have been adopted from Schwartz et al. (1984).

Treatment of Anorexic Families

As in individual therapy, the treatment of each anorexic family needs to be tailored to the needs of that family. There are no easy answers and no recipes for the treatment of anorexic families. Nevertheless a number of guidelines and principles of treatment may be identified.

The treatment process might involve the following procedures:

1. *Differentiation*. Family members are motivated toward differentiation. This should be done early in the treatment process so that the symptom is not reactivated by old family patterns.

2. *Challenging themes*. The framework of themes that maintain the symptom is challenged. Family themes such as ''closeness'' lead anorexic families into severe power struggles and unending disputes.

3. *Restraining*. In individual sessions it may be desirable for the therapist to take a re-

straining position by asking the client, ''Are you sure that you are ready to give up this behavior that has become such an important part of your life?'' Anorexics have become intimate with their symptom, and to leave it may seem frightening to them.

4. *Symptom separation*. Food is a safe battleground where family members can indirectly express their feelings of hostility toward each other. To remove the symptom would result in the loss of an important source of interaction with significant others. To alleviate this concern, the therapist might track the family's attempts to solve the problem, empathize with the family's frustrations and ineffectiveness, and give the family a ''vacation'' from these efforts.

5. *Developing personal control*. Statements such as, ''You will be in control of your symptoms when you are in more control of your life and relationships,'' help the client to frame the problem as a life-style problem rather than a medical concern to be remedied by some pills.

6. *The use of directives*. The therapist might ask the client to become depressed for specific periods each day about the issues he or she should feel depressed about. The family members are asked to remove themselves from the client so that he or she may have privacy and become depressed.

Other directives may be given to help the client develop a sense of personal control, autonomy, and individuation. Still other directives may help the client break rigid patterns of interpersonal interaction.

7. *Intensification*. The process of challenging themes and interaction patterns is intensified. Having established trust, rapport, and a therapeutic relationship with family members, the therapist may now take a more firm position with the family and challenge destructive patterns of interaction.

8. *Redirecting energies*. Family members are helped to break old themes and dysfunctional patterns of interaction and to redirect their energies more satisfactorily.

9. *Reframing*. Family members are helped to view the symptom as an attempt to show concern for family closeness rather than an oppressive and destructive underlying attitude.

10. *Forming independence*. Once the family members have learned to deal with each other directly, it should be possible for the anorexic to begin the process of developing independence from the family, such as finding a career, making friends, and launching from the family in a satisfactory manner.

11. *Developing alternative behavior and thought patterns*. By tracking old patterns and internal conflicts, the anorexic may begin to discover alternative behaviors and interactions. The therapist should encourage and support the client in practicing these new behaviors.

12. *Prescription of rituals*. The therapist may exaggerate the symptom to the point of absurdity by prescribing the symptom or behaviors associated with it. This may involve preparing very appetizing food and then throwing it away, and having friends and relatives observe the ritual.

13. *Community networks*. It is important for members of the family, including the anorexic, to develop relationships in the community. This, however, should not result in moving dependency from family members to dependency upon community members, friends, or significant others.

14. *Consolidating Change*. The therapist may help the client deal with feelings of isolation, dependence, protectiveness, and self-deprecation by prescribing a relapse and then dealing with the themes and interactions that result from such a relapse.

References

Bandler, R., & Grinder, J. *Reframing*. Moab, Utah: Real People Press, 1982.

Fisch, R., Weakland, J., & Segal, L. *The tactics of change*. San Francisco: Jossey/Bass, 1982.

Haley, J. *Problem-solving therapy*. San Francisco: Jossey/Bass, 1976.

Madanes, C. *Strategic family therapy*. San Francisco: Jossey/Bass, 1981.

Minuchin, S. *Families and family therapy*. Cambridge, Mass.: Harvard University Press, 1974.

Minuchin, S., & Fishman, C. *Family therapy techniques*. Cambridge, Mass.: Harvard University Press, 1983.

Minuchin, S., Rosman, B., & Baker, L. *Psychosomatic families: Anorexia nervosa in context*. Cambridge, Mass.: Harvard University Press, 1978.

Schwartz, R. C. Bulimia and family therapy: A case study. *International Journal of Eating Disorders*, 1982, 2, 75—82.

Schwartz, R. C., Barrett, M. J., & Saba, G. *Family therapy for bulima*. Unpublished manuscript, University of Illinois College of Medicine, 1984.

Selvini-Palazzoli, M., Boscolo, L., Cecchin, G., & Prata, G. *Paradox and counter paradox*. New York: Jason Aronson, 1978.

CHAPTER 3

COUPLE AND FAMILY DYNAMICS

3.1 INTERACTION PATTERNS OF COUPLES

Individuals in close relationships such as marriage often develop consistently repeating interaction patterns. Some patterns, such as sequences of love making and support, facilitate satisfaction in marriage. Other patterns such as blaming/placating or sequences of conflict, are dysfunctional and distressing.

In this section we discuss the nature of interaction patterns as repetitive communication sequences between members of a couple. Descriptions of interaction patterns are abundant. Examples include ''games people play'' such as: ''I'm right, you're wrong,'' ''I don't want to discuss it,'' ''It's all your fault'' (Berne, 1964).

Games are social rituals that are repetitive dyadic maneuvers which combine defensive and offensive tactics and are used to avoid intimacy with the partner. Furthermore games are well defined with predictable outcomes and patterns that repeat over time.

a couple in which the roles of the members are similar. An example is ''cross-complaining,'' in which a complaint by one individual is met with a complaint by the other. Asymmetrical communication patterns occur when members of a couple take different, mutually complementary roles in the interaction. In a blaming/calming interaction, one member of a couple blames, while the partner's role is to calm and placate the blamer.

Asymmetrical interactive patterns are evident in many family interactions and are often discussed in the clinical literature. Psychoanalysis views these patterns as complementary character defenses or complementary needs. A person high in the need for dominance may choose a partner who is low in this need and so readily submits.

Some interaction patterns may be satisfying to a couple while others may involve differences that polarize and cause misunderstanding. Misunderstanding between the couple will arise when one member perceives that his or her needs are not being met. In such a situation, serious conflict will occur unless the couple has the skills necessary to negotiate a resolution of the unsatisfying interaction.

Symmetrical and Asymmetrical Patterns

Interaction patterns are of two kinds: symmetrical and asymmetrical. Symmetrical communications are sequences between members of

Dysfunctional Asymmetrical Patterns

Asymmetrical patterns that are dysfunctional to the relationship polarize the couple and bring out the worst behavior in each member. Each spouse tries to change the behavior of the other by use of coercive control, although the style of coercion may differ. For example, he may nag, she may withdraw; he may blame, she may use guilt induction. Such interactive patterns may become rigid over time and very difficult to change.

In systems theory such interaction is termed a positive feedback cycle and is characterized by increasing polarization as the partners of the relationship try to extricate themselves through coercive activity. In family Structural terms, although such a couple may appear distant and disengaged, its members, in fact, are emotionally enmeshed with each other.

As the couple continues to fight, the members become increasingly emotionally involved with each other and lose their sense of personal identity. They begin to define themselves in terms of the other instead of examining their own personal behavior and motives. Such members of a couple need to extricate themselves from their struggle and develop a more differentiated ego structure.

Attributional Processes

As the distress in the relationship increases, the couple tends to search for causes of the trouble. Usually each perceives the behavior of the partner as responsible for the distress. Thus each attributes the partner's unsavory traits as the source of the problem, but fails to see his or her own role in the development and maintenance of the difficulty. One of the causes of the conflict is that couples tend to view interaction as linear, instead of circular. By being helped to punctuate the sequence as circular, the members come to different conclusions about the conflict. In a circular sequence, both spouses contribute to the coercive pattern.

A number of clinically used asymmetrical patterns may be identified in the literature. Sullaway and Christensen (1983) identify the following patterns: introvert/extrovert, flirtatious/jealous, assertive/nonassertive, more/less involved, repress/express emotions, less/more devoted to partner, dependent/independent, relationship/work oriented, emotional/rational, demand/withdraw, leader/follower, and cautious/committed. These asymmetrical patterns may not necessarily lead to conflict in the marriage. However, they may become "perverse" and lead to misunderstanding between the members of the couple.

Games

In some ways similar to the transactional patterns, couples may also play games that represent dyadic maneuvers that combine offensive and defensive tactics (Berne, 1964). In Adlerian terms the games are representative of a "lifestyle" (Dreikurs, 1967) or in TA terms, they reflect a "life script" (Berne, 1964). Fundamentally, however, games describe a number of stylized, conflictual, interactive patterns that are often present in dyadic relationships.

A number of such games have been identified. Some of them, adapted from the work of Mozdzierz and Lottman (1978), are presented here together with a list of the rules that govern them.

Game No. 1: "This is War!"

This is an open, explicit, and manipulative game. By use of a verbal club, each partner engages in an escalating cycle of attacks, counterattacks, and retaliation. The transaction, however, is a deception because it covers up the underlying motive of revenge, which may be hurt feelings. The rules of the game are:

1. Hurt your spouse's feelings more than you are hurt.
2. Attack your spouse at his or her weakest point.
3. Attack your spouse's family, friends, occupation, and so on.
4. Never intimate something nice about your spouse.

Game No. 2: "I'm Right. You're Wrong!"

This is a very popular game and can be played with many variations. The rules of the game are:

1. Both participants must claim exclusive possession of the real facts and deny the possibility of each other's access to them.
2. Statements are never presented as impressions or feelings, but as absolute facts.
3. Any third party 'in attendance' will be made judge or referee, whether a therapist, child, or relative.

Game No. 3: "I've Got the Debit. You've Got the Credit."

A ledger is kept of the balances in the interpersonal transactions so that one spouse always feels cheated. The rules of the game are:

1. Assume that your spouse will always try to short-change you.
2. A spouse's enjoyment must never be shared; insist that it be counterbalanced by your own opportunity for fun.
3. Always keep tabs on the activities of your spouse.

Game No. 4: "Pay Attention"

Both spouses can play this game. It involves a mutual shouting contest or a one-sided nagging affair. The goal is desperately to seek intense involvement with the spouse. Being ignored by a significant person is considered equivalent to not existing. If positive attention seeking fails, the person may turn to negative behaviors such as physical abuse or attempted suicide. The rules of the game are:

1. Never be silent in the presence of your spouse.
2. Always announce what you are going to do, for example, "I think I will sit down for a while."
3. Constantly ask permission from your spouse.
4. Require your spouse's assistance in everything you do.
5. Cultivate habits that annoy your spouse, such as arranging his or her clothes or books.

Game No. 5: "I Don't Want to Discuss It."

This game makes one spouse invincible. The spouse cannot lose the game because he or she is playing it by himself or herself. By the disdain the spouse shows, he or she takes the one-up position. The spouse is too mature, rational, or moral to engage in the conflict. Usually the game is played to avoid losing another battle. The rules are:

1. Never show irritation at the remarks of your spouse.
2. Whenever possible employ some method of dissociation: turn your head, close your eyes, leave the room.
3. Can be played even if you are wrong and cannot or will not admit it.

Game No. 6: "It's All Your Fault."

This game is encountered most often when one spouse has demonstrated symptomatic behavior and becomes the identified patient. The other spouse is then free to assume no responsibility. The rules are:

1. Strike first! The attacker has the advantage while the spouse moves to a defensive position.
2. Accuse your spouse of total liability for the issue. As long as the spouse is on the defensive, he or she is unable to score points.
3. Obtain the consensus of family, friends,

and relatives that the problem lies with the spouse.

4. Never consider what your part is in the situation.

Game No. 7: "Where Would You Be Without Me?"

One spouse develops the position of superiority or by simultaneously declaring his or her own unselfishness, and goodness and the other spouse as weak, worthless, and ungrateful. The purpose of the game is to defend against perceived inferiority. The wife might, for example, remind her husband that, ''I wash your clothes, fix your meals, raise your kids, lie to your boss, etc.'' The rules are:

1. Marry someone who is lazy, unattractive, uneducated, or from a lower social class. This act of benevolence can be traded for an entire marriage of demands.

2. Assume total responsibility for your spouse, if not in the present, at least in the past.

3. If the spouse questions your sacrificial qualities, take the spouse home to his or her conflictual family or home, and then constantly remind him or her of what you observed and what you saved your spouse from.

Recognizing Games in Therapy

1. Pronouns used in speech. The spouse's use of pronouns such as you, she, or he is directing attention away from his or her behavior and is indicative of a game.

2. Alliance maneuvers. When a spouse tries to align with the therapist against the other spouse, game behavior appears evident.

3. Impressions presented as facts. When feelings are presented as fact, a game is present. For example, ''He treats me as dirt,'' is a powerful weapon against the other spouse.

4. Feelings of the therapist. When the therapist feels frustrated, angry, and ineffective, a game is probably going on in the session.

Dealing with Games

1. Distinguish facts/impressions. Problem solving is increased by having each spouse transform his or her accusations by using prefatory phrases such as ''I feel'' or ''It seems to me.''

2. Enactment. Have couples act out their games; have them described and the implications assessed. New patterns are then learned.

3. Address all comments to the therapist. If a couple gains control of the session through game behavior, the therapist could interrupt the session and ask that all comments be directed to her or him.

4. Prescribing the symptom. Whenever the therapist finds he or she cannot intervene in the system, it may be appropriate to prescribe the symptom. Thus the implicit rules are made explicit and the couple is requested to act out that behavior.

The net effect of this is that the labeling devalues the prize of superiority. The ''winner'' has not achieved his or her position of ''one-upmanship'' and his or her behavior now seems silly.

References

Berne, E. *Games people play*. New York: Grove Press, 1964.

Dreikurs, R. *Psychodynamics, psychotherapy and counselling*. Chicago: Alfred Adler Institute, 1967.

Mozdzierz, G., & Lottman, T. Games married couples play. Manuscript, Vancouver, 1978.

Sullaway, M., & Christensen, A. Assessment of dysfunctional interaction patterns in couples. *Journal of Marriage and Family*, 1983, *45*, 653–659.

3.2 THE ROLE OF SYMPTOMS

Symptoms form an important component of family dynamics in family systems theory, but are interpreted differently than in individual or psychodynamic therapy theory. Psychodynamic theories view symptoms as idiosyncratic entities resulting from conflicts within an individual and between various parts of the individual psyche. Family system theories, on the other hand, view symptoms as the result of conflicts within the family as a unit.

While there are differing views on the role of symptoms, there is general agreement in family theory that symptoms develop to help balance or alleviate stress between family members within the family system. Thus symptoms are observed as behavioral, physical, or emotional signs of disorder or dysfunction in the family resulting in symptomatology such as alcoholism or delinquency.

Role of Symptoms in Homeostatic Relationships

All families develop patterns of behaving as well as patterns for responding to stressful anx-iety-producing situations. Homeostasis is the self-maintaining device that operates to return a family to equilibrium when it is unbalanced. For example, if a thermostat is set so that the normal temperature of the house is 68°F, then when the temperature drops below 68°F, the heating system will automatically turn on. If, on the other hand, the temperature rises above 75°F, the air conditioning system will automatically turn on, thereby lowering the temperature (Goldenberg & Goldenberg, 1980). A visual picture might be helpful as in Figure 3.2.1.

When a family member's behavior exceeds the normal range of behavior as defined by family rules, a crisis occurs and the homeostatic mechanisms attempt to reestablish equilibrium. Symptoms are some of the homeostatic mechanisms that are used to relieve stress, bringing the family back into the normal range of behavior (see Figure 3.2.1).

In Figures 3.2.2 and 3.2.3, the mother and father are evidencing a stressful relationship. The son begins to act in a delinquent manner. This behavior focuses the parents attention away from themselves, relieving the stress in their relationship, and onto the son. They gather around him to deal with his problem. As the son gets better, the focus of concern and anxiety returns to the parents' relationship which becomes stressful once again, thus retriggering the son's delinquent behavior.

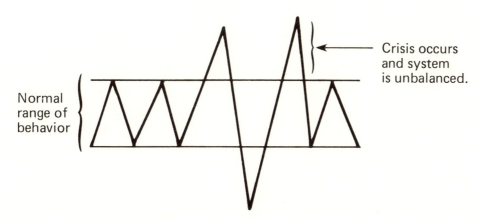

Figure 3.2.1. A cybernetic system

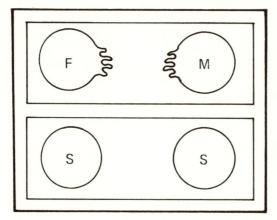

Figure 3.2.2. A conflictual spouse system

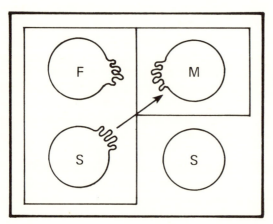

Figure 3.2.3. Parent–child triangulation

Symptoms and the Life Cycle

Both Structural and Strategic family theorists see a strong connection between the inability of the family to work through a development stage and symptomatic behavior. For instance, if members of a family are having difficulties coping with the stage where adolescents begin to leave home, the stress might trigger symptomatic behavior.

Minuchin (1981) gives the example of a family with a 17-year-old daughter who was not attending school and was failing classes. When the family gathered for therapy, Minuchin observed that the mother was distant and uninvolved, while the daughter took charge of the family, introduced the siblings, disciplined, and so on. He deduced that the daughter was taking on a parent role in a disorganized family and was having trouble separating from the family. Thus because of her heavy parenting responsibilities, school was of secondary importance.

Structural Perspectives

Structural family theory views the family as an organism with regulatory mechanisms that operate in times of stress or pain. Structuralists understand symptomological behavior as the regulatory mechanism or safety valve in the family system (Minuchin, 1981). As stress enters the family system, the system reacts. If this reaction continues, forming a pattern, symptomological behavior results.

Usually the symptom focuses on one person, who acts as the reliever of the stress for the family as a whole. The family then looks at this person as the individual who has the problem in the family (the identified patient or LP). The therapist, however, sees the whole family as acting out symptomological behavior, not just the IP. It is the task of the therapist to help the family redefine both the nature of the problem and its view of the IP.

Strategic Perspectives

Strategic theories of family dynamics view symptomological behavior as a protective solution in which the identified patient sacrifices himself or herself for the sake of establishing equilibrium in the family. Though the sacrifice is meant to be a positive offering, it usually ends up making the stress in the family worse. The symptom is often a kind of unconscious contract between two or more members of the family that has an interpersonal function within the family system. The symptom has a homeostatic or regulatory effect in the family, couple, or individual, and develops when a pattern of behavior becomes rigid and seemingly unalterable by any means except by symptomatic behavior.

An example of a symptomatic behavior is the continuing dysfunctional behavior of parents coping with a growing family. The couple's relationship is under much stress while the couple is trying to work out the parenting roles. If the stress continues, one of the children might begin to act in a particularly dysfunctional way. For example, the child might become increasingly ill or begin to skip school and fail classes. The parental focus then shifts from the stress to helping the child get well or return to more normal school attendance and grades. Thus by the child sacrificing health and school work, the stress between the parents is eased.

In Figure 3.2.4 a graphic representation of

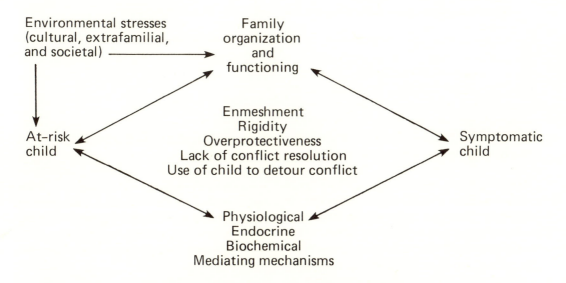

Figure 3.2.4. Model of symptom formation

symptom formation is presented. Note that there is no beginning or end point, that the symptom can be activated at any point and has feedback mechanisms operating at several places. The child and other family members regulate each other according to family rules to form a homeostatic system.

As can be seen from this discussion, symptoms play an important role in helping us to understand Structural and Strategic theories. While the particular focus is different, the basic understandings are similar in all system theories. Symptoms are assigned the role of reducing anxiety in the family system.

References

Goldenberg, H., & Goldenberg, I. *Family therapy: An overview*. Monterrey, Calif.: Brooks/Cole, 1980.

Gurman, A., & Kniskern, D. *Handbook of family therapy*. New York: Brunner/Mazel, 1981.

Depression and Marital Conflict

Depression is usually viewed as a symptom of individual pathology. It is assumed the problem resides within the individual, that is his construction of reality, or on physiological factors, or intrapsychic processes. In contrast to such a perspective, the Structural-Strategic understanding of depression focuses on the relationship dimensions that is on friends, family, peers and employer. Depression is reviewed as a symptom of interpersonal dynamics.

In line with this viewpoint, Bandura (1977) points out that a person's behavior influences others and their actions in turn influence the individual. Thus a person who is depressed tends to withdraw from significant others. These then respond with rejection and criticism. When this occurs, the depressed person increases his withdrawing behviors leading to even more severe feelings of self-rejection and self-criticism.

Coyne (1976) has proposed an interactional systems model of depression which fits into a structural-strategic framework. Research (Gotlib and Robinson, 1982) from this perspective has shown that after only three minutes of interaction with a depressed stranger, naive persons are significantly more negative in their verbal and non-verbal behavior. This research demonstrates that the behaviors of depressed persons is aversive and powerful in inducing negative mood shifts and generating guilt in others. Similarly, in marital relationships, the partner of a depressed person may temporarily reduce his demands, even while becoming increasingly impatient, hostile and withdrawing. The depressed person in turn becomes increasingly aware of the escalation of the aversive feelings he or she receives and consequently elicits further expressions of distress, thereby strengthening the pattern of depression.

Coyne et al. (1984), in a review of the literature, point out that depression is strongly associated with marital disturbance, which is characterized by dependency, inhibited communication, resentment, and friction. Couples that include a depressed partner tend to have extended periods of inhibited communication, tension punctuated by arguments with intense negative affect, and then withdrawal marked by little constructive problem solving. The aversiveness and futility of attempting to solve the interpersonal problems encourage the couple to avoid confrontations until an accumulation of unresolved issued precipitates another major conflict.

Treatment of Depression

Tricyclic drug treatment has a significant impact on the symptoms of depression, but more than a third of the patients given antidepressant drugs fail to comply or they drop out. Furthermore tricyclics have little effect on the interpersonal problems accompanying depression (Coyne, 1984).

Behavior therapy and cognitive therapy are shown to have a lower dropout rate than antidepressant medication and to have better results in various outcome studies. These therapies use a highly structured approach, have a goal-attainment focus, and emphasize constructive behavior change and the involvement of the environment as an alternative to negative self-preoccupation (Beck et al., 1979).

Marital Therapy

Marital therapy, without or in combination with antidepressant medications, may have the advantage of focusing on the disturbed relationship that accompanies depression. While such therapy must be tailored for each couple, there may be some common themes and treatment procedures that can be utilized. It is assumed from a Structural–Strategic perspective that depression arises from the ineffective movement through life transitions and the accumulation of mishandled conflicts and interpersonal problems with the key members of the social environment. These inappropriate coping mechanisms need to be modified so that the client's distress can be alleviated. Thus the therapeutic interventions are not focused on the depression but on more effective ways of interpersonal problem solving.

Structural–Strategic Treatment of Depression

Four assumptions underly the treatment of depression using a Structural–Strategic paradigm. These are:

1. Depression is a symptom that is characterized by recursive patterns of problem-maintaining behavior.
2. A highly anxiety-provoking experience such as an affair, a threat of separation or divorce, or the death of a loved one may be associated with the depression.
3. Three intertwined general themes will emerge during the treatment of a couple where one partner is depressed: (a) frustration from the

couple's attempt to deal with the marital problems; (b) distress generated by the depression; and (c) efforts made by the couple to modify or cope with the distress.
4. Treatment may mean doing what the couple has already been doing but with new energy and intensity.

Treatment Techniques

Coyne (1984) has identified a number of therapy techniques that can be used in couples therapy where one member is depressed. These are:

1. Joining.
2. Enactment of the problem-solving efforts that produce hurtful exchanges. The therapist might point out how the spouses' efforts and positive motives are misconstrued, and how the harder they try, the worse the depression becomes.
3. Use of metaphors such as, "Perhaps you are like two porcupines trying to get close to each other, and you are getting stuck on each other's quills."
4. One-down therapist position since an active and expert position may produce a passive, help-rejecting, and complaining stance from the couple. This often occurs when the therapist uses an active problem-solving orientation.
5. Positive connotation in which the therapist might commend the couple for passion, commitment, and romanticism, and the rejection of a dreary existence. A couple with fewer of these virtues would not be struggling so hard. Whenever a conflict is initiated, the struggle is positively connoted as an attempt to improve a banal relationship.
6. Prescription of continued arguments given in plausible terms and requiring no more than a variation on what they have already been doing.
7. The use of ritual by suggesting that the fights not occur spontaneously but that they be planned. Before the fight occurs, the couple clearly establishes how the attacker should proceed. There should be painstaking attention to

detail, and the defender should provide copious constructive criticism of the attacker's performance. The therapist, before the end of the session, might acknowledge that the ritual is a sacrifice with uncertain rewards.

8. Improving the sex life of the couple is usually an important part of couple therapy. Couples with a depressed member generally do not have a satisfactory sexual relationship. Depression seems to inhibit sexual desire.

9. Reframing; for example, framing depression as an active, dignified, even if costly practice of establishing intimacy. This may be done by use of a metaphor: "You are like a canary in a coal mine, registering serious problems in the relationship for both of you, and at the same time showing how miserable you can be, while still maintaining the relationship." (p. 36)

10. Cautioning against improving too rapidly with the statement, "Every silver lining has a dark cloud attached to it. Improvement must be undertaken slowly and even then problems are likely to arise." (p. 37)

11. The use of the family map to assist couples from becoming enmeshed in each other's lives. The emotional overinvolvement of the partners tends to aggravate the conflicts and prevents individuation.

12. Defining depression in positive terms; for example, the therapist might agree with the couple that the depression is a way of protecting the spouse and the relationship.

13. Pretending or jamming, which is a tactic of breaking up patterns of behavior in which one partner ritualizes new behaviors by making small changes, and then asks the other partner to guess what those changes were. Each session is begun by this guessing game, but neither the depressed person nor therapist can reveal whether the guesses are correct.

References

Bandura, A. *Social learning theory*. Englewood Cliffs, N.J.: Prentice-Hall, 1977.

Coyne, J. C. Toward an interactional description of depression. *Psychiatry*, 1976, *39*, 28–40.

Beck, A., Rush, A., Shaw, B., & Emery, G. *Cognitive therapy of depression*. New York: Guilford, 1979.

Coyne, J. C., Kahn, J., & Gotlib, I. Depression. In T. Jacobs (Ed.), *Family interaction and psychopathology*. New York: Pergamon Press, 1984.

Coyne, J. Strategic therapy with depressed married persons: Initial agenda themes and interventions. *Journal of Marital and Family Therapy*, 1984, *10*, 53–63.

Fisch, R., Weakland, J. H., & Segal, L. *The tactics of change*. San Francisco: Jossey/Bass, 1982.

Gotlib, I. H., & Robinson, A. L. Responses to depressed individuals. *Journal of Abnormal Psychology*, 1982, *91*, 231–240.

3.4 DEFINITION OF FAMILY THERAPY TERMS

There are a number of terms and concepts that are important in gaining an understanding of Structural–Strategic therapy. This glossary is a quick reference guide to clarify these terms and concepts.

affect   The feeling tone accompanying an idea or mental representation. If an affect is completely suppressed, it may appear not as an emotion but rather as a physical change such as perspiration or psychosomatic condition.

alignment   A joining of persons or groups having similar interests, values, or ideals, or a common purpose, and so forth.

boundaries   Delineations between parts of a system or between systems. The boundaries establish the system rules and define who participates and how.

cohesion   The degree of emotional closeness or distance in the family.

community involvement   The involvement a person has in the community in terms of social, religious, political, volunteer, sports, or similar activity.

differentiation   Recognition of a state of difference from others that allows for self-direction and self-regulation. The result of differentiation is autonomy.

disengaged   A transactional style that is opposite to enmeshment with regard to boundary functioning.

Members of disengaged subsystems function autonomously but have a skewed sense of independence. They also lack feelings of loyalty and belonging; neither do they have the capacity for interdependence since they find it difficult to request support when in need.

Symptoms of disengagement are: very low emotional bonding, high independence of family members, open external boundaries, closed internal boundaries, weak coalitions. Also, time apart from family is minimized, space is maximized (both physical and emotional), individual friends are seen alone, and decision making, interests, and recreation are individual and outside of the family.

emotional cutoff   Insulation of self or cutting self off emotionally from family members. A way to deal with unresolved fusion to family of origin.

enmeshment   An extreme connectedness within the family. Enmeshment can be anticipated if emotional bonding is high, if there is a high level of dependence between family members, if external boundaries are closed and internal boundaries are blurred, if ''alone'' time or ''private'' space is minimized, if *all* family decision making is jointly orchestrated, and if interests and recreational activities must be shared by entire family. Enmeshment describes families in which members are overconcerned and overinvolved in each other's life.

invasiveness   Degree to which members speak for one another or make ''mind-reading'' statements.

marital commitment   Degree to which self is identified with marital relationship.

marital external pull forces   External forces pulling marital dyad apart; for example, in alternative attraction, desirability of singlehood, means of self-support, liberal sex-role ideology.

marital external "push" forces   External forces keeping marital dyad together; for example, in feelings of obligation, moral prescription, primary group affiliation, community stigma, legal and economic restrictions, sex ideology, religiosity, large number of children.

marital congruity   Consensus of perceptions and feelings about the relationship.

myths   Legendary narratives that represent part of the belief system of a person or explain a practice or natural phenomenon. Myths are a way of orienting oneself to life; they give meaning to relations with self and others, they carry moral values of a person and a society, and they enhance and codify beliefs. All families have family myths. A myth is a belief or an acceptance of a way of doing things for no better reason than that it was done so in the past, such as boys must be strong and not cry.

masked/distorted message   A message that is disguised and unclear. The greater the lack of clarity in a message, the greater the confusion and ambiguity it creates.

message—clear direct   Communication is obvious and undisguised, and aimed at the person for whom it is intended.

message—double   A set of contradictory messages from the same person to which an individual must respond. His or her failure to please is inevitable whatever response is made to a double message.

network   Refers to the psychosocial support system surrounding a person or family unit; it includes friends, employers, associates, school contacts, church, and community contacts.

oscillating balances   In relational ethics the concern with the balance of equitable fairness between people. The long-term oscillating balance among family members indicates whether the basic interests and needs of each are taken into account by others. Relational ethics is founded on the principle of equitability, that everyone is entitled to have his or her welfare interests considered in a way that is fair from a multilateral perspective.

projection system   Describes the way the undifferentiation of the parents is transmitted to a child. The process is one in which parental emotionality defines what the child is like because the parent's emotional reactiveness is projected into the personality of the child. *Or* projection is an unconscious act or process of ascribing to others one's own ideas or impulses.

power structure Refers to the relative influence each family member has on the outcome of an activity. The power distribution in a healthy family is flexible. There is a casual freedom to express individual differences and to negotiate role structure and role expectations and to reevaluate past experience.

roles An expected behavior pattern that accompanies a social position, as in a family. Roles are defined by many conditions: past history; present history; ideas about future; interaction within the family, with extended family, and with one's culture. Roles are also defined by one's own growth experience.

role complementarity The degree of harmony in the meshing of social roles in a family system. Patterns in a family system that permit each member to "give in" without feeling he or she has "given up." For example, both husband and wife must yield part of their separateness to gain in belonging. The acceptance of mutual interdependence (complementarity) in a (symmetrical) relationship may be handicapped by the spouse's insistence on independent rights.

role clarity A general feeling of knowing what behavior is expected of any specific role such as that of father, mother, husband, daughter, son.

role flexibility Refers to the family's ability to change the structure of role relationships in response to new developments, unique situations, and/or stress.

role fulfillment The degree of satisfaction realized as one functions within a specific role, such as wife, husband, parent, or child.

rules—family A metaphor coined to identify a witnessed pattern of repetitive action. All families function under a set of family rules. Rules can be explicit or implicit, rigid or flexible, many or few.

triangle Formed with a two-person emotional system is under stress and recruits a third person in order to lower the intensity and anxiety and gain stability. A family's emotional system is composed of a series of interlocking triangles. An example of the process of triangulation is as follows: As tension increases in the relationship between husband and wife, harmony is preserved by one partner absorbing the relationship problems. This "uncomfortable" partner resolves the dilemma by moving toward relationship fusion with a third person, for example, mother to daughter.

CHAPTER 4

FAMILY AND COUPLE ASSESSMENT

4.1 A STRUCTURAL–STRATEGIC MODEL OF FAMILY ASSESSMENT

Traditionally much of the clinical assessment literature has been oriented toward the individual client and the intrapsychic meaning of the behavior. In recent years, however, there has been increasing attention devoted to the interpersonal aspects of an individual's behavior, especially in the interaction with other family members. This shift in emphasis toward interpersonal interaction has paralleled the development of family therapy.

In the model presented here, a system for identifying family patterns based upon a Structural–Strategic theoretical framework is proposed. The assessment system is designed for family therapists and provides a schema by which to locate family interactions along predetermined dimensions. The emphasis of the scale is upon relationships among dimensions and on positioning family behavior at some point within multidimensional space. Although efforts are made clearly to define and delineate the dimensions, an overlap and interaction may occur. It is expected that further research will refine and modify the dimensions used in this scale. The scale is presented in the Instrumen-

tation chapter of this handbook.

Assessment as defined here is the working hypothesis that the therapist evolves from his or her experiences and observations upon entering and joining the family. To assess means to identify the family dynamics through the use of the family interview. It is in this participatory experience of face-to-face encounter that the therapist empathically "feels into" and "sees into" the family.

Methodology of Family Assessment

The methodology of family assessment involves continuous observation, feedback, and interpretation of relevant events. The client/therapist relationship stimulates in the therapist a progression of hypotheses arising from his or her knowledge of psychodynamic, behavioral, psychosocial, and systemic processes, and by past personal and professional experience. These hypotheses are constantly put to the test, amended, and verified in the ongoing process of therapy.

Family assessment differs radically from the process of assessment and diagnosis in psychiatry. A psychiatric assessment involves gathering data from or about a client and assigning a label to the accumulated information. In contrast to this, a family assessment runs parallel to the therapy process. Thus assessment and intervention are interdependent activities. Since the family is an ever changing organization, the assessment changes as the family changes.

Family assessment involves the active process by the therapist of gathering data and entering into the feeling, acting, and thinking of the family. This process involves deliberately joining the system and imaginatively experiencing the pain and joys of the family. On the basis of this encounter, a family profile can be developed and hypotheses about family dynamics generated.

The assessment process consists of two steps: (1) data gathering, and (2) problem description.

Step 1. Data Gathering

The assessment process begins by the therapist asking the family to describe the problem(s) that brought them to therapy. It is important for the therapist to obtain an accurate picture of the nature and history of each problem. In doing so the therapist explores the interpersonal interactions, historical perspectives, precipitating events, and who is mainly involved with the problem and how.

In exploring the problem, the therapist should utilize the dimensions of the Structural–Strategic Family Assessment Scale. The therapist should obtain information on the dimensions identified in the scale.

In doing an exploration of the presenting problems, other issues will arise and be defined as difficulties. By use of paraphrasing and summarizing skills, the therapist feeds back to the family an understanding of the presenting problem. Each problem identified by the family is summarized and reflected back to the family for verification.

Step 2. Problem Description

Using the Structural–Strategic Family Assessment Scale, the family is assessed after the

first or second session on the eight dimensions, including developmental stages, family life context, structure, flexibility, resonance, communication, marital dynamics, and individual pathology. The assessment focuses on detailing effective and ineffective functioning on each dimension. By use of subscale profile analysis, it becomes possible to determine aspects of overall family functioning that influence the emotional and/or physical health of family members.

The assessment is based on (1) the family members' reports, (2) the observed interactions that occur between family members, (3) and the confrontation and clarification of contradictions between stated information and observed behavior and between information offered by different family members. The therapist's impressions are condensed and reflected back until the family agrees that an honest appreciation of the family's functioning has been obtained.

The therapist should be careful to gather firm evidence to support the hypothesis before putting it forward to the family. If the therapist has a hunch without strong evidence, it should be put forward as such, and the family should be asked for an opinion as to the validity of the impression. This approach prevents the therapist from moving into areas without evidence, and yet allows him or her to test clinical hunches arising from clinical intuition. Such a method engenders the family's confidence in and respect for the therapist's objectivity, impartiality, and regard for data. It also encourages the family to take seriously its role in the therapy process. If there is substantial disagreement between the family and therapist, the therapist can make the statement, ''O.K., we disagree in this area, so let's agree it is a problem and move on to another area of concern.''

The assessment should, while taking the presenting problem seriously, focus on the overall family dynamics and avoid developing formulations based only on data related to the presenting problem. The assessment should be approached tactfully, directly, and honestly. All issues should be discussed openly. Family dynamics are then reflected back to the family members so that they understand their strengths and weaknesses. Strengths are emphasized, since this is trust building and supportive, and assists the therapeutic process that follows. The concepts, however, are simplified as much as possible so that family members understand the dynamics and do not fear the psychological labels and jargon.

4.2 A STRUCTURAL–STRATEGIC ASSESSMENT SCALE

The Structural–Strategic Family Assessment Scale is based on the work of Structural and Strategic family theorists (Haley, 1980; Madanes, 1981; Minuchin, 1978). We have drawn heavily from the thinking of such schools of therapy as the interactional view of MRI, the Structural family approach, the Milan approach, and the communications perspective. The assessment schema is designed to present a distillation and refinement of some of the Structural–Strategic thinking regarding family dynamics and therapy.

The purpose of this scale is to provide a schema by which families may be assessed so that family workers may develop more effective therapeutic plans. Before proceeding with therapy, it is essential that the therapist understand the family system, its strengths, problems, and dynamics. From our viewpoint family assessment is interwoven with family and marital therapy and intervention and involves a careful delineation of the family issues.

The family assessment scale presented here is designed to assist family therapists understand the complex interactions within the family. It may also be used to monitor the results of family therapy. This may be done by comparing the family profile developed by the therapist during the first and second sessions with the family profile after five or more sessions of intervention. This type of comparison may be used to indicate the direction or movement of the therapy process.

In developing the proposed family assessment scale, an effort was made to meet the following criteria: (1) The framework for assessing the families should be comprehensive and inclusive enough to encompass Structural and Strategic understandings of family dynamics. These understandings are drawn largely from the family literature and personal experience with families. (2) The dimensions of family functioning should be well defined and differentiated so that they are useful in discriminating between various family interactions and patterns. (3) The assessment procedure should be clinically oriented, meaningful, and practical, so that it can easily be used as a guide to the therapeutic process.

Scale 1: Family Developmental Issues

The family developmental scale is based on the notion that each stage is potentially a life-crisis event that must be resolved if adaptive growth is to continue.

Stage 1, premarriage, involves dating and making a choice and commitment to one spouse. This stage includes taking a risk and developing a mutually satisfying and reciprocally agreeable relationship with another person.

Stage 2, marriage, involves two tasks, ending each spouse's primary gratification with his or her own parents and redirecting these energies into the marriage.

Stage 3 includes the birth of the first child and childbearing. This stage requires the solidification of the marriage as well as the establishment of parental roles. A frequent difficulty in this stage is the sacrificing of marital roles to parental roles.

Stage 4 involves the individuation of family members. This stage includes the broad mid-range of family life in which the task is the continual modification of roles and the evolving individuation of each family member.

Stage 5 refers to the actual departure of the children. The primary task of this stage is the reworking of parental roles pertinent to becoming parents of adult children.

Stage 6 involves an integration of loss. It includes the acceptance of social, economic, and physical changes that occur in old age.

Family Development and Dysfunction

Several different views are held regarding the role of developmental stages in generating family dysfunction. Some family theorists suggest that family pathology arises from a combination of life stage events plus external circumstances. Other clinically oriented theorists propose that family dysfunction emerges from the construction and dynamics of the family system itself and that developmental stages simply color the expression or define the nature of the symptom.

The two perspectives emphasize different intervention strategies. The first puts the emphasis upon environmental manipulation as well as therapy with individual members. The second perspective views the family as a system and conceptualizes family dysfunction as a symptom of family dynamics. It is this latter view that most clearly represents our thinking in this handbook.

Scale 2: Family Life Context

This scale addresses the context in which the family resides. More specifically the concern is with the factors in the ecological environment that sustain, enhance, or impair the operations of the family, including such mechanisms as environmental reinforcement, modeling, identification, and social learning. This scale focuses on the extent to which children in the family have valued adults available to them who engage them in progressively more complex joint activities and have resources and incentives available to them to engage in complex activities such as community sports and cultural events.

The developmental potential of a family context depends on the extent to which third parties present in the setting support or undermine the activities of those actually engaged in interaction with the child. These support systems include family and community networks that enhance and nurture the family system.

The family life context also involves an examination of relations between settings and their relevance for developmental processes. The scale raises the question, "What are the interconnections between those settings in which the child actually participates, such as home, day care center, preschool, and school?"

An assessment about what is functional and dysfunctional in a family rests upon an understanding of the family in its social context. Such issues as religion, culture, societal expectations, and parental standard must be understood to make an adequate analysis of family dynamics.

Scale 3: Family Structure

The family structure scale rests on the belief that the whole and the parts can be properly explained only in terms of the relations that exist between the parts. The emphasis is upon the links that connect one part of the whole to the other and thereby form the family structure.

"Codes" exist within the structure that regulate the human relationship. The structuring force in the family is an innate and determined mechanism, which is transmitted from generation to generation.

Each system has a regulating code that is expressed through the transactions that occur. The structural dimensions present in all transactions include boundary alignment and power. The ability of the family to function well depends on the degree to which the family structure is well defined, elaborated, flexible, and cohesive.

A goal of family therapy is to change the dysfunctional underlying systemic structure. The problems in the family are sustained by the current structure of the family and its ecosystem. Identifying the problem means looking for the point in the operation of the structure at which the system fails to carry out its function.

Scale 4: Family Flexibility

The family flexibility scale is concerned with the degree to which the rules of the system are sufficiently open to allow for the adequate exchange of information between systems and within the system itself. The boundary of a system regulates information exchange through the operation of the system rules that define who participates in the family and how. These rules dictate who is in and who is out of an operation. Rules also define the roles which those who are in will assume toward each other and the world outside.

Family flexibility also includes the common dysfunctional behavior called "violation of function boundaries." This concept refers to the inappropriate acceptance of roles and responsibilities of other family members. An example of this is the parental child who assumes responsibility for parenting siblings.

Scale 5: Family Resonance

The family resonance scale is designed to measure the sensitivity the family has to the needs of its members. The openness, fluidity, and permeability of the family, the expression of affect, and the level of tolerance of differing beliefs describe family resonance.

The concept of enmeshment and disengagement are essential to an understanding of family resonance. At the enmeshment end of the continuum, the family is seen to be characterized by undifferentiated or fluid boundaries. The family members function as if they are part of each other. Disengaged family members, on the other hand, have very little to do with each other because the family boundaries are firmly delineated and rigid. The family members tend to go their own way with little overt dependence upon each other for their functioning.

Scale 6: Family Communication Processes

The family communication scale is designed to identify the patterns of communication in the family. The assumption of the scale is that the manner of communicating will elucidate the underlying interactional patterns of behavior. The focus is on the messages members send to each other.

The messages, even the simplest ones, are regarded as having multiple aspects or levels. These levels may be congruent or incongruent with each other. If incongruent, they may be incongruent in certain highly specific ways. Also, the various levels may be congruent or covertly labeled. The person to whom the message is directed has the option of responding to different aspects of the message. The particular level that is characteristically responded to may be significant.

Analysis of family communication also leads to insights concerning family laws and rules. The laws are consciously held values that are related to the values of the family's cultural environment. Rules are hypothetical constructs formulated by the observer to account for observable behavior in the family. The family may be totally unaware of them. The therapist's function is to make explicit the family rules so that the family has an option to change or modify them.

Scale 7: Marital System

This scale is based on the assumption that the parents are the chief architects of the family. If the parental subsystem is dysfunctional, it will seriously influence the child subsystem. Parenting patterns, modeling behavior, and the family climate are strongly influenced by the dynamics within the spouse subsystem.

The Marital System Scale identifies some of the assessment dimensions of importance in marriage. The degree of vitality, commitment, and satisfaction in the marriage are significant indicators of family functioning.

Scale 8: Individual Issues

This scale is designed to focus on the individual within the context of the family and social structure. By focusing on the individual, effort is made to identify individual problems in addition to family system functioning issues.

References

Aponte, H.J., & Van Deusen, J.M. (1981). In A.L. Gurman & P.D. Kniskern (Eds.), *Handbook of family therapy*. New York: Brunner/Mazel.

Epstein, N. B., & Bishop, D. S., (1981). Problem-centered systems therapy of the family. In A. S. Gurman & D. P. Kniskern (Eds.), *Handbook of Family Therapy*. New York: Brunner/Mazel.

Haley, J. (1976). *Problem solving therapy*. San Francisco: Jossey-Bass.

Haley, J. (1980). *Leaving home: The therapy of disturbed young people*. New York: McGraw-Hill.

Madanes, C. (1982). *Strategic family therapy*. Washington: Jossey-Bass.

Minuchin, S. (1974). *Families and family therapy*. Cambridge, Mass: Harvard University Press.

Minuchin, S., & Fishman, H.C. (1981) *Family therapy techniques*. Cambridge, Mass: Harvard University Press.

4.3 THE TRIAXIAL MODEL OF FAMILY ASSESSMENT

The triaxial model of family assessment has been developed by Tseng and McDermott (1979), and presented here as one model of family assessment. It was developed to capture the dynamic, multidimensional aspects of family life. Dysfunctions within the family might affect one area of family life with the remainder functioning adequately. The triaxial model attempts to assess family dysfunctions on a broad, deep, and flexible level, and accurately to reflect the pattern of family dynamics.

The model looks at families in three dimensions or axes. The first is the area of family development, in which the family life cycle is translated onto a longitudinal scale. The second axis is the intrafamily or family subsystem. The third is the family group dysfunction, which views the family as a group and its involvement in the larger social context.

Family Development

The first axis addresses the problems that can occur as a family goes through the different stages of development. The first stage is couple development. The difficulties are in couples establishing their marriage in the areas of communication, roles, power, boundaries, and unconscious expectations, and in separating from their families of origin. These difficulties may occur at the beginning of the marriage, but can reoccur at any stage.

In the second stage, dysfunction may occur with the birth of the first child. In such instances parents have difficulty in establishing and/or shifting between spouse and parent roles. They may develop symptoms based on unconscious expectations or fears regarding the child. Such couples fail to account for the disruption to their life-style that a child can bring. Usually these difficulties occur at the birth of the first child, but they may also occur at the birth of subsequent children.

The third stage, childbearing family dysfunction, may develop as a consequence of difficulties encountered in making room for and rearing the young children. Areas of difficulty may include the family organization and the family atmosphere. Difficulties may occur as the couple and the children cope with issues of separateness/togetherness, and the solving of triangular alliances.

The fourth stage is maturing family dysfunctions. Difficulties may arise as the children move into and through adolescence. Issues of separation of the children from the parents are intensified, and family roles change and are redefined. Parents may have difficulty in letting their adult children go. The parents may have difficulty in reestablishing their own marriage relationship (empty nest syndrome).

The fifth stage is contracting family dysfunction. Problems may develop as the parents age, come into retirement, and face the loss of a spouse. There may be difficulties in readjusting to a new pattern of living, and in coping with loneliness and insecurity. Parents may also encounter difficulties in coping with, relating to, or feeling isolated from their children's lives.

Within the developmental axis, there are both complications and variations in the traditional family structure. The first is the interrupted family in which there has been separation or divorce. Difficulties may arise in coping with the split, either in the desire to be separated or to remain attached. Problems in resolving feelings, usually negative, may continue, as well as difficulties in working through the custody arrangements for the children.

A second difficulty may be the single-parent family. Problems may develop around the presence of only one parent as a result of divorce, separation, or death. Difficulties may lie in the support, care, and discipline of the children. Problems may also develop in the area of the child's sexual identity (developing without the same-sex parent being present).

Reconstructed families (step families) may encounter difficulties in establishing new role divisions between parents, stepparents, and children, and between various groupings of children. Previous family issues may resurface as well.

A fourth difficulty may be the chronically unstable family. Problems develop because of a continuous lack of stability and/or roots in the family. This may develop from frequent separation/divorce or from frequent moves. The areas most likely to cause difficulty are confusions in role divisions, boundary issues, and a lack of competency and stability among family members.

Family Subsystem Dysfunction

The second axis is that of family subsystem dysfunction. The attention is focused on the various groupings within the family subsystems. The purpose is to identify the particular family members involved in the dysfunction. There are three subheadings under this axis: spouse subsystem, the parent–child subsystem, and the sibling subsystem. There are categories within each of these subheadings.

The spouse subsystem dysfunction is concerned with the ability of the couple to work out the marriage relationship. It is here that the most dysfunction within the family occurs. There are five different areas of dysfunction that typically may take place in the spouse subsystem.

The first is the complementary dysfunction and involves two people who have dysfunctional complementary behavior and/or character. This relationship is unbalanced but often stable because the couple's needs are met. Examples are dominant/submissive, emotionally detached/affection craving, powerful/dependent, and sadistic/masochistic. These relationships usually are structured with the couple in a one-up/one-down relationship.

The second area of dysfunction is the symmetrical dysfunction and is a relationship characterized by conflict. Each person has the same desire and tendency to control the relationship. Power is the issue. Their similarities result in constant competition and rivalry.

The third is the dependent dysfunction where both spouses are dependent, helpless, and immature. This relationship has a built-in catch-22; if the couple separates, one or both may be unable to function as individuals. Thus they stay together.

The fourth area is the disengaged dysfunction and is a relationship characterized by distancing in which interaction and emotional involvement are limited. However, the couple stays together for social or religious reasons, or simply because its members are too apathetic or passive to change their accustomed routines.

The fifth area of dysfunction is the incompatible dysfunction and is characterized by widely different interests, personalities, value systems, and life-styles. Quite often there are wide differences in age, education, and occupation that result in continued chaotic attempts at working out husband and wife roles.

Parent–Child Subsystem

Dysfunctions in the parent–child subsystem center around the difficulties between parents and children. The focus may be centered on the parent, the child, or the parent–child dysfunction.

The first category is parent-related dysfunction and involves the behavior or character of a parent that interferes with parenting. Some examples of this are faulty expectations from the child, inappropriate child-rearing techniques relative to the child's age, inadequate parenting behavior, and extreme favoritism toward one child.

The second category is the child-related dysfunction in which the difficulty lies within a child. The child may have an organic, maturational, developmental, neurotic, or psychotic dysfunction, and may disrupt the family and the family system.

The third category is the parent–child interrelational dysfunction in which disturbances in the relational interactions between the parent and child occur. Some typical examples are an overattachment of the parents to the child, an overattachment of the child to the parent, a controlling parent with an inhibited child, and a parent–child relationship where both parties are hostile and rejecting.

The fourth category is the parent–child triangular dysfunction in which a child becomes intensively involved with one parent, resulting in a triangular conflict.

The fifth category is sibling subsystem dysfunction in which the problems are primarily between the children. Some examples are destructive rivalry or competition, various coalitions against the parent(s), and overly close identification and lack of differentiation between siblings.

Family Group Dysfunction

There are two subheadings in this axis: structural/functional dysfunction and social coping dysfunction.

Within the structural/functional subheading are five categories, each of which includes: organization, role division, communication, emotional atmosphere, task performance, group boundaries, and integration.

The first, structural/functional dysfunction, is the underperforming family where the parents are immature and lack the ability to lead the family. The family is poorly organized, has weak communication, and ineffective decision making, and tends to perform inadequately.

The second category is the overstructured family, which has at least one perfectionistic parent. The family tends to be highly task oriented with a focus on discipline and achievement. Though orderly and structured, emotional involvement and warmth are lacking.

The third category is the pathologically integrated family, which has inappropriate role divisions and assignments. The interrelationships are misdirected and unbalanced.

The fourth is the emotionally detached family in which family members dislike or are dissatisfied with each other. There seems to be an underlying sense of anger or hostility between them, resulting in limited emotional involvement. The family stays together because of external reasons such as financial pressure and social or religious expectations.

The fifth category is the disorganized family, which is characterized by multiple problems in group functioning. Some of these include vague, ineffective communication, unclear role division, and chaotic organization.

The second subheading is that of social coping dysfunction where the family seems unable to cope in relationship to other families. There are three categories in this subheading.

The first category is the socially isolated family, which is overly isolated from the community and has little contact with members of the extended family.

The second is the socially deviant family, which is in revolt against the community mores. Such a family does not conform to prevalent social standards and demonstrates deviant goals.

The third category is the special-theme family, where the life of the family is controlled by commonly held themes, myths, secrets, or cultural beliefs. Usually the family theme is developed by both parents and shared by the whole family. The theme is usually unique to this family and is not shared with other families. Also, it is common for a family member, usually a child, to be designated by the family as the ''carrier'' of the family theme.

Reference

Wen-Shung Tseng & McDermott, J. Triaxial family classification. *Journal of the American Academy of Child Psychiatry*, 1979, *18*, 22–43.

CHAPTER 5

COMMUNICATION

5.1 CYBERNETIC MODEL OF FAMILY INTERACTION

A systems-oriented approach to family therapy views the whole family as involved in and contributing to the problem behavior of any single family member. A delinquent teenager, for example, may reflect a problem in some particular aspect of family organization, such as interpersonal and subsystem boundaries, attachments and coalitions, regulatory mechanisms, family rules, collective beliefs, and goals (Tomm, 1980).

The degree of regulation and control in family interaction patterns is an aspect of family organization, and of particular interest to cybernetic theory. Cybernetics is a scientific discipline devoted to the investigation of communication and control in both mechanical and living systems. This section briefly explores the contribution of cybernetic theory to our understanding of family interaction patterns.

Feedback

Cybernetic theory makes explicit the mechanisms that promote homeostatic stability in our relationships. One such regulatory mechanism that has considerable influence on our interactional patterns is feedback. Feedback monitors the consequences (output) of an interaction and directly influences further regulation of that interaction in an ongoing manner. Positive feedback is said to operate when the consequences of an output serve to increase the same output. For example, if tailgating and honking at a slow driver in front of you result in the driver going even slower, positive feedback has occurred. Positive feedback thus is deviation amplifying or escalating. Negative feedback, on the other hand, is said to operate when the consequences of an output serve to decrease that output; thus, in our example, if tailgating and hoking at the driver succeed in "speeding the driver up," then negative feedback has occurred. Negative feedback, therefore, is deviation minimizing or homeostatic.

Both positive and negative feedback processes are important for a relationship to maintain itself in a steady state or equilibrium. There are various patterns of interplay (e.g., see Figures 5.1.1 and 5.1.2) between positive and negative feedback that serve to preserve a relationship in homeostasis; in fact these patterns of control tend to become quite stable and predictable (Tomm, 1980), and can lock a marriage or family relationship into a treadmill of habitual and destructive interactions. Tomm maintains that "for any substantial change to occur in a relationship, the regulatory limits [as determined primarily by feedback] must be adjusted so that a new range of behaviors is possible or an entirely new pattern can emerge" (p. 8). Feedback regulation is especially activated around the organizational elements of family beliefs and rules.

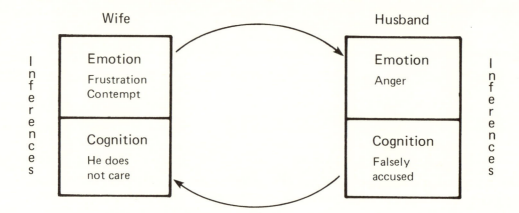

WIFE'S BEHAVIORAL OUTPUT

Verbal: "You just sit around all day!"
Nonverbal: Raises voice, lowers brow, face flushes.

HUSBAND'S BEHAVIORAL OUTPUT

Verbal: "Ah, quit your bitching!"
Nonverbal: Sneers, turns away.

**Figure 5.1.1. Diagram of cyclical marital
conflict**

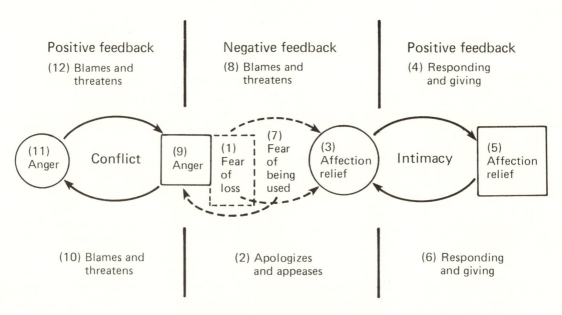

**Figure 5.1.2. Positive and negative
feedback loops in marital conflict**

Our interactional patterns are often complicated and difficult to "understand." Geometric forms, therefore, are currently in use to help visualize them. Tomm (1980), for example, has developed the circular pattern diagram, a technique for "mapping" interactional patterns that we shall use to illustrate the role of feedback in relationships. Figure 5.1.1 is a circular pattern diagram of a marital conflict. The scenario is of a working wife who comes home from a long day at work to find the house in a mess and her unemployed husband watching television. The following points can be made:

1. The circle implies an interaction pattern that is stable, repetitive, and self-regulatory.

2. The connecting arrows represent information relayed to another person through behavior. The behavioral output of one person becomes perceptual input to the other. All behavior communicates at multiple levels; for example, there is verbal and nonverbal behavior. It is nonverbal behavior that primarily regulates and controls ongoing interpersonal relationships. Nonverbal behavior also yields clues that are important for making accurate and appropriate inferences. A raised voice, lowered brow, and flushed face, for instance, may reflect anger and frustration. If verbal and nonverbal behaviors are incongruent, an inference should be based on nonverbal behavior, since verbal communication is more easily "managed" to create a certain impression (Tomm, 1980).

3. Inference is how the behavioral output of one person is perceived by the other. A cognitive (thinking) inference and an emotional (feeling) inference are made. The cognitive inference reflects the idea, concept, or belief that is used to attribute meaning to the perceptual input, whereas the emotional inference refers to a motivational response that is activated in the individual and 'drives' the behavioral output.

4. The husband's snide remark serves as positive feedback to the wife's criticizing, because it reinforces and amplifies her critical behavior. Likewise, the wife's behavior serves as positive feedback to the husband's sneering be-

havior. Each round of positive feedback will escalate and intensify the conflict.

We have said that, according to cybernetic theory, positive feedback is deviation amplifying, and that the marital spat we have just examined should thus develop into total war before too long. While "vicious circles" often do escalate, cybernetic theory suggests that, in fact, relationships manifest stable maintenance patterns, not rapidly escalating ones. Tomm (1980, p. 11) explains:

Each behavioral pattern has certain limits which are governed by rules of the system. That is, as positive feedback escalates the pattern, a point is reached at which negative feedback is activated to resist further change in the same direction.

Figure 5.1.2 illustrates how positive and negative feedback will interact to regulate a marital conflict and preserve homeostatic stability in the relationship. The fear of loss (1) on the husband's part, in this case, limits the conflict by activating conciliatory behaviors such as apology and appeasement (2), negative feedback for the conflict.

By "giving in" the husband defuses the conflict and attempts to stimulate relief and affection (3) in his wife. The wife expresses her relief and affection through responding and giving behavior (4), and her husband responds in kind (5, 6), thereby activating positive feedback and returning the relationship to homeostasis. If, after the couple "cools down," the wife (7) becomes suspicious of being used ("His apology was only a ploy to stop the argument so that he wouldn't miss more of his hockey game") and begins to blame and threaten again (8), another round of conflict will ensue (9, 10, 11, 12). In this case her blaming and threatening behavior (8) constitutes negative feedback for the intimacy cycle. The diagram as a whole, therefore, may be seen as a conflict–intimacy interaction pattern: the couple experiences successive rounds of conflict and intimacy, and positive and negative feedback preserve both the pattern and the homeostasis.

Summary

The circular pattern diagram will help the family therapist think systemically. Rather than thinking of a family problem in linear (cause/effect) terms and embarking on a witch hunt for the guilty party, therapists will think of the problem in circular terms as involving the entire family circle in some way. Thus therapists will maintain their impartiality and systemic orientation.

Furthermore, when parts of a circular process are not readily evident, therapists can focus their attention and intervention on discovering the missing links. From this perspective, Tomm (1980) suggests that "significant but nonobvious regulatory behaviors are more likely to be elicited and identified" (p. 14). The behavioral feedback generated by all family members concerning a particular problem will provide the family therapist with a doorway into the family's beliefs, rules, and structure.

Reference

Tomm, K. Towards a cybernetic systems approach to family therapy at the University of Calgary. In David S. Freeman (Ed.), *Perspectives on family therapy*. Vancouver: Butterworth, 1980.

5.2 THE PROCESS OF COMMUNICATION

Communication might well be called the circulatory system of human relationships. It is the medium through which relationships grow or wither. It is the process by which the content of the relationship is transferred between people. Family therapists, such as Jackson, Weakland, and, perhaps most notably, Satir, have in the past concentrated their efforts in family therapy on the process of communication.

This section focuses on the area of communication and feedback. We briefly describe modes of communication, congruent and incongruent communication, and finally communication roles or stances. These concepts are referenced to various skill training exercises found in the training exercises section of this manual.

Verbal and Nonverbal Communication

Communication involves sending, receiving, processing, and interpreting and sending return messages. Communication is a double-level process. The first level is the "verbal," that is, the words and content of the message. The second level is the "nonverbal," which may interpret or qualify the verbal level, and involves gestures, body language, tone of voice, posture, intensity, and context.

A person is said to be congruent when the verbal and nonverbal levels of communication correspond to one another, that is, when what you hear from a person matches what you feel from that person. When the two levels do not match, a person receiving these incongruent messages consciously or unconsciously feels uneasy or anxious.

An example of incongruent communication might be helpful in understanding this concept. We may recall someone with a sarcastic sense of humor who communicates anger in a humorous yet biting manner. We laugh, but feel confused or uncomfortable. There is a hurting sting behind the humor. To illustrate how confusing this anger feels, imagine a sheepdog putting his paws on your shoulder and licking your face while at the same time urinating on your leg. One is not sure which message to believe, the humorous verbal message or the nonverbal, angry message.

Communication can become one or both of the following rigid and incongruent forms, namely, mystification and the double bind.

Mystification

Mystification occurs when, in the example given, the receiver of the sarcastically humorous comment inquired as to the meaning of the message, and was told that there was no negative intention in the message. The resulting confusion would be mystification. Laing (1965) talks about mystification as a way in which some families deal with conflict by obscuring, confusing, and masking what is going on. This does not necessarily reduce the inner conflict, but just obscures the true nature of it.

Double Bind

The double bind develops when a person is given two mutually exclusive messages. To respond positively to one message is, therefore, to respond negatively to the other (Goldenberg & Goldenberg, 1980). An example is the "come here—go away" actions of some people. But it goes one step further. Along with this conflicting message is a verbal message that asks why a person did not come here. This behavior is frequently visible in families where schizophrenia is present. Perhaps the classic example is given by Bateson et al. (1956, p. 25).

A young man who had fairly well recovered from an acute schizophrenic episode was visited in the hospital by his mother. He was glad to see her and impulsively put his arm on her shoulders, whereupon she stiffened. He withdrew his arm and she asked, "Don't you love me anymore?" He then blushed, and she said, "Dear, you must not be so easily embarrassed and afraid of your feelings."

Bateson et al. report an immediate resumption of violent behavior when the youth returned to the ward. In many families the results of incongruent behavior are not so drastic, but incongruent communication disrupts trust and understanding.

Communication is not an isolated singular event, but develops into distinct patterns. Bandler et al. (1976) have developed a circular model of communication that has five stages. This model is helpful in understanding the pattern that communication follows, in seeing where and how it becomes incongruent, and in observing what congruent communication looks like. This communication model is presented in the following.

Stage 1: *Communication*—A message is sent by the communicator at the verbal and nonverbal levels. The message may or may not be sent consciously by the sender.

Stage 2: *Experience*—Describes the ways the message is received through eyes, ears, skin, and so on. The message may or may not be received consciously by the receiver.

Stage 3: *Conclusion*—Involves the receiver's understanding of what the message means.

Stage 4: *Generalizations*—This is the way the receiver connects the message to past experiences.

Stage 5: *Response behavior*—Involves the way the receiver responds to the message that is communicated back to the sender.

Table 5.2.1 developed from materials by Bandler et al. (1976) reveal how congruent and incongruent patterns are formed. The model also indicates how to break out of the dysfunctional communication pattern.

Communication Stances

Virginia Satir (1972) has identified five categories, or stances, of how people react under stress. Four of the five are dysfunctional and are hooked in with the calibrated communication cycle. The fifth is the leveling response, which is connected with the functional feedback cycle of communication.

Placator

The first category is the "placator" or people pleaser (Satir, 1972). This person is always

Table 5.2.1
A Comparison of the Qualities of Congruent and Incongruent Messages

Incongruent Message	*Congruent Message*
Stage 1: The message sent is incongruent, but the sender is unaware of incongruency. The sender is aware of only certain parts of the message that are verbal.	*Stage 1*: Usually no incongruent messages are sent; the verbal/nonverbal match. In the event that the sender is incongruent, receiver will recognize that fact and have the freedom to change the message.
Stage 2: The receiver has the task of understanding the incongruent message. Usually the receiver will selectively choose which part of the message to accept. If aware of the incongruency, the receiver will regard the sender as insincere or deceitful. If the sender is aware only of messages that do not conflict, then he or she will accept conflicting messages at an unconscious level and become uncomfortable. Usually will deal only with verbal messages at a conscious level.	*Stage 2*: If the sender is congruent, then no problem. If not, the receiver can gracefully call attention to the incongruent message, asking for clarification without causing the sender to feel defensive or attacking his or her self-worth. The freedom to comment is the key point. If the receiver is unaware of the incongruency of the message, he or she will feel uneasy and will have the freedom to explore the source of the uneasiness.
Stage 3: Given the task of understanding incongruent message, the receiver will typically respond in one of two ways: (a) If only aware of nonconflicting messages, will accept the preferred message at the conscious level and the incongruent message at the unconscious level. (b) If the receiver is aware of the incongruent message, he or she will think the sender is either insincere, manipulative, or malicious.	*Stage 3*: If the message is congruent, there is no problem in understanding its meaning. If not, the receiver will either recognize the incongruency of the message and will gracefully comment on it, offering specific feedback, or will be aware of his or her experience and will comment on the uneasiness he or she feels. As in stage 2, the receiver is able to comment in such a way as to avoid creating a defensive response from the sender.
Stage 4: Incongruent messages trigger recall from past experiences, and the receiver filters new messages through them. The past experiences usually are from one's family of origin and are responses to a specific set of messages or feelings of confusion to incongruent messages. An example might be if a parent has sent messages of anger accompanied by pointing a finger. When the receiver sees the pointed finger, he or she concludes the sender is angry whether or not this is so. Typically this association is rigid, with the receiver having no means to check out the accuracy of the assumption.	*Stage 4*: Receiver is aware of both present and past experiences such that if an incongruent message triggers a past experience, he or she is aware that he or she is not responding in the present moment and will comment on that fact. The options are to explore the unfinished past business or to continue in the present. Again the key is the receiver's awareness of what is going on and the freedom to choose how and when to respond.
Stage 5: Receiver recycles the incongruent communication, reinforcing and strengthening the pattern. Unless therapists are congruent, they may become enmeshed in the clients' communication patterns instead of helping them to become more congruent.	*Stage 5*: Either the receiver will have detected the incongruent message and commented on it, or will be aware of feeling confused and will comment on it. If neither of these, the receiver will communicate back to the original sender an incongruent message. If aware of what is going on, the original sender will have the freedom to comment on the incoming incongruent message, thus breaking the cycle.

agreeing, apologizing, and pleasing. The bodily representation might portray a stance of helplessness. The person's inner feelings are of worthlessness, inadequacy, and lack of control.

Blamer

The second stance is the "blamer" (Satir, 1972). This role involves being the boss or commanding general and finding fault with everyone and everything. The person is harsh, loud, domineering, and superior, and puts down others with words that are accusing in nature. The body is tight, with pointing finger, and there is internal loneliness and a feeling of failure.

Computer

The third stance is the "computer" or superreasonable person who is analytic, emotionally distant, cool, and flat-voiced. The body is stiff, straight, held aloof and motionless, but the person masks feelings of helplessness inside.

Distractor

The fourth stance is the "distractor" or mascot. The key word to describe this person is "irrelevant." He or she interrupts, and often assumes the role of a comedian, thereby relieving tension. Physically, his or her body might be seen as going in all directions, angular and generally in motion. He or she feels as if no one cares, and is afraid and lonely.

Leveling

The fifth response is the "leveling" or congruent response. For this person the verbal and nonverbal communications match. When people evaluate or criticize others using the leveling response, they deal only with the specific behavior of the other persons and not with his or her worth as a person.

The skills of leveling are to be found in the section on active listening. The person who relates from a leveling role is in touch with the totality of personal being, namely, heart, mind, body, feelings, and will.

This section discussed the process of communication and feedback. Specific attention was given to the two communication cycles, congruent and incongruent, in order to see how healthy communication takes place, is reinforced, and can be changed. In addition five communication responses were identified and explained.

References

Bandler, R., Grindler, J., & Satir, V. *Changing with families*. Palo Alto, Calif.: Science and Behavior Books, 1976.

Bateson, G., Haley, J., Jackson, D., & Weakland, J. Towards a theory of schizophrenia. *Behavioural Science*, 1956, *1*, 251–264.

Goldenberg, H., & Goldenberg, I. *Family theory: An overview*. Monterrey, Calif.: Brooks/Cole, 1980.

Laing, R. D. Mystification, confusion, and conflict. In I. Boszormenyi-Nagy & J. L. Framo (Eds.), *Itensive family therapy: Theoretical and practical aspects*. New York: Harper & Row, 1965.

Satir, V. *Peoplemaking*. Palo Alto, Calif.: Science and Behavior Books, 1976.

5.3 BASIC COMMUNICATION SKILLS

The previous section dealt with the overall process of communication and feedback. This part deals with some of the skills that are essential to the art of communication. We present an overview rather than a full discussion of communication. Many volumes and workbooks have been developed on basic communication skills and we will not attempt to duplicate this work. The skills of acceptance, attending, and empathy are discussed below.

The precursors to communication involve a person's attitude or stance toward another person. To a large degree, the precursors are nonverbal, although they do have verbal components. Precursors lay the foundation for communication, without which the verbal aspects of communication may not be believed. While these precursors to communication involve attitudes toward others, they also involve skills that can be learned.

Acceptance

The concept of acceptance is important. Gordon (1970, p. 31) states: "Acceptance is like the fertile soil that permits a tiny seed to develop into the lovely flower it is capable of becoming. The soil enables the seed to become the flower. It releases the capacity of the seed which is within the seed, to grow."

When people feel genuinely accepted, they are more able to risk change and growth with less likelihood of acting defensively or fearfully. Often nonacceptance is used to motivate performance, but this runs counter to our human needs for acceptance.

Many people believe that acceptance is a passive attribute, like a state of mind, an attitude, or a feeling (Gordon, 1970). But in order for acceptance to be like fertile soil, it must be demonstrated and communicated.

Acceptance Skills

Acceptance skills might be categorized under nonverbal and verbal aspects. To do nothing and to listen passively can be a demonstration of acceptance. To not intervene (do nothing) in a situation might say to a person that he or she is acceptable. Similarly, continually interfering, checking up, and offering advice can communicate nonacceptance or at least that one's be-

havior is suspect. For example, parents interfering in the child's playing activities can communicate a message that the child is engaged in unacceptable behavior and can reduce the child's ability to make and work through mistakes (Gordon, 1970).

Similarly, to listen quietly to another person without breaking in with advice, questions, and criticism is to communicate that the other is valuable, particularly when he or she is working through a problem. Listening gives individuals the freedom to work through personal issues.

An example might be a friend's frustration with a boss. He or she starts by berating the boss, the job, and the impossibility of working in the situation. A listener's tendency would be to intervene with advice about how to get along in the situation, minimizing the severity of the situation, and exhorting him or her to change. This would result in short-circuiting the person's opportunity to work through the issue fully.

Verbal Acceptance

Verbal acceptance can be communicated by using such words as: "I see, oh, you don't say, how about that, tell me more, let's discuss it, I'm listening, seems like it's important to you," and others (Gordon, 1970). These communicate acceptance by drawing the other person out without interpreting the situation. It communicates interest in what others have to say and gives permission to say it.

Attending Behaviors

The skill of attending can be viewed as an aspect of acceptance. This skill involves how to make oneself available to another. Attending has physical and psychological aspects.

Egan (1975) deals with attending behaviors in detail. Physical attending has to do with how we relate physically to another person. If we turn our bodies away, it suggests that we either do not care what another person is saying or that they are not worth being involved with, or both.

Our physical presence can suggest involvement: facing the other person squarely, maintaining eye contact, open posture (not having arms or legs crossed), leaning in toward the other, and being relatively relaxed. Psychological attending involves listening to verbal and nonverbal messages and picking up the messages; this includes an awareness of the ways in which verbal messages are delivered (tone of voice, inflection, etc.). Often a verbal "no" may really mean "yes" because of the nonverbal cues that are expressed.

When an individual attends well to another person, he or she communicates respect and support for the other person. Such communication conveys a sense of genuineness and sincerity that can be reassuring. Such skills can be readily learned.

Empathy

Another corresponding interpersonal skill is empathy. According to Egan (1975), empathy is the ability to:

1. Imaginatively enter another person's world through the person's frame of reference and get a feeling for what his or her world is like.
2. Communicate to a person in a way that shows understanding of the person's feelings.

Primary Empathy

Egan (1975) develops two levels of empathy that are progressive in nature. The first, which he calls "primary," involves communicating to the client an initial basic understanding of his or her experiences and the feelings that go with them. At this level the helper does not try to probe deeper into the client but only reflects what the client has explicitly revealed. When this is done well, it allows the client to move forward in exploring other issues. An example may be helpful (Egan, 1975, p. 78):

Client: I don't think I'll make a good therapist. The other people in the program are much brighter than I am. I'm beginning to see my deficiencies more and more as I move through the practice sessions and I don't really know if I have what it takes to help someone else. Maybe I need to work more things out for myself.
Therapist: You're feeling pretty inadequate, and it's really getting you down—enough to make you want to give up.
Client: And yet I know that "giving up" is part of the problem. I'm not the brightest, but I am not absolutely dumb. And I have been picking up some of the skills in the practice session. I'm like a kid. I want everything right away.

Advanced Empathy

Advanced empathy explores not only what the client expresses, but also what he or she implies, leaves unstated, or expresses unclearly. These are the covertly expressed issues as opposed to the overt ones responded to on the primary level. Again an example is provided (Egan, 1979):

Peter explores his feelings and behavior to a certain point but seems to skirt delicate issues at the core of the problem in his life. He also shows signs of fatigue and frustration during therapy. The therapist puts all of these clues together and the following dialogue ensues.
Therapist: Peter, it seems that you're skirting some of the issues that bother you the most. Maybe running away is more work and more depressing than facing them squarely. It's very painful for you to put yourself squarely on the line.
Peter: I knew that had to be said sooner or later. I don't know what I'm afraid of. It's stupid of me to invest my time in therapy and then not make the most of my time.

The criterion for the good use of empathy is that it causes the client to push forward in exploring personal issues.

There are some potential difficulties in using advanced empathy. There is always a danger of using it too soon. One might confuse, scare away, or anger the client by initiating advanced empathy too soon. The therapist should wait until the client has established trust and rapport.

Authenticity and Genuineness

Another problem area is feigning understanding. This happens when a therapist gets lost in what the client is saying. This can happen to anyone at some time. The difference is how the therapist deals with this. The therapist should not fake understanding but admit it and work to get back in touch with the client. By doing so the therapist demonstrates genuineness, authenticity, and caring (Egan, 1975).

One of the potential problems of therapy is being a ''parrot''; that is, simply repeating exactly what the client is saying. Parroting involves feeding back the words of the speaker without relating the words to the feelings. The goal in empathy is to communicate understanding that gets at the essence of the issue, allowing for growth and the development of new meaning.

Questioning

Finally we discuss the area of questioning. Therapists often ask too many questions that tend to be a substitute for empathy (Egan, 1975). Often the questions are asked in a closed rather than open manner.

Closed Question: Are you having problems with your father?
Open Question: In what ways are you upset by your father's actions?

Closed questions tend to elicit yes or no answers, and do not serve the purpose of opening up areas that need to be understood by means of empathy. Questions that simply pile up information are not helpful. The goal of information is action.

References

Egan, G. *The skilled helper* (2nd ed.). Belmont, Calif.: Brooks/Cole, 1982.
Gordon, T. *P.E.T.: Parent effectiveness training*. New York: Peter Wyden, 1970.

5.4 ACTIVE LISTENING SKILLS

This section discusses the skills of active listening. The skills described in the previous section are some of the foundation skills that make active listening possible.

Active listening skills are ways of involving the receiver as well as the sender in meaningful conversation. Too often people tend to preach, give advice, exhort, and judge each other, thus closing down the desire to disclose a problem or work on it, or even to feel good about the person to whom they are revealing the problem.

Active listening skills have been used as the focus of the helping approach advocated by Gordon (1970), Egan (1975), and others.

Active listening can be effectively used when someone presents a problem that needs exploration. That is, it is the other person's issue, not yours. Active listening should not be used when the problem is yours, or when the other person does not really want to talk about his or her feelings, or when either the presenter or the receiver does not have sufficient time to explore the question, or when specific information or help is not what is being asked for.

Feedback

The first aspect of active listening is feedback. A person has a message. He or she communicates it to the receiver, who uncodes it and responds. It might look like Figure 5.4.1.

The mother feeds back her understanding of the message to the child. If the mother misinterprets the message, she may, for example,

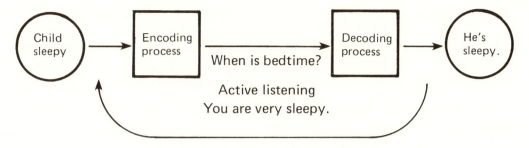

Figure 5.4.1. The process of active listening.

*Adapted from Gordon, 1970, p. 51

think that the child is asking about bedtime in order to be able to go out and play. By checking the meaning of the message, she will be able to clarify the content and feelings the child is communicating.

In this example the mother was wrong because the issue was that the child was sleepy. By checking out the message, the mother was able to understand the child's issues and accurately answer those needs. In this case, since bedtime was a while off, she offered some support and understanding.

Active Listening Values

The values of active listening are to:

1. Help people become less afraid of negative feelings.
2. Promote relationships of warmth and acceptance.
3. Promote problem solving by the person asking for help.
4. Influence the person to be more willing to listen to thoughts and ideas.
5. Keep "ball" or energy in the other's court so that he or she can work on personal issue.

Gordon (1970) also lists what he calls typical ways that people deny active listening. He calls these ways the terrible 12:

1. Ordering, directing, commanding
2. Warning, admonishing, correcting
3. Exhorting, moralizing, preaching
4. Advising, giving solutions or suggestions
5. Lecturing, teaching, giving logical arguments
6. Judging, criticizing, blaming, disagreeing
7. Praising, agreeing
8. Name calling, ridiculing, shaming
9. Interpreting, analyzing, diagnosing
10. Reassuring, sympathizing, consoling, supporting
11. Probing, questioning, interrogating
12. Withdrawing, distracting, humoring, diverting.

When not practicing active listening, these 12 ways of relating tend to be used to answer questions, put people down, and "fix" them without having heard their concerns. The 12 ways of relating demonstrate a lack of trust and acceptance, a disregard of feelings, and a lack of worth. A person does not necessarily wish to communicate the negative messages mentioned, but unfortunately does.

"I" Messages

When you are the person with the problem, how do you communicate this without causing a defensive reaction in the receiver or without attacking his or her self-worth? Many therapists, including Gordon, have advocated the use of "I" messages, as opposed to "you" messages.

Much of the time, when frustrated, upset, angry, or confused, we tend to blame others for our feelings. We put the responsibility for negative feelings onto others. It is quite evident how easy it is for another person to feel attacked, put down, and defensive, and thus less willing to work for a solution to a problem.

A husband, for example, comes home from work, is tired, and wants to rest for a few minutes before entering into the activities at home. His wife immediately starts making demands on him, or wants to talk about her day. The husband might typically respond with something like, "You are always bugging me," which causes a defensive reaction in the wife. His real feeling is one of being tired. If, on the other hand, he says, "I am very tired and would like to rest," the issue can be resolved quickly. The communication is open and honest. The wife is free from defensiveness. By actively stating his needs, a mutually agreeable solution can be negotiated.

If the communication gets hooked into "you" messages, the use of active listening can break the cycle. To return to the example, suppose the husband reacts to the wife's demands by blaming her for bugging him. She might actively listen to him by asking if he is tired and inquiring about his needs. Thus the negative interaction cycle might be creatively blocked.

Ways to Communicate Feelings

It should be remembered that active listening and talking can be used to describe positive as well as negative feelings; to encourage as well as to communicate a problem. Hollinbeck and Mease (1971) have developed acronyms that are helpful in remembering how to communicate feelings. They are DESI (negative feelings) and DEE (positive feelings) messages.

D—*describe* specifically the behavior you feel is negative
E—*express* the feelings you have related to this behavior to the person
S—*suggest* alternative behavior
I—*involve* the person in the process of choosing an alternative behavior

and

D—*describe* specifically the behavior you feel is positive
E—*express* your feelings about that behavior to the individual
E—*encourage* the individual to continue desirable behavior

References

Egan, G. *The skilled helper* (2nd ed.). Belmont, Calif.: Brooks/Cole, 1982.

Gordon, T. *P.E.T.: Parent effectiveness training.* New York: Peter Wyden, 1970.

Hollinbeck, R., & Mease, W. *Family communication systems.* Minneapolis: Human Synergistics, 1971.

CHAPTER 6

CONFLICT RESOLUTION

6.1 AN INTEGRATED MODEL OF CONFLICT THEORY

Tom and Mary are in their mid-30s. They have been married for approximately five years, and have one child. Over the past year, their relationship has been steadily deteriorating. Mary recently returned to her career as a legal secretary after a five-year absence, and has begun a small business venture. Tom works as a machinist at a nearby industrial plant.

Mary has been experiencing a growing excitement about her job and business. She has been making new friends, enjoying a few parties with co-workers, and earning a lot of money. Earlier in her marriage, Tom was her best friend and virtually her only source of companionship. Recently, however, Mary has noticed a growing boredom with her marital relationship and an increasing attraction to other men.

Tom, on the other hand, has become more demanding in terms of Mary's commitment to their relationship. He is glad that Mary seems so much more exuberant and excited about life, but resents the fact that her new occupations mean less time for him. A frequent "bone of contention" is the length of time that Tom and Mary should spend together as opposed to time apart from each other with friends.

A Multidimensional Perspective

Rank and Le Croy (1983) have illustrated the possibilities of utilizing a multiple theoretical perspective in the analysis and intervention of family conflict. They suggest that the combination of several theoretical perspectives, when brought to bear on a specific family topic such as conflict, may yield differing though complementary insights, thereby providing the therapist with greater flexibility in handling a particular problem.

This section describes a multiple theoretical perspective on family conflict consisting of social exchange theory, symbolic interactionism, and conflict theory, and applies this perspective to the family scenario described.

Social Exchange Theory

Social exchange theory is based on an economic metaphor. Marital and family interaction is like the business interaction of the stock exchange, which consists of mutual barter for the exchange of rewards. Exchanges may include a variety of commodities, resources, or skills (Rank & Le Croy, 1983). Like any good stock broker, we attempt to maximize profits and minimize costs in our social exchanges so that we obtain the most profitable outcome; that is, Reward − Cost = Profit (Rank & Le Croy, 1983). The motivation and goal of our behavior are, therefore, the maximization of profit through a bargaining process with the exchange partner(s).

There is, however, a limit to our profit making, beyond which we will not pursue self-gain (Rank & Le Croy, 1983). Furthermore, we evaluate the rewards and costs of our relationships according to a standard (level of comparison), which represents what we feel we deserve. When the outcome of a particular relationship meets this standard, we are satisfied, but when it falls below the standard, we may explore more satisfying alternative relationships.

Symbolic Interactionism

A shortcoming of social exchange theory is that it fails to specify what constitutes a reward or cost. How do we come to determine what a reward or cost is? Symbolic interactionism addresses this issue. This theory suggests that we learn to interpret and value certain items and skills as rewarding through interaction with our social environment (Rank & Le Croy, 1983). Individual differences arise as to what constitutes a reward or cost due as a result of the influence of such variables as social class, religious background, and peer group. As we move through the social structure, acquire new peer groups, and pass through the family life cycle, our values may change, and thereby create an evolving conception of what is rewarding and costly.

Our evaluation of exchange outcomes is rarely static, but tends to be in a state of flux that corresponds to our changing definition of reward and cost.

Conflict Theory

Conflict in our relationships is experienced when we undergo a change in our conception of what is rewarding or costly, and when we begin to sense inequity in a particular social exchange. At this point conflict theory offers another complementary perspective to social exchange theory.

Conflict theory assumes that conflict is natural and inevitable in human interaction. Rather than conflict being viewed as disruptive or negative, and, therefore, to be avoided, it is viewed as an ongoing part of life that needs regular attention and resolution. In fact if there is adequate problem management in a relationship, conflict can strengthen the relationship and make it more meaningful and rewarding. Furthermore the family, like all other social institutions, may be seen as a system geared toward the regulation of conflict.

Marriage and family relationships "reflect a perpetual situation of 'give and take,' a state of affairs within which order and interpersonal harmony can be maintained only through negotiation" (Sprey, 1979, p. 142). One source of conflict is a perceived unequal exchange between partners in a relationship, an idea already discussed in connection with social exchange theory.

In response to conflict, an individual either may leave a relationship, or attempt to resolve the conflict. Conflict resolution requires three essential components (Beckman, 1979, p. 61):

1. Open communication.
2. Accurate perceptions regarding the degree and nature of conflict.
3. Constructive effort to resolve conflict, which, at minimum, includes each partner being willing to consider the other's point of view and alternative solutions, and to compromise if necessary.

Case Example

The multiple perspective described may be applied to Tom and Mary's situation in the following manner. (See Figure 6.1.1.)

Mary has been learning new things about herself through her interactions with others

(A2). She has been experiencing a change in her values and perceptions of rewards and costs. For example, she is beginning to value experiences and relationships outside the domain of her family. Furthermore her interactions with others have caused her to reassess her relationship with Tom (B). Consequently she no longer feels that the relationship with him is equitable (C).

Tom, on the other hand, has had fairly consistent values and perceptions (A1). His concepts of rewards and costs have not shifted. What was once a satisfying and equitable relationship for him, however, has now changed as well (B). He feels neglected by Mary for the first time, and, therefore, would agree with her that their relationship has become inequitable (C), but for different reasons. It is clear that neither spouse is experiencing the level of profit enjoyed upon first getting married. This, in turn, has led to increasing conflict between them (D).

This conflict inevitably will result in some form of reorganization (E), involving negotiation to reestablish equity in the marital exchange, trial separation, or even divorce (Rank & Le Croy, 1983).

Intervention

Social exchange theory provides a way of describing Tom and Mary's current marital exchange. At present they do not have a compatible standard (level of comparison), and hence there is unequal interest in and reinforcement derived from their relationship (B, C).

One intervention at this point would be to help the couple find ways of increasing possible exchanges with each other. Symbolic interactionism provides a way of explaining how and why Tom and Mary are èxperiencing inequity in their marital exchange. The therapist, for example, can explore with the couple how Mary's interaction with her friends and co-workers has changed her standard and shifted her concepts of reward and cost.

Finally, conflict theory directs the therapist to teach Tom and Mary conflict management strategies, so as to maintain their relationship in the midst of inevitable conflict. Beckman (1983) suggests that to handle conflict effectively, the couple must (1) be able to identify contentious issues, (2) get beyond defensive and emotional reactions, (3) implement problem-

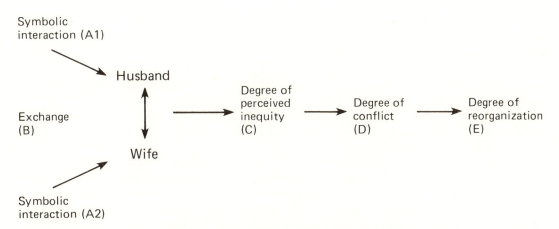

Figure 6.1.1. A multiple-perspective model.
(From Rank and Le Croy, 1983, p. 445.)

Adapted from *Family Relations Journal*, July 1983, p. 445.

solving procedures, and (4) have sufficient commitment to wait for equitable exchanges in the future.

By combining the three theories, not only is there greater insight into relational dischord, but a more effective and flexible treatment may be obtained. For example, our analysis has revealed multiple points of entry (A, B, C, D) into Tom and Mary's situation. At each point various modes of intervention are available to the therapist.

References

Beckman, L. T. Couples' decision-making processes regarding fertility. Cited by Mark R. Rank & Cray W. Le Croy, Toward a multiple perspective in family theory and practice: The case of social exchange theory, symbolic interactionism, and conflict theory. *Family Relations*, 1983, *32*, 441–448.

Rank, M. R., & Le Croy, C. W. *Ibid.*

Sprey, T. Conflict theory and the study of marriage and the family. Cited by Rank & Le Croy. *Ibid.*

6.2 ANGER: A BRIEF OVERVIEW

Anger is often expressed destructively in our society. Consequently it is often regarded as a taboo, and we do not instruct people how to express it appropriately. Richardson, in his book *Statistics of Deadly Quarrels*, claims that in the 126 years between 1890 and 1945, people killed each other at a rate of one every 68 seconds in wars, skirmishes, quarrels, or murders. A total of 59 million people were killed during this period.

War, murder, and vandalism are examples of the expression of destructive anger that are obvious to the public. Other examples, such as child abuse or wife beating, are concealed within households. This section examines the nature and function of anger and concludes with a discussion of anger management as it applies to marriage.

The Nature of Anger

Anger is an emotional experience. Augsburger (1976) defined it beautifully when he wrote:

Mind and body, head and gut, appraisal and arousal, are interdependent parts of the whole called "experiencing." Experiencing unites symbolized awareness (cognition) and physiologized awareness (emotion). Emotion requires both a state of physiological arousal and a cognitive assessment of the situation. Neither of these alone will induce emotion.

Cognitive assessment of the situation may produce physiological arousal. For example, a basketball coach may see a team member fouled and experience an injection of adrenalin and increased heartbeat. However, the coach may not be aware of these physiological changes because physiological signals precede cognitive awareness.

Anger as Innate Response

Anger may be viewed as a physiological arousal, as a biological inborn response, and as an interpersonal frustration or fear. Heinrichs (1976) encapsulates the development of anger as an innate response in the following statement.

Beginning as an undifferentiated protest in response to internal physiological discomforts and external stresses, anger becomes increasingly an affect which is object-oriented and arises in response to specific qualities of interpersonal relatedness experienced by the individual.

Anger Defined

Mace (1976) suggest that anger is not a primary emotion, but is triggered by other emotions, especially frustration and fear. Anger, for example, may be triggered by frustration when physical and psychological needs are not being met.

Anger may also be triggered by fear. Fear warns us of danger; we may react in fear by running away as fast as we can, or we may react in anger by preparing to fight with all our resources. This "fight or flight" reaction pertains to psychological as well as physical threats. For example, when someone makes a cutting remark that threatens our self-esteem, we may withdraw (fear response) or strike back with a cutting remark of our own (anger response). Anger as an innate response is a biological and psychological experience that facilitates need attainment and personal preservation.

Anger as a Learned Response

The way we have learned to perceive situations controls how we experience internal arousal. Our perceptions of a situation determine the labels we give to physiological arousal since our physical sensations are the same for anger, sadness, euphoria, or fear. Schachter and Singer (1962), who injected subjects with epinephrine (a stimulant) to produce inner arousal, discovered that the subjects identified their internal arousal from cues in the external situation. This experiment supported the viewpoint that emotion is the joint product of two factors, namely, physiological arousal and cognitive appraisal (inferences), and is appropriately called the two-factor theory of emotion. The following is Schachter and Singer's (1962, p. 33) formulation of the two-factor theory.

Given a state of physiological arousal for which an individual has no immediate explanation, he will "label" this state and describe his feelings in terms of the cognitions available to him.

Anger as a Personal (Intrapsychic) Phenomenon

A personal view of anger maintains that it is the product of factors within the individual. For example, the anger of one marriage partner toward the other is construed as a personal problem more than an interpersonal one. The angry reaction may be seen as a displacement of frustration experienced in other areas of life, a release of pent-up aggressive energy, a projection of the spouse's self-hate, an emergence of primitive sadism, an expression of narcissistic rage or oral demand, a displacement of anger originally experienced toward parents or siblings, or even a manifestation of basic hatred toward women or men.

Anger as an Interpersonal (Interpsychic) Phenomenon

An interpersonal view of anger maintains that anger is the product of a dysfunction in our present relationships. In the case of a marital spat, the anger of each spouse is attributable to interpersonal factors more than personal ones. For example, when a relationship is considered to be unequal in some way (as delineated by social exchange theory), anger and frustration will likely be experienced.

The Function of Anger

As a psychological and physiological response to a threat to the self concept or physical being, or to frustration of need satisfaction, anger has several functions. Anger energizes the body to defend itself against threat, or to overcome obstacles when attaining needs. This aroused state may result in greater than normal physical prowess and perceptual awareness.

In the context of relationships, anger stimulates the expression of negative feelings and unsatisfied expectations of the other person(s). As such it is essential to a warm intimate relationship (Bach & Wyden, 1969).

Mismanaging Anger

There are at least two categories of people pertinent to anger expression: the "stuffers" and the "venters."

Stuffers

Dismissing or denying anger, so characteristic of stuffers, leads to delayed awareness, and can generalize to screening out all emotions. Anger that is acknowledged, but not expressed directly at the triggering incident, is expressed indirectly. The vehicle of this indirect expression may be self-hate, psychosomatic pathology, or fractured interpersonal relationships. Thus anger can be related to a host of different pathological symptoms in personal and interpersonal spheres.

Modow (1977) emphasizes the physical damage caused by repressed anger. He refers to three defense mechanisms, defined more clearly by Heinrichs (1976). They are (1) denial of anger, (2) suppression or conscious hiding of anger, and (3) repression of anger. Anger turned inward may cause gastrointestinal problems such as gastric ulcers, respiratory ailments such as asthma, skin disorders, nervous disorders such as tics, and some types of hypertension.

Venters

Just as "stuffing" anger can generalize to screening out all emotions, so the inappropriate "venting" of anger can generalize to other feelings also. Thus positive feelings become toned down, delayed, and possibly inexpressible when anger is vented indiscriminately. Relationships become strained and estranged, disagreements become blow-ups, and blaming behavior increases. Tarris (1982, p. 131) vividly critiques the ventilation theory of anger management as follows:

It seems to me that the major affect of the ventilationist approach has been to raise the generational noise level of our lives, not to lessen our problems. I notice that the people who are most prone to give vent to their rage get angrier, not less angry. I observe a lot of hurt feelings among the recipients of rage. And I can plot the stages in a typical "ventilating" marital argument: precipitating event, angry outburst, shouting, recriminations, screaming or crying, the furious peak (sometimes accompanied by physical assault), exhaustion, sudden apology or just sullenness. The cycle is replayed the next day or week. What in this is "cathartic"? Screaming? Throwing a pot? Does either action cause the anger to vanish or the angry spouse to feel better? Not that I can see.

Tarris points to research that suggests that aggression inflames anger and that "talking it (anger) out" only rehearses anger.

Managing Anger Effectively

If both stuffing and venting anger have undesirable consequences, how then shall we manage it? According to Mace (1976, p. 131), "What causes marriages to fail, over and over again is the incapacity of the couple to cope with their own and each other's anger."

Reflection

Earnest Harburg of the University of Michigan suggests an anger management strategy called "reflection" (Tarris, 1982). Reflection involves waiting until we have calmed down, and then attempting to reason things out. An underlying assumption is that the most successful way of dispelling anger is to understand why we behaved in a certain way. This assumption has been supported by research comparing a reasonable explanation for annoying behavior with two methods of venting anger.

We may, however, raise an objection to this approach, on the grounds that it requires the angry individual(s) not to be very angry. Suppose we feel like making a cutting remark or bursting with rage? Clearly the reflection approach may need supplementary measures for some couples at certain times. Those couples who have great difficulty in calming down and resisting the urge to vent their anger immediately may have several needs. They may need to relive unresolved conflicts from the past and, in so doing, will tap and release residual anger so as to be free to deal with current anger incidents. They may also need to learn about the dynamics of current conflicts and how they compare with well-established conflict patterns derived from their respective families of origin. They may further need training in how to fight fairly during an angry incident.

Fair fighting for Feuding Couples

Specific details of anger management therapy for feuding couples vary, but the general model remains the same. It is to involve the couple in an experience of each aspect of the conflict so that the couple can learn to have a fair fight (Bach & Wyden, 1969) and resolve the conflict so that both partners' needs are met (Gordon, 1975); that is, both partners are involved unless one partner has an excess of residual rage to ventilate. Such a person would need to work through this anger before effective anger management could occur at the interpersonal level.

It is necessary fully to experience and express anger before resolution of the conflict can be negotiated. Bach and Wyden (1969) insist that very few couples know how to have a fair fight, and, therefore, never resolve conflicts. They encourage couples to fight in therapy, and

often use a rating scale to assess the fairness of the fight. After the fight these ratings are communicated to the fighters, with the expectation that insight will create openness to change. They then continue to teach basic rules for fair fighting, with specific application to the couple. Satir (1972) uses body sculpting to the same end. She might ask the husband and wife to assume the posture typical of their fighting styles and hold it for a minute or so. Then she encourages them to hold their feelings and work toward open, straightforward communication styles. In both cases the communication aims are the same: to create awareness of the harmfulness of present communication patterns and develop new constructive patterns of interaction and communication in which negative feelings are dealt with and individual needs are met.

Resolving Anger Empathically

Once both partners are expressing their anger openly, honestly, and directly, the stage is set for the resolution phase of anger. Gordon (1975) has proposed a system of conflict resolution that features the following. The disputing parties identify their feelings and needs with "I statements," listen empathically to each other, and negotiate a settlement that satisfies the needs of everyone concerned.

Although seriously estranged couples may need a good deal of "fight training" first, Gordon's no-lose system is helpful if the parties meet two prerequisites. First, the problem and each party's needs are clearly defined. Then everyone involved brainstorms nonjudgmentally for potential solutions. After brainstorming each solution is appraised to see if it meets all the stated needs. The process continues until a solution agreeable to all is found. After a trial period, the effectiveness of the solution is assessed. Eventually this system reduces the number of anger incidents in a relationship, because needs can be expressed openly and are usually satisfied.

The Smouldering Fire

An important task in the resolution stage of anger is to share hurt feelings. L'Abate (1977) argues that "just dealing with anger is not enough"; for underneath "the smoke" of anger there is the "smouldering fire of hurt feelings" (p. 13). According to L'Abate, these hurt feelings "may be related to unresolved grief, past frustrations and failures, feelings of inadequacy, present loneliness, or poor self-esteem" (p. 13).

Different Strokes for Different Folks

Different couples have different needs. Some couples may comfortably adopt the reflection approach in anger management, whereas other couples may need to supplement this approach with fair-fight procedures. In either case the reflection approach may be further supplemented by Gordon's (1975) system of conflict resolution when couples are attempting to reason things out.

References

Augsburger, D. *Perspectival approach to anger management training.* Symposium at meeting of the Christian Association for Psychological Studies of the Western Association of Christians for Psychological Studies, Santa Barbara, Calif., June 1976.

Bach, G. P., & Wyden, P. *The intimate enemy: How to fight fair in love and marriage.* New York: Morrow, 1969.

Gordon, T. *Parent effectiveness training.* Scarborough, Ont.: New American Library, 1975.

Heinrichs, D. *Psychoanalytic approach to anger management training.* Symposium at meeting of the Christian Association for Psychological Studies and the Western Association of Christians for Psychological Studies, Santa Barbara, Calif., June 1976.

L'Abate, L. Intimacy is sharing hurt feelings: A reply to David Mace. *Journal of Marriage and Family Counseling*, April 1977, 13–16.

Mace, D. R. Marital intimacy and the deadly love–anger cycle. *Journal of Marriage and Family Counseling*, April 1976, 131–137.

Modow, L. Do you have any of these symptoms of repressed anger? *New Woman*, Jan.–Feb. 1977.

Satir, V. *People making.* Palo Alto, Calif., Science and Behavior Books, 1972.

Schachter, S., & Singer, J. E. Cognitive, social, and physiological determinants of emotional state. *Psychological Review*, 1962, *69*, 379–399.

Tarris, J. Anger management. Unpublished manuscript, Vancouver, B.C., 1982.

6.3 RESOLVING CONFLICT IN MARRIAGE

Marriage is the most intimate of all human relationships, and as such holds the greatest potential for conflicts. The manner in which conflicts are handled determines whether they are harmful or damaging to the marriage. Couples who learn to value their conflicts can utilize them to improve their communication skills and thereby grow in intimacy. A couple's intimacy grows when conflicts are faced openly and resolved in the painful but rewarding process of growing understanding and compromise of differences.

The following discussion of several practical facets of conflict resolution in marriage does not pretend to be comprehensive, but to provide some helpful guidelines. (*This material was adapted from a Burnaby mental health pamphlet.)

Necessary Attitudes for Effective Resolution of Conflict

Both partners must be willing to listen to each other's complaints and to accept feelings, however vehement they feel about them. A related attitude is a commitment to honesty, a willingness to be transparent and thus vulnerable to the marriage partner. This implies a deep involvement in the quest for greater intimacy in the relationship, without fear of attack or loss of acceptance. A continual struggle is necessary to lower the wall between partners that limits their closeness and communication.

It is also necessary to come to the inescapable realization that enduring love is more than feeling or tender emotion; it is also action. Couples must not only feel, but act in love. This kind of love moves the relationship beyond the 50–50 philosophy. True love may be experienced only beyond that point. Anything up to 50 is merely barter.

There must be a strong desire to resolve differences and make compromises so that the outcome of conflicts will leave both parties satisfied with the resolution. In marriage, conflicts must not be seen as win–lose propositions, because when one partner seeks to win, both lose.

Ground Rules for Successful Conflict Resolution

Keep to the here and now Do not use yesterday's problems as today's ammunition. ("He who forgives an offense seeks love, but he who repeats a matter alienates a friend.") Phrases such as "you always . . ." and "you never . . ." usually confound the issue by implicitly bringing up past failures.

Keep to one issue Identify and discuss only one specific issue, which is the center of the conflict. Do not bring in other issues because of a need to defend yourself or to attack your partner.

Use "I" messages Express your feelings using "I" rather than "you." It is less threatening to say, "I feel very angry when I work hard to fix a meal like this and it doesn't get eaten right away," than to say, "Why do you have to come home without telling me?" The first is a statement of feeling about an objective situation. The second is an attack on your partner.

Avoid character analysis Do not attack your partner's character; talk about behavior rather than personalities. "It is hard to keep the bedroom clean when dirty clothes are left on the floor" is better than "Why did I have to end up with the town slob?" "He who belittles his neighbor lacks sense."

Do not counterattack If your spouse initiates a legitimate complaint, do not respond with something like, "Well, you're just as bad, look what you did when . . ." Accept reproof graciously.

Avoid mind reading Do not attempt to analyze your partner's attitudes or motives. The "why" behind a person's behavior is not the issue; the issue is the behavior itself. We have no right to judge another's motives. If you sense a problem in this area, check it out by asking your partner.

Deal with conflict quickly Do not put off confrontation if it means harboring resentment toward your spouse. Such feelings may be buried alive! They will inevitably be expressed in some manner; if not honestly and directly, then dishonestly and indirectly.

Keep emotions appropriate The expression of emotions during the attempt to resolve a conflict is usually helpful, if it is appropriate to the size of that conflict. However, the unrestrained venting of anger may be destructive.

Don't try to win When one partner wins, the other loses, and when one loses, both partners lose. The goal should be to find a mutually satisfactory solution to the problem at hand, so that both partners come out as winners. This is especially true in marriage.

Establish belt lines Each spouse should tell the other what kinds of remarks constitute "hitting below the belt," that is, comments that are too hurtful or damaging for the other to be able to handle. Avoid below-the-belt statements at all costs. If your partner is hitting below the belt during a conflict, call him or her on it immediately.

Call foul when a rule is broken These rules and others agreed upon form the ground rules for handling conflict. When one partner breaks a rule, the other should call foul. This is a signal that the ground rules must be reestablished and followed.

A Suggested Procedure for Handling Conflicts

No single procedure will be acceptable or ideal for every couple, or even for the same couple at all times. However, the following guidelines provide several key elements helpful in developing a method of conflict resolution. Although the procedure may seem cumbersome and somewhat artificial, it has proved of great value to those who have taken the time and effort to learn it. As part of a couple's communication skills, it becomes a natural and helpful method of resolving conflicts so that both partners come out winners.

In this description partner A designates the initiator of the conflict and partner B the receiver. For purposes of illustration only, partner A is the wife and partner B is the husband in the following description.

Step 1

Partner A feels a need for conflict resolution.

Goal   To determine whether conflict can be resolved alone. Then ask yourself a few important questions: Is this issue a one-time event that can be handled by myself, without going to my partner? Am I willing to be honest as well as loving? Have I identified the true issue, or is my complaint a trivial one that hides a deeper grievance? Am I ready to present a specific request for change?

Step 2

Partner A announces her intention.

Goal   To open the issue. Partner A may open the issue with a statement such as, ''I have a problem I need to talk over with you.'' You may or may not want to state the issue at this point. Timing is crucial. If this is not a good time, an appropriate time and place should be negotiated and specifically stated.

Step 3

Partner A states the conflict. (This step begins the actual discussion and attempted resolution of the conflict.)

Goal   An adequate statement and understanding of the issue. Two matters are shared at this step—what is wrong and how you feel about it. Keep your statement short and simple, so that you do not overload the communication channels. Throughout this step, partner B listens carefully and gives feedback at frequent intervals. That is, he states in his own words his understanding of what is wrong and how partner A feels about the problem. This is very difficult for most people to do but is perhaps the most important skill for good conflict resolution. It is crucial that partner B not counterattack or attempt to defend himself at this stage of the conflict.

Partner B's task here is simply to listen and to feed back understanding. A great advantage of this is that partner A's feelings will usually be greatly diminished if she is able to express them in an accepting atmosphere and have them acknowledged by her partner. This in no way implies that he agrees with her. However, just having one's feelings acknowledged as real and valid is a great help in resolving them.

When partner A is convinced that the issue is clear to partner B and her feelings are understood, they may go on to the next step.

Step 4

Partner A proposes a solution to the conflict.

Goal   A proposal and understanding of possible solutions. In this step the initiator states what she wants in order that the problem be corrected. She states clearly her request, the basis for it, and realistic ways her spouse can meet this request. She attempts to tell what is at stake or what it would mean to her to have it resolved, and how it might benefit both of them.

As in step 3, partner B gives feedback to indicate that he understands exactly what partner A wants. It is not enough to say, ''I understand.'' Unless he actually describes in his own words what his partner desires, it is impossible to ascertain the accuracy of his perception. When partner A is sure that she is understood, the couple may go on to step 5.

Step 5

Partner B responds to partner A.

Goal The expression and understanding of partner B's response to the issue and the proposed solution.

This is partner B's opportunity to tell how he feels about the issue and about the proposal for a change. He also should keep his discussion simple and in short steps, waiting for frequent feedback from partner A along the way.

Partner B has three options at this point. He may agree with the request; he may disagree completely; or he may suggest a compromise solution. A compromise solution may be a totally new proposal or an agreement to go along with partner A's proposal if she concedes to counter requests from him. If an agreement is made at this point, a contract for change is agreed upon and the couple may proceed to step 7. If no agreement is reached in a short time, the couple should go on to step 6.

Step 6

Take an intermission (optional).

Goal To allow for extra time if necessary before final decision. At times it is very helpful to take time out in a conflict, to agree to let the matter rest without further discussion for a period of a day or two. A solution is often much easier to reach after a time to cool down. A specific time should be designated for coming back to the issue.

Step 7

Ask for and grant forgiveness.

Goal To resolve any resentments held by either party. Unresolved feelings of anger or resentment need to be dealt with. Before a conflict can be resolved, those feelings must be taken into account. In this step both partners ask for forgiveness from each other. Asking for forgiveness does not necessarily imply that you intentionally wronged or were totally wrong yourself; only that your actions or words have hurt your partner, and that you want your partner to be free from any resentments that have come about as a result, so that the relationship may be restored. Also, this decision means that you are giving up your right to your feelings and the right to bring up those acts or situations that caused the feelings. This step is a willing and significant act of love on the part of both partners. "He who forgives an offense seeks love . . ."

Step 8

Review the conflict

Goal To learn from the experience and review the solution. This is a time to rethink the conflict alone. Ask yourself such questions as: What have I learned from this conflict? Did I abide by the ground rules? Have all hurts been forgiven?

Another aspect of this step is to review the situation after a week or so to determine if the solution is actually working out to the satisfaction of both partners. If it is not, the subject is to be reopened and alternative solutions sought.

Summary

This approach will seem cumbersome and awkward to many. However, those very characteristics force the couple to concentrate on the process of resolving the conflicts. It slows that process down to enable the couple to work at it step by step. It admittedly is a process that requires sustained effort to master and generally necessitates the aid of a trained therapist. In many cases the rewards are worth the effort.

Reference

Author unknown. Resolving conflict in marriage. Burnaby Mental Health, Burnaby, 1978.

CHAPTER 7

FAMILY ISSUES

7.1 INCESTUOUS FAMILY SYSTEMS

When family life fails, the inevitable consequence is a tendency toward dehumanization of human behavior.

Nathan Ackerman

Incest is a serious family problem in contemporary society. While there are no firm estimates of the incidence of incest, large-scale United States studies of child sexual abuse report that one in four girls and one in ten boys will be sexually molested before the age of 18.

Definition of Sexual Abuse

Sexual abuse is incest if the abuser's relationship to the child is one of kinship (father, older brother) or is kinlike (mother's live-in boyfriend, regular babysitter). Thus this class of abusers is distinguished from others who may be authority figures of another sort (teachers, club leaders) or may be strangers.

Myths About Incest

Contrary to common belief, incest is not limited to certain geographic areas and social classes. Incest occurs in all socioeconomic groups and is present in all occupational groups and settings. Furthermore incest is not a one- or two-time occurrence in the life of a victim, but often takes place from early childhood into the teens. The typical incest relationship is initiated between the ages of 5 and 7 and lasts a minimum of two years before it is discovered. Cases of children experiencing incest with their fathers as early as 2 or 3 years of age are not uncommon.

Although it is sometimes assumed that sexual involvement with a family member is less harmful than sexual relations with a stranger, the fact that incest occurs in the context of a caring relationship makes the experience even more traumatic. Rape by a stranger is quick and brutal. It allows for a straightforward reaction of anger and hate. But the violation of the psychological or emotional bonds that exist among family members leaves scars that are deep and lasting. The victim grows up distrusting adults, especially men, and the long-term consequences often appear when young women who have been raped as children try to form a satisfactory relationship with men. Giaretto (1976) maintains that 20 to 30 percent of children who visit mental health clinics have been victims of incest and that one out of four females involved in incest has suffered serious side effects.

The Myth of the Seductive Daughter

There is a widely accepted belief that the victim of incest invites sexual advances from the offender. The daughter, it is argued, turns her father on in order to gain some personal advantage. Some clinicians and lay people believe that girls are naturally seductive and adept at the art of involving their fathers in an incestuous relationship.

Although some children have active sexual fantasies and adults can use these fantasies to develop sexual relationships, it is the adult's responsibility to assess the short-term and long-term potential harm and not to throw better judgment to the wind and sexually exploit the child.

Mother's Responsibility for Incest

The view that the mother is responsible for permitting the incest situation to develop, because she chooses to ignore or deny that it is happening, is widely accepted. But most mothers do not know that the daughter is being victimized by the father because he has threatened the daughter and sworn her to absolute secrecy. Where the mother suspects incest is happening, the father and daughter usually strongly deny the existence of such activity.

Mothers are sometimes blamed for the father turning to the daughter for sexual fulfillment because the wife is cold and unresponsive. The father often uses this as an excuse to justify his behavior, and the daughter may accept this version of what is happening in the marriage. Many incestuous fathers, however, are having an active sex life with their wives and at the same time exploiting their daughters. Incest is not simply a matter of sexual dissatisfaction in the marriage.

Profile of Incestuous Family Members

Although many incestuous fathers appear competent and successful, they usually suffer from a poor self-image and lack confidence in relationships with adult women. Consequently, the father may turn to the daughter for affirmation and acceptance. Sometimes he sees in his daughter the person his wife was when the marriage was new.

Daughters who become involved in incestuous relationships tend to have negative feelings toward their mothers and ambivalent or positive feelings toward their fathers. They often see their mothers as cruel, unjust, and depriving. Herman and Hirschman (1981), in a study of adult women, found that although these women expressed disappointment with and contempt for their fathers, they felt a keen sense of betrayal by their mothers.

Daughters in incestuous relationships often assume the role of surrogate mother and carry out many responsibilities in the home. They usually suffer from a low self concept and a feeling of inadequacy. Their basic need for love and affection can be easily exploited.

Mothers tend to have a disturbed, even hostile, relationship with their daughters. The estrangement between them is often present prior to the development of the sexual relationship. In some cases the mother is incapacitated by a physical or mental illness and the daughter perceives the mother as weak, dependent, and ineffectual.

Profile of Incestuous Families

Thorman (1983) points out the following specific dysfunctions found in most cases of father–daughter incest.

1. There is unequal distribution of power, with the father dominating the family.

2. There is unresolved conflict between the spouses, with both partners feeling isolated and lonely.

3. Adult–child role reversals are seen.

4. Mother is physically or psychologically absent.

5. Family members are socially isolated.

6. Conflict is resolved through scapegoating.

7. Communication is confused.

8. Family members lack autonomy.

9. Family affect is not supportive to family members.

10. The family lacks adequate stress-coping mechanisms.

Psychodynamics of Incest

Incest follows a well-defined pattern of psychodynamics among the three key family members—father, mother, and daughter. Each member plays a role in the incestuous relationship. The father usually appears quite well adjusted and functions adequately in most areas. He is often inhibited and rigidly devoted to his role as family man and determined to fulfill his sexual needs within the marriage, even though this may mean turning to his daughter.

The wife is typically disenchanted with her husband and not interested in affirming her husband's needs. She is often resentful of her daughter's attractiveness, turns to interests outside of the family to fulfill her own needs, is away from the home much of the time, and counts on her daughter to take her place.

The daughter views her mother as a model of femininity and then begins to relate to her father as a wife, particularly if the father responds favorably. She does not refuse her father's advances and expects him to draw the line and set limits. She initially protests his sexual invitations, and when he fails to carry out his protective role, she feels betrayed by her father. The daughter, at this point, experiences a double bind: If she turns to her mother for protection, the mother may accuse her of lying and charge her with seducing her father; if her mother accepts the story, she may refuse to take effective steps to stop the incest. Some mothers tell their daughters that the secret must be contained, or else the father will be sent to prison and the family will be destroyed. Thus a conspiracy of silence is developed; to do otherwise would disgrace the family. As Armstrong (1979) contends, generation after generation of women have learned that "you don't talk about things like that!" Silence, however, perpetuates the problem. Breaking down the secret may, in contrast, reduce the incidence of incest and treatment for the family can be initiated.

References

Armstrong, L. *Kiss daddy goodnight*. New York: Pocket Books, 1979.

Butler, S. *Conspiracy of silence*. San Francisco: New Glide Publications, 1978.

Firestone, S. *The dialectic of sex*. New York: William R. Morrow, 1970.

Geiser, R. *Hidden victims*. Boston: Beacon Press, 1981.

Giaretto, H. Treatment of father–daughter incest. *Children Today*, July/Aug. 1976.

Herman, S., & Hirschman, L. *Father–daughter incest*. Cambridge, Mass.: Harvard University Press, 1981.

Meiselman, K. *Incest*. San Francisco: Jossey-Bass, 1979.

Thorman, G. *Incestuous families*. Springfield, Ill.: Charles C. Thomas, 1983.

7.2 FAMILY ATMOSPHERE: SOME COMMON THREADS

There is often a prevailing mood or atmosphere that runs throughout the structure of a family (Dewey, 1971). The purpose of this section is to describe a series of common family "atmospheres" or "moods," and the kind of interactions that precipitate the prevailing atmosphere. When a negative family atmosphere is prevalent, the energy that moves within the family is blocked and has a limiting impact on all interactions. From a Structure–Strategic perspective, the therapist does not try to change the family atmosphere directly, but attempts to modify the underlying interactions, and thereby remove the blocks to the energy flow within the family. When that occurs the family atmosphere will change.

Common Family Atmospheres

Labeling

The interaction patterns can be arranged in such a way that a family member feels that he or she no longer is part of the family. Lebeling often occurs where the rejected person is seen as "bad" because of negative behaviors. The remainder of the family members (and possibly one specific person labeled as "good") tend consistently to stereotype the "bad" person in a negative light. Whether or not the "bad" person perceives himself or herself as such, in an accurate or inaccurate manner, it is nevertheless necessary to change this person's image in the family. It is helpful to separate the actions of the "bad" person from the way the "individual" is perceived. Reducing the status of the "good" person also has a leveling effect.

Authoritarian

Whenever a person or a subsystem within the family has all the influence, there is an authoritarian theme. Persons outside of the authoritarian subsystem have little influence and must obey on command without question. Persons who respond to authoritarianism tend to have little creativity, and are very sensitive to opinions of others.

Those who reject the authoritarian subsystem may make overt aggressive responses and develop devious ways to break away. This could occur in the sibling subsystem or on the part of a spouse who has little influence. Balancing the level of influence with the family can reduce the authoritarian structure. Parents in rigid family structures have difficulty in sharing family influence with their children. This becomes a serious matter as children mature and are ready to leave home. For example, a 20-year-old "boy" may have an 11 p.m. curfew set by his parents.

Victim

The "suffering saint" is a person who perceives himself or herself as victimized and having no influence, but simultaneously controls the family from a point of weakness. Being critical of others and at the same time declaiming self-righteousness are characteristics of the suffering saint.

This situation is seen in chemically dependent families, where the spouse of the dependent person is the saint. When the dependent is cured, the saint may develop "illness," or if the marital relationship ends, the suffering saint again forms a relationship with a chemically dependent person.

Chaos

A chaotic atmosphere has inconsistent rules and roles. There is confusion among children and parents alike. Persons in this atmosphere develop instability, a lack of desire to pursue tasks independently, and a general lack of ability to maintain human relationships. To produce change, rules and roles need to be made explicit, behavioral tasks accurately defined, accountability for assigned responsibilities encouraged, and achievements acknowledged in order to reduce chaos and bring family stability.

Enmeshed

Lack of individuation occurs when persons are not encouraged to develop their own identities. The family members are overinvolved with one another. They are not allowed to give opinions on a topic or to perform difficult tasks such as fixing an object after the majority of the repair has been completed.

The mood within the family is one of suppression. Overt expenditures of energy cannot be displayed. Persons exposed to this atmosphere for long periods of time are unable to express personal thoughts, do not have self-confidence, are very dependent, and will avoid close relationships. These disadvantaged persons require opportunities for responsibility, encouragement to exert influence in a variety of tasks, and training in communication skills.

Families with a repressive atmosphere often have a pessimistic outlook on life. In this atmosphere the persons feel helpless and hopeless and appear to lack sufficient energy and insight to change the family system.

Materialistic

The family with a monetary success orientation holds relationship issues in low esteem and places a high value on what can be gained monetarily outside of the family system. This is not necessarily indicative of families that have many material things. The focus of a family pursuing monetary success is: "If only we had . . . , it would solve our problem." Both monetarily "poor" families and "wealthy" families may evince this mood. Members of such families often lack creativity, are not able to enjoy what is available to them, and believe that there is something tangible that is the key to success. In these families there is a need to develop relational skills and to know the warmth of friendships.

Competitive

A competitive atmosphere is dominant in some families. Members are continually trying to be categorized as superior to others within or outside the family. The objective is to be "better than" rather than "the best I can be." Within the family this may be evidenced by role dissatisfaction, conflict over what roles are most important, and accusing others of not fulfilling their roles. In extreme cases a person may attempt to show his or her superiority by being "the worst" at something, if that person finds that he or she has no chance of being "the best."

Combatative

In the combatative atmosphere, there is constant bickering and criticism among family members. Children often learn this behavior from their parents and have it reinforced as the parents relate to the children in a similar manner. As the children interact with each other, chaos can develop.

Concern for fairness becomes a major issue. The exercise of power is one of the major issues in this family. The children have learned from their parents that power is of utmost importance. Family members need to learn how to share power with others, respect other persons' opinions, and realize that significance need not be gained through the exercise of power.

Reference

Dewey, E. Family atmosphere. In A. Nikelly (Ed.), *Techniques for behavior change*. Springfield, Ill.: Charles C. Thomas, 1971.

7.3 HUMAN SEXUALITY: THE IMPORTANCE OF THE DESIRE PHASE

Human sexuality has undergone a period of expanding study and research. The pioneering efforts of Masters and Johnson (1970), for example, were the first major attempts to describe the human sexual response. Their work marked the beginning of the scientific study of sexuality, and has generated further empirical investigations by others.

As data about human sexuality have accumulated, it has been necessary to adjust the overall conceptualization of human sexuality. A unitary view of sexuality, for example, was replaced by a biphasic view. That is, instead of viewing the human sexual response as a single event that passed from desire to excitement, and finally to orgasm, two separate phases were distinguished, namely, excitement and orgasm. This conceptual separation logically led researchers to separate the disorders associated with the two phases in males and females, and to develop treatment techniques and interventions appropriate to each phase.

Biphasic Response

The biphasic concept represented a significant theoretical advance in the field, leading not only to important clinical developments (i.e., separating phase disorders), but also to greater therapeutic success (Kaplan, 1979).

The understanding of the sexual response and its dysfunctions, however, was still incomplete, and current clinical data were still insufficiently accounted for until the recent recognition of a third and crucial phase, the phase of sexual desire. It certainly makes good sense that if a person has a problem with sexual desire in the first place, then all the treatment techniques and strategies in the world pertinent to the phases of sexual excitement and orgasm will prove unhelpful. If a person does not want sex to begin with, who cares about the mechanics of orgasm?

Triphasic Response

Kaplan (1979, p. 4), therefore, proposes that:

The human sexual response is composed of three separate but interlocking phases which are each vulnerable to disruption in a specific manner by multiple physical and psychic pathogens, and which produce a variety of disorders that are responsive to specific and rational treatment strategies.

This section briefly examines the physiology (physical aspect) and specific disorders of the sexual desire phase.

Sexual desire is "an appetite or drive which is produced by the activation of a specific neural system in the brain" (Kaplan, 1979, p. 9), that is, the sensation of sexual desire has a biological basis. Kaplan (1979, p. 10) explains:

Sexual desire or libido is experienced as specific sensations which move the individual to seek out, or become receptive to, sexual experiences. These sensations are produced by the physical activation of a specific neural system in the brain. When this system is active, a person is "horny," he may feel genital sensations, or he may feel vaguely sexy, interested in sex, open to sex, or even just restless. These sensations cease after sexual gratification, i.e., orgasm. When this system is inactive or under the influence of inhibitory forces, a person has no interest in erotic matters; he "loses his appetite" for sex and becomes "asexual."

Disorders of Sexual Desire

There are two common disorders of the desire phase: hypoactive sexual desire (HSD) and inhibition of sexual desire (ISD). Hypoactive sexual desire is indicated by loss of interest in sexual matters, or "sexual anorexia." The sexually hypoactive person behaves as if his or her sexual circuitry is operating on a poor battery. The sex drive is at a low ebb because of lack of activity in the sex centers of the brain.

Inhibition of sexual desire has similar symptoms, but they are caused by deliberate inhibition of the brain's sex centers. The person with ISD has, in effect, turned off his or her sexual circuitry. In HSD, then, the sex drive is diminished because it is not being generated in the first place, whereas in ISD, it is being suppressed due to psychological conflict. Both HSD and ISD are to be differentiated from normal asexuality and low sexual desire. "Normal asexuality" occurs when people are born with sexual appetites somewhat lower than average. Low sexual desire is attributable to various life circumstances, such as crisis, danger, and sickness, or to nonneurotic celibacy, or to the personal unattractiveness of the partner (e.g., extreme obesity).

These disorders are prevalent sexual dysfunctions. One report estimated that 40 percent of the clients applying for help with sexual problems were suffering from ISD (Kaplan, 1979). Unfortunately HSD and ISD are also highly intractable. Kaplan (1979, p. 53), for example, estimates that "only 10 to 15 percent of patients suffering from ISD are cured within the average fourteen sessions which are traditional in sex therapy."

Hypoactive Sexual Desire

Hypoactive sexual desire is often the result of physiological factors, this is, of disturbances in the sex centers of the brain. In such cases sex therapy is inappropriate. The most common physiological factors are depression, severe stress states, certain drugs and illnesses, and low testosterone levels. On the other hand, inhibition of sexual desire is often the result of psychological factors.

Inhibition of Sexual Desire

The immediate cause of ISD is the deliberate suppression of sexual desire, albeit involuntary and unconscious. People with ISD suppress their sexual appetite by evoking or focusing on negative, antierotic thoughts, feelings, or images. In this way they literally make themselves angry, fearful, or distracted, and so mobilize natural inhibitory mechanisms that are meant to suppress sexual desire when it is in the best interests of the person (e.g., in dangerous or emergency situations).

On an evening when lovemaking is in the air, a husband focuses on an unpleasant quality in his wife, criticizes her for it, and succeeds in illiciting a heated argument. Not surprisingly any flicker of passion in him is quickly extinguished. Normally people do not allow such negativity or distraction to intrude upon their sexual pleasure. In fact they tend to select thoughts and images that will enhance their sexual desire, and screen out whatever will diminish their desire. Negative, antierotic mental activities may be viewed as unconscious defense mechanisms that are triggered by underlying psychological conflicts.

According to Kaplan (1979, pp. 38–39), antierotic mental activities can be associated with the following.

Fears of success, pleasure, and love; intense performance fears; fears of rejection; neurotic power struggles based on infantile transference towards the partner; fears of intimacy; deep sexual conflicts that have their roots in the patients' early development; and anger caused by poor communication between the couple.

Stuart (1980, p. 344) gives his own list of psychological factors.

. . . Stress, conflict, depression, fear, and anxiety, as well as traumatic sexual experiences such as rape and incest . . . Sexual ignorance, religious prohibitions, low self-esteem, distressed couple communication, hostility and destructive interactional patterns, and excessive demands and fatigue. . . .

Marital Therapy

Marriage and family therapists tend to view sexual difficulties as more a function of interpersonal, relational problems than as a function of individual, intrapsychic ones. They ask themselves, therefore, how sexual problems reflect dysfunctions in the marital system. They will want to know, for example, if sexual dysfunction is symptomatic of such dynamics as a power struggle; a coalition or triangulation involving a child or someone outside the family; a violation, slurring, or confusion of personal boundaries or roles; or an inadequate completion of a particular stage in the family life cycle. Clearly not only one factor underlies the symptom, but a multiplicity of interwoven issues.

References

Kaplan, H. S. *Disorders of sexual desire*. New York: Brunner/Mazel, 1979.
Masters, W. H., & Johnson, V. E. *Human sexual inadequacy*. Boston: Little, Brown, 1970.
Stuart, R. B. *Helping couples change*. New York: Guilford Press, 1980.

7.4 STAGES IN AN AFFAIR

Marlow (1983) points out that couples whose relationship has undergone an affair often undergo a more or less regular sequence of stages in their adjustment to the event. These stages involve disclosure, grief, discovery, and relationship creation.

Movement through the stages is different for each member of the couple. People define their own path as they struggle with the issues of the relationship. Some couples are able to work through the stages while others never completely resolve the affair. Some couples work at each stage separately while others work on several stages at a time. The stages are useful conceptualizations since they provide specific boundary markers that identify the territory the couple has covered and give meaningful perspective to the specific events within the resolution process.

Disclosure

The key feelings of this stage are anger and guilt, regardless of whether the affair is discovered or is confessed. Confession of an affair usually occurs as a result of unbearable guilt. Whether or not the couple remains stuck at this stage depends in large part upon how each member of the couple deals with his or her feelings.

When couples initially enter therapy, they are often involved in a repetitive blaming/defensive interaction. This bitter debate usually identifies one member as "guilty" and the other as the "injured" party. When the accusations and counteraccusations are not overt, the cycle may be expressed by the withdrawal of one or both members of the couple.

Therapy should be designed to move deeply into the affective components of the event so that no secrets remain. This process usually results in understanding "self" and the "other" partner and a growing realization that each partner is overcome with a profound sadness. During this stage the guilty partner may open up to reveal hidden anger. The injured party may remove the angry mask and cry. In response the guilty partner may also cry as a reflection of deep emotions.

Grief

The tears that the couple share is the beginning of the grief stage. Grieving, when expressed mutually, can be supportive and nurturant to the relationship. The injured partner may grieve the loss of trust with the words, "I can never trust you again!" As this partner moves deeply into the loss of trust, connections may be made by the therapist of similar loss experiences that may reflect early childhood developmental deprivations that have not yet been resolved. Growth, as a result of making past and present connections, allows the partner to realize that trust is a function of self. The innocent partner begins to assume responsibility for the lack of trust while the guilty partner grieves the loss of the lover.

Too many people do not feel entitled to express this feeling of loss to their spouses and choose to keep silent about it, or, alternatively, to express it only to their ex-lovers. This expression of deep feelings and understanding may result in the affair being resumed. To avoid this the therapist should encourage the partners to share these feelings of loss. The honesty opens up communication between the partners and may lead to a resurgence of the blame/defense cycle. The full expression of their feelings allows them to move on to deeper experiences of relationship and remove the stuck quality of their interactions. They are now ready to grow as a result of the experience and learn the meaning of the affair for them.

Discovery

The experiences associated with the stages of disclosure and grief prepare and predispose the couple to transform the crisis created by the affair into an opportunity. As a result of the grieving process, new awareness may be gained connecting the experience of loss with childhood deprivations. Following this awareness of how each person creates his or her own reaction to the affair, the partners may be willing to suspend their judgements and to take responsibility for their emotional and behavioral reaction patterns. Each partner can then take responsibility for the affair. The "innocent party" can ask, "What did I do to predispose or even invite my partner to choose an affair?" The guilty party can ask, "How was I protecting myself and avoiding my partner by choosing the affair?" (Marlow, 1983).

Relationship Development

The final stage, although it is part of the previous stages, concerns itself primarily with rebuilding the relationship. Some of the considerations which appear to be important in this stage include:

1. Keeping agreements. The partners have a need to build trust. This can best be done by clearly defining behavioral expectations through the development of an operational agreement about their relationship for the future.

2. Establishing closeness with clear boundaries between the partners. Each partner learns to listen before reacting and judging the partner. Each partner has the right to psychological and physical "space" while at the same time enjoying intimacy.

3. Honesty. Honesty is a necessary companion of developing trust. Truth must come out regardless of the consequences.

4. Choosing responsibility. Instead of blaming, each partner needs to assume personal responsibility for his or her actions. The counterproductive repetitive cycles of blame/defense need to be blocked as new interactions are created. Such transformations make it possible to rebuild the relationship or to terminat it without undue difficulty. Such termination may lead to a mutually agreed upon separation and divorce. Working through the affair by use of the stages identified earlier makes the divorce process a much more humane and constructive endeavor. Alternatively the marriage may be rebuilt and the relationship restored as the spouses acknowledge their grief and move toward reconciliation, forgiveness, and acceptance. [This section is an adaptation of the Marlowe (1983) article.]

Reference

Marlowe, K. After the affair. *CATSEF Newsletter* (Toronto), 1983, *3*, 3–4.

CHAPTER 8

STRUCTURAL–STRATEGIC THERAPY SKILLS

8.1 SKILLS OF JOINING

This section considers some of the ways of beginning family therapy sessions or joining with the family. Minuchin and Fishman (1981) suggest that therapists should be able to enter into therapy spontaneously with families. By this they mean that having learned and assimilated the skills and techniques of therapy, the experienced therapist "forgets" them in order to be able to respond to the dynamics of the family. The skills become second nature and flows out of the personality of the therapist in response to the family.

The Therapist and the Family

A family that comes for therapy in most cases will look to the therapist to lead, but the therapist must earn that right. The therapist will have to learn how to accommodate, support, suggest, and follow the family. He or she will be buffeted by the storms as entry is made into the family, but must remain the helmsman. Sometimes the therapist will be more aware of the buffeting, and other times less aware. The family will usually have a presenting issue, often in the form of an "identified patient" (IP), who, after much effort at helping, they see as the source of the problem.

The experienced therapist recognizes that (1) the whole family is acting in a dysfunctional manner, not just the IP; and (2) the ability of the family to be free and explore a problem is curtailed by its focus on the presenting problem. It is the therapist's role to enter the family and redirect the emphasis from the presenting problem without losing the rest of the family.

Joining

Joining is both an attitude and a technique. One might view joining as forming an umbrella of safety for the family under which the therapeutic dialogue takes place. The therapist lets the family members know that they are understood and that he or she is working for and with them. The therapist also needs to maintain the freedom to confront the family and to help the family accommodate to him or her.

The therapist should be able to respond differently in different circumstances with different families. He or she should be able to choose to be loud or quiet, to be verbal or nonverbal, to use different patterns of speech, to boister or pamper, and to talk more with specific family members than with others. In all cases the therapist should observe the family responses, as well as changes in himself or herself to these responses. Much of what goes on in joining goes on beneath the surface, or verbal level of communication.

Use of Proximity in Joining

Joining can take place from three different areas or positions of proximity: close, median, and disengaged. Specific joining techniques are adapted to these areas.

1. *Close*. The therapist affiliates with family members, and may even form coalitions with one or more of them. Confirmation is a valuable tool because the therapist is looking for positive things to say, reinforces people where possible, reframes negatives, and helps to build up self-esteem. These behaviors often help the family members to see each other in a new light. This is helpful because people make observations about others that tend to confirm their view about them, ignoring the other facets.

The therapist also identifies areas of pain, difficulty, and stress. He or she lets the family know that he or she is aware of these areas and will deal with them sensitively. This helps the family view the therapist as a source of family and personal self-esteem, while at the same time it establishes the therapist's right to withdraw approval if the situation warrants.

2. *Median*. The therapist joins the family in a way that is more distant than the close position. The primary way of joining in the median position involves active listening and tracking. This process allows the therapist to get in touch with the way the family processes the interactions. A danger the therapist faces is to become overly locked into the content of the most verbal family members and to ignore the behavior of the remaining family members.

Tracking is the technique of helping family members tell their experiences while the therapist offers comments that clarify, capsulize, interpret, and deal with the process of the in-

teraction. The therapist gains helpful insight by being aware of how and whom he or she tracks. Does he or she focus on one particular person to the exclusion of others? Does he or she feel protective or hostile toward any members? What pressure is he or she feeling from the family and how is he or she responding to it? The therapist notes these pressures and responses.

3. *Disengaged*. In this position the therapist joins the family more in the role of a coach or director than as a participant. The therapist leads from his or her role as an expert in creating contexts that help the family feel a sense of competence and hope for change. From a position of distance, the therapist can observe the patterns of interaction and engage the family in exercises that bring out familiar patterns of interaction (enactment), force the family members into unfamiliar patterns of interaction (role play), and give them a clearer picture of the dynamics (mapping, floor plan, sculpting).

These exercises are change producing, and help the therapist join the family by increasing family leadership in the family. By being disengaged, the therapist is able to see the family's world view; that is, the family values, rules, and myths. The therapist helps the family members understand how they order or frame their experiences, how the communication patterns support their interactions, and which phrases are meaningful to them. The therapist uses these phrases either to support how the family experiences reality or to construct an expanded view of reality that will allow the family to grow and change.

Problems in Joining

It is more difficult to join with people who have different value systems, personalities, ways of communicating, or simply a different chemistry. In these cases, referring the family to another, more compatible therapist is desirable, but not always possible.

The frustration the therapist experiences with a family might lead to a more confrontive relationship, resulting in a greater sense of helplessness for both the therapist and the family. To acknowledge this condition is often helpful in creating feelings of closeness between the family and therapist, and may result in more effective problem solving in the family.

Reference

Minuchin, S., & Fishman, H. C. *Family therapy techniques*. Cambridge, Mass.: Harvard University Press, 1981.

8.2 SKILLS OF RESTRUCTURING

Minuchin and Fishman (1981) have presented the following family and marital therapy techniques as helpful tools in restructuring the organization and function of the family.

Enactment

Enactment is the process in which the therapist constructs an interpersonal scenario within the therapy session whereby the family lives out its dysfunctional transactions. An enactment may result from questions the therapist asks or from observing transactions taking place in the session. There are at least three advantages to be derived from using enactment techniques:

1. More information is gathered about the family and more rapid joining occurs.
2. The family lives out its reality with greater intensity within the session. This challenges the family's assumptions about the nature of the problem. The family system opens up during the enactment.
3. Family members become involved with each other as opposed to only listening. The

concreteness of the situation offers opportunities to experiment with alternative transactions.

Minuchin and Fishman (1981) present enactment as a three-stage process.

Stage 1: Spontaneous Transactions

The therapist observes the spontaneous interactions and decides which of the dysfunctional ones to highlight or pursue.

Stage 2: Eliciting Transactions

The therapist has the family engage in scenarios in which they act out the dysfunctional interactions in the therapist's presence. The therapist may push, challenge, or question the process in order to intensify or clarify the interactions.

Stage 3: Alternative Transactions

The therapist suggests alternative transactions, which are then created in the session. This process can give the family a concrete experience of change and a sense of hope.

The therapist must be willing to be involved with the family but flexible enough to encourage changing and shifting family patterns.

Reframing

Families develop reference points, myths, patterns of behavior, and labels based on certain expectations and experiences of family members. This is known as framing. Some examples are: bright, witty, lazy, klutzy, all thumbs. Framing also occurs around significant family experiences that become part of a legacy.

Reframing is a technique therapists may use to give a family a new "therapeutic" view of reality. Usually reframing is a verbal altering of the patterns, myths, labels, and experiences to present a more positive view of reality. This can be done no matter how bad the label, experience, or symptoms. For example, child abuse by a father could be reframed as his desire to get close to his children. If the frame or picture the family has of itself is open to being changed, then new behaviors may emerge.

Focusing

Focusing is the skill of closing out new information and avenues of approach that the family presents in order to emphasize or highlight other areas. This technique is used to concentrate the energy on the focused areas so that specific change may result. Minuchin and Fishman (1981) compare focus to photography where the photographer can focus various lenses to highlight an aspect of the subject while relegating other aspects of the subject to the background. In therapy, the therapist receives a great deal of information, which must then be translated into a theoretical schema such as boundaries, hierarchies, and alliances. The schema helps the therapist make sense out of the data and provides a framework of meaning and strategy for change.

The therapist who is able to keep a direct focus can move deeply into an area, gather data, and move toward the desired change. This indepth exploration may, for example, open understanding about the rules that regulate family transactions and structure. Thus the therapist is able to bring about change within the family, which in turn fosters a sense of hope and trust.

There are, however, hazards in focusing. For example, one may develop "tunnel vision." The therapist should realize that focusing on one issue will ignore other areas, issues, and information. The therapist should be sensitive to family dynamics and continue to listen to the family interactions. Also, the therapist should be aware that information families disclose may be in-

formation they feel comfortable with and may not be very important. This phenomenon can trap the therapist into helping the family stay comfortable without changing.

Focusing can be helpful in changing the family's view of what is important and what is not. However, by focusing on specific and often small behaviors, the family can elevate the importance of these behaviors, and incorporate them into a greater theme.

As the family's view of reality shifts, family members may become uncomfortable. When this happens action is usually taken. Families will often oppose a theme because they have been programmed not to see it.

Minuchin and Fishman (1981) detail a case study of a family with children who are acting out in school and have been labeled by the mother and case workers as bad, lazy, and delinquent. The authors view the children as bright, creative, and curious, and develop the theme of Dr. Jekyl and Mr. Hyde to explain the seemingly contradictory behavior. This metaphor is repeatedly promoted until a new reality is created. Viewing the children as both good and bad provides the opportunity for the emergence of a new view of reality.

Intensity

Intensity is the level of impact, emphasis, repetition, or drama that is required to communicate a message to the family so it is both heard and acted upon. Intensity is the level of forcefulness required to secure the family's attention. The ability of family members to hear and act upon the therapist's message is selective, and grows out of the family's pattern and common history. Even families that are highly motivated for change hear within certain limits. The therapist's message may be blunted, deflected, or diffused by the normal range of the family's hearing and operational patterns. The therapist must get the family to hear the message by sending it more loudly than the family's level of hearing and/or areas of deafness.

How this intensity is achieved depends on

several factors. First, the style and personal characteristics of the therapist play a significant role. Some therapists build a sense of drama and intensity with quiet communication. Others are loud, expressive, and highly involved. Therapists should be aware of their personality and styles of working, as well as their sensitivity to the needs of different families in order to adapt effectively to a given situation.

Second, therapists need to recognize that to send only a cognitive message will in most cases be inadequate. Minuchin and Fishman (1981) remind therapists that the fact that their message is sent and/or is true does not necessarily mean that it will be received, much less acted upon by the family.

Third, therapists are often stymied by the rules of courtesy that govern their daily lives. If a level of intensity is reached that upsets people, they usually sense this and almost automatically lower the intensity of the message. Therapists, however, must learn to ignore the signals requesting a reduction in intensity to ensure that change in the family occurs.

There are various ways of developing intensity. At the beginning or opening stage, cognitive structures are used that are of lesser intensity. Higher levels of intensity are developed as the therapy process continues by creating scenarios that cause the family more directly and powerfully to experience its interaction patterns. Scenarios are also created to break the old patterns and replace them with new ones. Minuchin and Fishman list several of the most helpful scenarios.

Repetition of the Message

This involves repeating the message until the family responds to its importance. Repetition may involve both the structure and content of a sequence of behavior. Minuchin and Fishman (1981) provide an example of a young couple living in the home of the husband's parents, and planning to move out. On the day of the planned move, the husband slept until 2:00 p.m. When questioned, he said he forgot. The therapist continued to ask the question "Why didn't you move?" until the wife challenged the husband's desire to leave his parents. She decided she would move out alone. This activated the husband, who began to cry, asking her not to go without him. She said she did not really want to move without him. Two days later they both moved. It was the continued repetition of the message "Why didn't you move?" that heightened the intensity until deeper issues were heard and acted upon.

Repetition of Similar Messages

This involves developing and repeating messages that appear to be different but have a common theme running through them. Thus what appear to be disconnected events are linked together as components of a pattern. This strategy helps families develop an awareness of the depth and breadth of a pattern, such as enmeshment or distance.

Changing the Time

This involves changing the rhythm and timing of a normal interaction pattern. Changing the timing interrupts the normal pattern, and raises the intensity level. Minuchin and Fishman (1981) give the example of two family members who had short tempers with each other. They would blow up quickly and then disengage. If the therapist could facilitate the conditions so that the blow-up were lengthened (delaying the disengagement pattern), the resulting intensity would cause a change in the transactions.

Changing the Distance

This involves heightening or lessening the level of intensity by use of physical space in the therapeutic setting. Moving closer, moving away, turning toward, turning away, standing taller, and crouching down are some uses of space that transform patterns of interaction.

Resisting the Family Pull

The family may attempt to pull the therapist into the interaction pattern, thereby reducing the therapist's ability to change the pattern. By resisting this pull, the therapist raises the intensity level, facilitating family change. To continue with the example of the young couple, the therapist resists the family's pull, and accepts the husband's statement "I forgot." By being firm and continuing to ask "Why didn't you move?" the therapist creates the conditions for the family to change.

Boundaries

Boundary issues involve family subsystem membership and the degree of distance between members within a subsystem. Therapeutic strategies dealing with boundary issues help regulate the permeability of boundaries by examining issues such as closeness/distance between family members and subsystem alignments.

First, a therapist may study where the boundaries appear to be in a family and attempt to delineate them. Family seating patterns in the therapeutic setting give some indication of the nature of the affiliations within the family. The therapist may examine patterns, coalitions, overinvolved dyads, or triads by noting the manner in which the family communicates; that is, who supplies data, who fills in data for whom, who interrupts whom, and who helps whom. This information is not exhaustive but gives soft data that help the therapist develop a tentative map of the family structure.

Minuchin and Fishman (1981) identify two strategies for creating new boundaries. They are cognitive constructs and concrete maneuvers. Cognitive constructs are verbal phrases or instructions by which the therapist communicates to family members the nature of the boundaries and the process of developing new ones. For example, in the course of conversation, a family member may interrupt another and answer questions for that person. The therapist could delineate the boundary by noting it, and asking the

interrupting family member if he or she is always so helpful. The therapist could double-check this idea with the interrupted member. Minuchin (Minuchin & Fishman, 1981) has developed some stock phrases that serve this initial purpose. They include: "You take his voice." "If she answers for you, you do not have to talk." "You are the ventriloquist and she is the puppet." "If your father does things for you, you will always have ten thumbs." Minuchin suggests that therapists develop their own spontaneous phrases and metaphors to help clarify boundary issues.

Boundary issues are a concern when two family members are in a dysfunctional relationship that is balanced by a third member who detours, allies, or judges. This prevents the original two family members from dealing with their conflicts. The therapist may decide to separate the dyad from the third party in order to allow the dyad to work uninterrupted on its issues. This separation may be a simple verbal request asking the third party not to interrupt or asking the third party to leave the room. Alternatively the therapist might ask the third party to join him or her in observing the behavior of the dyad, thereby separating the third party from the dyad.

Concrete spatial maneuvers help to change the distance between family members. The use of space is recognized by people as indicative of psychological events and/or emotional transactions. Moving people around to form or break subsystems is helpful in reinforcing the cognitive structure. The therapist may also use physical gestures to reinforce the cognitive structuring.

Expanding the time of interactions strengthens the new boundaries in the family. Asking family members to relate by talking or doing an activity together for an extended time (20 minutes or more in a session) reinforces a new boundary. Assigning homework may also facilitate the development of new boundaries. To build closeness a therapist can ask a parent to do an activity with a child or children. To create distance between family members, a therapist might, for example, challenge a parent to develop an outside activity or hobby apart from a child with whom he or she is overinvolved.

Unbalancing

The goal of unbalancing is to change the hierarchical relationships and power issues within the family. Minuchin and Fishman (1981) recognized that while a family may delegate power to the "expertise" of the therapist, the family members expect to be treated fairly.

When family members change positions in the family hierarchy, they are often able to explore an expanded range of behavior. The changing of roles within the family hierarchy can upset the balance of the family and, therefore, the therapist should be strong enough to maintain the changed behavior until the family can incorporate it. This process can be stressful to the therapist as a result of the buffeting engaged in by the family.

There are three basic strategies (Minuchin & Fishman, 1981) the therapist can use in unbalancing the family. The therapist can affiliate with family members, ignore family members, or enter into a coalition with a family member. Joining is a part of the affiliating process in which the therapist affirms the strengths and confirms the self-esteem of a family member. To unbalance a system, the therapist uses the affiliation to alter the hierarchical structure in the family.

Usually the therapist affiliates with a family member lower down on the hierarchical scale. For example, a mother and daughter may have a conflictual relationship with the daughter missing school and disrupting the mother's life. The therapist may affirm the mother's struggle by emphasizing the daughter's exploitation of the mother. This activates the mother, who begins to make demands regarding the daughter's school attendance (Minuchin & Fischman, 1981).

Alternatively a therapist may affiliate with a dominant family member in order to intensify the sequence of events between conflicting family members until new boundaries are established that more fully meet the needs of all family members.

The strategy of ignoring family members is difficult because this goes against the grain of the therapist's training and requires the therapist to act as if certain people are invisible (Minuchin & Fishman, 1981). The experience of being ignored either activates the silent member(s) or promotes the overinvolved member to quiet down while others take their rightful place in the family. Therapists can expect hostility to be directed toward them by the ignored family member. The ignored family member might even try to enlist others in a coalition against the therapist. But even this action by the ignored family member causes a reshaping of the family hierarchies.

Finally, the strategy of participating with a family member(s) in a coalition against one or more members is a difficult one because the therapist must be able to exert expertise and power over and against the power of the "expert" in the family. The goal is to use the resistance of the "expert" so that change may come about. This may be stressful for both the family members and the therapist since they are pushed beyond their normal level of transacting.

Unbalancing promotes new hierarchial structures and new sources of power in the family. While the stress level may be high, the benefits can be worth the effort.

Complementarity

Often a most difficult part of family therapy is helping the family members, particularly the spouses, view their behavior in an organic, interrelated way. Most of our conditioning has been toward an individual autonomous model of self, as thus we are taught to take sole responsibility for our actions. Certainly the majority of psychological models lead us in this direction. While recognizing the value of being responsible, we need to view personal responsibility as occurring in a social context. Others play a role in our behavior, even as we do in theirs. A complementarity or interdependence exists in our relationships, with the parts forming a greater whole. This is especially true in the closeness of family relationships. It is often difficult for family members to see both the complexity and reciprocity of the relational patterns in the family because they are part of it.

How can a therapist challenge an individualistic and narrow mind set? Usually the family will diagnose one person as the patient. Minuchin and Fishman (1981) suggest several ways to develop a new diagnosis.

The therapist may reframe the issues by asking the identified patient (IP) to identify how other family members maintain his or her acting-out behavior. The therapist may expand the problem to include other family members as follows: "I am hearing you say that you and your son have an issue over control," or "You are telling me that you have a problem in the way you relate and that you wish things to change." Or the therapist may describe the IP as a healer in the family who carries the family pain. Responses such as these serve to block the usual responses to the client and to develop new patterns.

The therapist might confront the family's concept that one member alone can control the whole family (Minuchin & Fishman, 1981). The therapist might pursue the IP by asking questions such as, "If someone in your family outside yourself helped cause your problems, who would it be?" or "Who is involved with you in such a way as to support your problems?" The purpose of such questioning is to help the family see the concept of mutuality and context, and extinguish the view of individual ownership of the problem.

Minuchin and Fishman present an example of a couple in which the wife has all the decision-making power in the family, and the husband is asked how he worked out this curious arrangement. This strategy provides an expanded picture of the family as a system and blocks nonproductive repetitive patterns.

Finally, the therapist may develop an expanded context or framework of behavior by connecting individual behavior to a larger context. Thus families are urged to view their seemingly unrelated behaviors as part of a pattern or family rule.

Reference

Minuchin, S., & Fishman, H. C. *Family therapy techniques*. Cambridge, Mass.: Harvard University Press, 1981.

8.3 STRATEGIC THERAPY SKILLS

Strategic therapy focuses primarily on specific behavioral changes rather than on skill training or promoting insight into family dynamics. Strategic interventions are pragmatic and directive in nature. They are initiated using a planned strategy and are based on the belief that problems emerge from and are maintained by repetitive sequences or patterns of behavior. Therapists using Strategic skills intervene directly in the sequences of behavior, blocking the usual pattern while offering new options. The following are some of the skills used in Strategic interventions.

Reframing

Reframing in Strategic theory is similar to the skill identified also in Structural family therapy. The intervention is focused in two separate ways. The first is changing the nature of the problem or question. For example, Barker (1981) describes a family with problems related to a daughter. It became clear that giving a list of things to the parents to do to help their daughter was not effective. The therapist reframed the issue from problems with the daughter to whether or not the parents were willing to accept the consequences of taking a firm stand with their daughter. Thus reframing the issue opened up new possibilities for change as the perspective of viewing the problem changed.

Positive Connotation

The second way of using reframing is that of positive connotation. This is the skill of taking a negative behavior and labeling it as a strength. By using this skill, families can obtain a new viewpoint on an issue or family member. The dysfunctional behavior of a family member can be severe enough that he or she is labeled by the behavior. Other family members may see the dysfunctional member as a negative person. Feelings of helplessness and hopelessness develop in the light of these labels. Positive connotation can help family members view other persons or issues in a new and positive way.

Barker (1981) describes a family whose son was constantly taking apart radios and appliances. Nothing seemed to be able to curtail this behavior and the parents were driven to distraction by it. As the therapist noted and complimented the boy's curiosity and interest in how things worked, the boy brightened up immediately. The therapist acknowledged the parents' concern over their household appliances and suggested they find a source of used appliances for the boy. The symptoms ceased immediately after this plan was carried out. The parents were excited by the newly perceived "talents" of their son, as was the boy about himself.

Sequences

Sequences involve the twofold skill of observing the pattern or cycles that develop in a family and intervening in that pattern to facilitate change. The therapist blocks certain sequences and initiates new patterns. Haley in the videotape "Leaving Home" makes clear the patterns within a family involving a deaf 24-year-old son:

The son lives at home. He becomes abusive to the mother. The parents kick him out of the home. He abuses drugs and gets into trouble with the police. He is sent to the hospital for treatment. He is sent home where the pattern repeats itself.

The therapist entered the system by blocking the sequence of going to the hospital. This created a new option. The next time the son got into trouble, he was to be sent to jail. This blocked the cycle and the son no longer acted out. Then the therapist invited the parents to help the son move out in a positive affirming manner instead of kicking him out in a time of stress. The sequence was changed and positive behavior was established.

Directives

Directives are involved when the therapist moves directly with a family in creating interventions. This does not mean the therapist lectures or preaches to the family. There are six helpful steps for direct intervention (Barker, 1981).

1. Be specific in giving detailed instructions instead of general directives.

2. Involve other family members in helping a family member to keep the instructions. This is done in a positive manner without judging.

3. Set up a reward system.

4. Help family members develop different behaviors instead of merely asking them to stop a particular behavior. The "different" behavior should be incompatible with the behavior that is inappropriate.

5. Help family members change the sequence of their behaviors. Altering patterns is a way of changing outcomes.

6. The directness and/or forcefulness of the therapist's personality can create intensity that can move family members into action.

Metaphor

Metaphor use is described at length in an article in the section containing exercises. The Strategic use of metaphor helps people develop a picture of their present reality as well as of their desired reality. Changing a person's metaphor or view of himself or herself and the world often is a first step in developing new patterns of behavior.

Paradox

Paradox is very much a part of Strategic therapy. It needs to be stated that the use of paradox is not a separate technique, but a technique within a larger Strategic model. Neither is paradox to be used as a primary technique for change, but as a fallback when other methods are ineffective. Barker (1981) discusses three indications that would signal the need to use paradox. The first is that the family fails to respond to direct injunctions. The second is that the symptoms have become worse as repeated countermeasures were attempted. The third is that there is a lack of motivation with members of the family to do the work necessary to bring about behavior change.

Paradox is helpful with resistant families because the symptoms serve as a self-regulating mechanism within the family. To change the symptom is to leave the dysfunctional part of the system unregulated and thus exposed. This would heighten the resistance to change as a protective maneuver. Paradoxes help deflate the resistance by reframing the problem and skirting around the defenses of the family. By legitimizing the symptom and exposing the secret rules that the symptom mask(s), behavior change in the family is encouraged. Typically a couple might divert its conflict through a child's acting out, and would desire to have the symptom cease without changing the couple's behavior.

The following examples of the use of paradox show how families' defenses are disarmed, allowing for change to take place.

The first use of paradox is simply prescribing the symptom. This entails making a negative fear of experience positive, thus removing the problem.

The second use of paradox involves confirming the symptomatic behavior and positively connecting it with the system. Papp (1981) describes a case where a father, failing in business, was becoming apathetic. He gave signals that, if confronted, he would collapse. The son started failing in school. The wife diverted her anger and combativeness from her husband to the son. The therapist praised her for fighting with the son, who was more flexible than the father, and for protecting the father. The father agreed with this assessment. The mother exploded and began to fight directly with the father. The son was removed from his protective middle position.

The third use of paradox is similar to the second, but adds the element of regulating the symptom to a specific time and place; this adds

a note of absurdity to the behavior and diffuses its effectiveness. A therapist might positively reframe the behavior of a child who wets his pants regardless of the actions taken to stop the behavior as a way of getting the mother's love. Then the parents and child are asked to negotiate a time and place for the wetting behavior to take place. If the child wets his pants at the wrong time or place, he is told to wait. The therapist must not take credit for the reduction in wetting, but is to be concerned about the symptom until it goes away.

The fourth use of paradox is giving alternative instructions to the family. This is used when the resistance of a family is high. Barker (1981) describes a family whose daughter would not act responsibly at home. Nothing the parents tried worked to change her behavior. The therapist suggested that the parents work out the conditions of their daughter's staying home, and asked her to comply. If she refused, she was to be asked to leave home. Then the therapist told the parents that they would not be able to carry out this plan because their love for her was so strong. Therefore, they should work on an alternative plan of how to accept the status quo. The therapist carried out the first plan and the daughter moved out. The therapist desired the family to act out a plan, but knew that, if it was presented in a direct manner, the parents would resist. The use of alternatives with the ''impossible to carry out'' clause in the first plan motivated the family to change.

The fifth use of paradox is that of ''reversals'' (Papp, 1981). This method is effective when there are both compliant and defiant family members. The therapist asks the compliant person to change his or her attitude toward the defiant or resistant person. The therapist senses that the compliant person is able to act cooperatively. This suggestion is given without the defiant person present. The combination of the acceptance of previously unacceptable behavior and the surprise can create the conditions for change. This is especially helpful with rebellious children.

Papp (1981) gives the example of a rebellious teenager who was failing in school. The parents were quite angry at this behavior, but their anger only reinforced the rebellion. The therapist suggested that the parents openly accept and agree with their child's actions and to point out that they were relieved at the lack of school attendance because it meant the teenager would be in summer school. The parents then would not have to worry about what the teenager was doing during the summer.

There are four keys to the uses of paradox. The first is that the negative behavior is reframed positively. The second is that the seemingly absurd directions of the therapist must be given in a believable and forceful manner. The third is that the therapist must not take credit for the changes in behavior. Instead, until the changes are secured, the therapist should express shock that the changes are happening. Finally, in implementing the paradox, the therapist sets up the family to get angry at him or her and the family changes to prove to the therapist that it can change.

References

Barker, P. Paradoxical techniques in psychotherapy. In D. Freeman & B. Trule (Eds.), *Treating families with special needs*. Ottawa: Alberta Association of Social Workers, 1981.

Frankle, V. E. Paradoxical intention; a logotherapeutic technique. *American Journal of Psychotherapy*, 1960, *14*, 520–535.

Papp, P., Paradoxes. In S. Minuchin & H. C. Fishman, *Family therapy techniques*. Cambridge, Mass.: Harvard University Press, 1981.

8.4 STRATEGIC PATTERN INTERVENTIONS

Patterns may be changed or broken by addition, by repetition, by anything that will force you to a new perception of it, and those changes can never be predicted with absolute certainty because they have yet not happened.

Gregory Bateson, *Mind and Nature*, 1979.

The main focus of this section is on the interventions that may bring about change in patterns and in symptoms.

Symptoms tend to occur in patterns. They do not occur at all times, but at certain times of the day or night, with certain frequency, at certain intervals, at certain locations, and with certain persons and not with others. Symptoms have cognitive, physiological, and perceptual components and are characterized by observable behaviors (Bandler & Grinder, 1975).

Pattern Types

Clients may have personal patterns, which can be identified by observing certain phrases, analogies, metaphors, and verbal patterns that are characteristic of the client. In addition clients may have nonverbal elements that feed into the personal patterns. These may include breathing rate and depth, eye scanning movements, voice tone, body posture, muscle tone, and body symmetry.

Families may also have interpersonal patterns. These may be identified by observing who sits next to whom, who agrees with whom, who talks to whom, who touches whom, and so on. Patterns may also be defined by identifying the games that the families play, or by observing the patterns of symmetry and complementarity that may be present in the family.

Generic Intervention

O'Hanlon (1982) has identified 13 classes of intervention that delineate different options for interventions in personal and interpersonal patterns of perception, behavior, and experience.

1. Change the frequency/rate of the symptom/pattern.
2. Change the intensity of the symptom/pattern.
3. Change the duration of the symptom/pattern.

4. Change the time (hour/time of day/week/month/year) of the symptom/pattern.

5. Change the location (in the world or in the body) of the symptom/pattern.

6. Change some quality of the symptom/pattern.

7. Perform the symptom without the pattern; short-circuiting.

8. Perform the pattern without the symptom.

9. Change the sequence of the elements in the pattern.

10. Interrupt or otherwise prevent the pattern from occurring.

11. Add (at least) one new element to the pattern.

12. Break up any previously whole element into smaller elements.

13. Link the symptom/pattern to another pattern/goal.

System Transformation

Interventions are made in the dysfunctional personal or interpersonal pattern until an intervention is found that abolishes the symptomatic behavior. It is usually possible to find in the social milieu a new pattern that will challenge the symptom. Selvini-Palazzoli et al. (1978) make the point that because only some of the elements are fully absorbed and used by the system, others remain available and can be put to use in constructing a working family system. By destroying old rules, patterns, and sequences, new ones may emerge. If we change the rules, we change the organization and make possible a transformation of the system. New patterns may evolve and the symptom disappears.

Conclusions

Symptoms are not things but are patterns of personal and interpersonal behavior, perception, and experience. When the therapist gathers data

on the pattern of the symptoms, a difference that makes a difference can be discovered, and appropriate interventions made. The classes of intervention identified here can be used to generate new choices for intervening at personal or systemic levels.

References

Bandler, R., & Grinder, J. *The structure of magic.* Cupertino, Calif.: Meta Publications, 1975.

Bateson, G. *Mind and nature.* New York: Dutton, 1979.

O'Hanlon, W. Strategic pattern intervention. *Journal of Strategic and Systemic Therapies*, 1982, 4, 26–33.

Selvini-Palazzoli, M., Boscolo, L., Cecchin, G., & Prats, G. *Paradox and counterparadox: A new model for the family of schizophrenic transaction.* New York: Jason Aronson, 1978.

8.5 ERICKSONIAN INTERVENTIONS

Maladies, whether psychogenic or organic, follow definite patterns of some sort. A disruption of this pattern could be a most therapeutic measure, no matter how small the disruption.

Milton H. Erickson.

This section discusses three main Strategic functions identified by Milton Erickson (Erickson & Rossi, 1981) and which are useful in understanding the therapeutic process. These functions include: (1) mobilization of change-promoting forces; (2) creation of boundaries facilitating change; and (3) symptom modification and decontextualization (Omer, 1982).

The three strategic functions, however, do not always appear as independent stages or moves in therapy. They often appear as part of an interdependent process that is facilitated by specific tactics. An analysis of Erickson's cases usually discloses three strategic functions in the process of intervention. These have been identified by Omer (1982) and are presented in the following.

Mobilization of Change-Promoting Forces

As a method of intensifying the change-producing forces in a system, Erickson either (1) blocks negative feedback devices that attempt to establish equilibrium or (2) increases the magnitude of antihomeostatic forces, or both. The following two tactical moves are used by Erickson to achieve these results.

Capitalizing on Misery

People usually seek help when they see their situation as unbearable and incapable of bringing about change. By allowing the misery to become even more intense at the beginning of therapy by revealing the depth and darkness of the bottomless pit of misery, the client is more motivated to change. (This is an example of positive feedback.)

The Pressure-Cooker Technique

Erickson, attempting to bring about change, blocks the client's normal outlets and intensifies the naturally growing urges that point to a direction for change.

Creation of Boundaries Facilitating Change

In many societies significant life changes are accompanied by rites of passage. An important component of these rites is raising boundaries between the old situation and the new one.

Friends, relatives, and the community generally are called on to witness the change that has occurred. The old is replaced by the new. There is a discontinuity in the behavior.

Erickson uses many therapeutic moves that are designed to be ''change milestones,'' or markers, or brackets in the process of growth, and which distinguish the ''past'' from the ''now.'' The following are some tactical moves that serve a boundary-creating purpose.

The Dramatic Overture

Erickson, with flourish and fanfare, acknowledges a break with past behaviors and interactions. This recognition may involve a change in therapeutic procedures or some symbolic act performed by the client.

Precommitment

An opening marker facilitating change may be a solemn demand for a precommitment to unconditional acceptance of the therapist's prescriptions.

Achieving Closure

By sealing the therapeutic process, Erickson crystallizes the change process. When symptomatic changes have taken place, Erickson will block the client's return to obsessive patterns of the past.

Symptom Modification and Decontextualization

Erickson's approach to symptomatic behavior may be best described by the concept of utilization. By this is meant an attitude of ''going with'' the symptomatic behavior in order to steer its course, resulting in significant symptom changes and gradual disappearance.

This method works by encouraging the symptom, or by creating an alliance between the therapist and the client's symptomatic behavior. This is not achieved by simply prescribing the symptom, but by encouragement that is linked to immediate modification of the symptom or a modification of the symptom context.

In other words, Erickson creates an ecological impossibility for the symptom's persistence and generates a new environment for the purpose of extinguishing the symptom.

Other tactics used by Erickson include the following.

1. Gradual symptom modification.
2. The divide-and-rule technique.
3. Modifying the spatial context.
4. Modifying the interpersonal context.
5. Modifying the affective context.
6. Modifying the cognitive context.

These tactics are more fully discussed by Omer (1982).

References

Erickson, M. H., & Rossi, E. L. *Experiencing hypnosis*. New York: Irvington, 1981.

Omer, H. The macrodynamics of Ericksonian therapy. *Journal of Strategic and Systemic Therapies*, 1982, *5*, 34–44.

8.6 SUGGESTED INTERVENTIONS TO REDUCE RESISTANCE

Held (1982) suggests that the following interventions may be designed, among other things, to reduce the resistance of the client system and thus increase the therapist's impact and effectiveness.

Resist Becoming Triangled

Triangles, whether cross-generational or perverse, tend to perpetuate problems rather than alleviate them. A coalition is a solution that creates more problems than the anxiety and isolation it was designed to diminish.

The therapist who consistently takes one member's side against the other is becoming "triangled" into the system's conflict. Once triangled into the system, the therapist becomes a regular member of the system and maintains the dysfunctional patterns. A coalition should be distinguished from an alliance. A coalition always involves two parties in opposition to or to the exclusion of a third party. Alliances are simply a teaming up of two parties on the basis of common interests, with no third party involved.

Proceed Slowly

Therapists should avoid pushing their client for too much change too quickly since this will increase client resistance. Clients should have the chance to request assistance rather than have help thrust upon them. The therapist treads a delicate balance between making his or her competencies apparent and not appearing presumptuous. There is always the danger of proceeding without sufficient information, of leaping in and creating resistance to change. Finally, change often comes about by small increments.

Take a "One-Down Position"

It is often advisable in therapy not to present oneself as "knowing all" and in control, but in a one-down position. This allows others to bring forward information without feeling threatened by the "expert."

Positive Connotation, Reframing, Prescribing the Symptom

Positive connotation involves connoting the family members in positive terms, or reframing the pathology as the system's pursuit of health, caring, or problem solving.

Reframing is a technique defined as a method of changing a conceptual and/or emotional response or viewpoint and placing it into another frame that fits the ''facts'' of the same concrete situation equally well or even better, thereby changing its meaning. In other words, it is restating a situation so it is perceived in a new way.

Paradoxical instructions involve prescribing behavior that appears in opposition to the goals being sought in order actually to move toward them. This means going with the resistance, rather than confronting it.

Reference

Held, B. Entering a mental health system: A Strategic-Systemic approach. *Journal of Strategic and Systemic Therapies*, 1982, *3*, 40–49.

CHAPTER 9

TRAINING EXERCISES

9.1 METAPHORS

The use of metaphors and other symbolic language is often helpful in unlocking patterns, structures, perceptions, and feelings in individuals, couples, families, and other groups of people. The word metaphor is derived from the Greek, and means "to carry from one place to another". Bunny Duhl (1983, p. 124) discusses the use of metaphors as "the transposing of an image or association from one state or arena of meaning to another, highlighting similarities, differences and/or ambiguities . . . metaphor is the linkage of meaning—that which connects any two events, ideas, characteristics, modes." Metaphors can be verbal, spatial, imagistic, and kinesthetic, and can be formed in such diverse modes as painting, music, dance, sculpting, and film.

How Metaphors Can Be Useful

It is by imaging or pictoral language that people can make connections between their inward and outward realities. How people perceive their reality has a great deal to do with how life is lived. Conversely, if people can develop a different perception or metaphor of reality, they can begin to live out this new reality. Much of the therapeutic process is helping peo-

ple recognize and change their metaphors about themselves, relationships, and situations.

Often it is difficult for people consciously to be in touch with their images. Part of the therapist's task is to help people discover both their metaphors and the process by which they were developed. Much of the information, patterns, and structures in individuals, couples, families, and groups can be very threatening to divulge. Nevertheless exploring symbolic language can be fun as well as a nonthreatening means of self-exploration.

Exercises

The following section provides examples of exercises that can be used in training and therapy. This is by no means an exhaustive list, but is meant to be representative of exercises that can be used. The exercises range from the simplest to those that are more complex. They may be used to break down barriers between people, and to help them discover each other in an enjoyable manner.

Introductory Games

These games involve the description of oneself by means of a metaphor such as a car, animal, musical instrument, color, or weather system, wherein the analogy or connection between the self and analogy is made. There are different ways to do these exercises. The first is a straightforward one where people describe themselves using one or more analogies. Members of the group or family can each write the metaphors on pieces of paper and put them into a pile in the middle of the group. One by one the papers are read and the members try to guess who wrote each of them. The member who wrote a particular metaphor will elaborate on its content.

The group or family also might choose a person who is willing to participate. The remaining members of the family or group pick a metaphor they believe best represents that person. Then the chosen person describes the metaphor he or she sees himself or herself as and why. The group processes this and moves on to the next member.

More Focused Games

Bunny Duhl (1983) gives the example of each person in a group choosing an animal to represent how he or she learned in a structured setting. Each person is then asked to go around the room being that animal. Then the person is asked to sit down and explain why he or she chose this particular animal and what it represents in terms of personal learning style. The metaphors allow a person to see the self as a totality and to make connections using the imagery of the metaphor. The process is playful, explorative, and nonthreatening. For example, a person may see himself or herself as an eagle soaring above the terrain, checking out the territory. When ready the person picks his or her prey, swoops down, grabs it, and soars away (Duhl, 1983). One can explore facets of the metaphor such as the fact the eagle is alone. Does this mean you study alone? Who soars (studies) with you? And so on.

Another game (Duhl, 1983) requires everyone to think of two labels or nicknames they had when they were children—one that seemed positive and one that seemed negative. Participants go around the room and introduce themselves by their labels only, saying nothing else.

They give the positive one first and the negative one second. Participants sit down and examples of labels are written on the blackboard. As this is going on, they are asked:

1. Whether people see any labels from others that they could have applied to themselves.
2. What memories and associations each person had as he or she introduced himself or herself and heard other labels.
3. Whether each person could have chosen other labels that would have been just as accurate for use in this exercise.

The exercise is then processed with the participants divided into small groups.

Still another game requires participants to give a metaphor for their internal and external reality. Examples might be:

1. A crippled bird inside and a file clerk on the outside.
2. A caring nurturing father figure inside and a bulldozer on the outside.

Couple Metaphors

Each member of the couple uses a metaphor to describe his or her image of the relationship. An example of such a metaphor is an old Ford, well worn outside, but still running fairly well. The car, while not flashy, is functional and the wife does not have to pay much attention to it. The husband feels the battery has run down and always needs recharging. The engine is starting to misfire occasionally. Finally, the husband is tired of trying to keep the car going. It gets a flat tire, which represents the husband finding a new relationship with another woman. Many friends then gather about to fix the tire, but no one pays any attention to the engine or the battery; this surprises the husband, who sees these issues as being far more crucial than the flat tire.

After the metaphor is given, the couple talks about its meaning; clarifying, changing, and adapting. Then the other members describe their images. The value of the exercise is in generating images that reveal facets of the relationship that may not be evident and providing a setting and context for interventions by the therapist.

Family System Metaphors

Couples come out of families to form families; a marriage, therefore, might be seen as the joining of two family metaphors. You might go back one more generation to say that there are four sets of metaphors (the grandparents) that go into a marriage. It is often helpful to have the whole family develop and/or use a common image to describe its interrelationships. Warren Rule (1983) describes the use of the "pie" metaphor. He discusses the analogies to families: (1) parts (slices) make up the whole; (2) nourishment; (3) varying the ingredients affects the outcome; (4) varying the cooking (process) affects the outcome; (5) crust can hide what is beneath the surface; (6) pie must be preserved or it will perish; (7) recipes can be passed on for generations. He cites many different questions that can be asked and pictures drawn. Some examples are:

1. The pie represents the family's problems: Who gets the biggest slice?
2. What size of slice should each person get vis-à-vis his or her contribution to the problem(s)?
3. Who is not getting his or her fair share of the pie? The pie contains the nourishment the family needs.
4. What ingredients in the pie need to be changed in order for everyone to enjoy it more?
5. What key ingredient is missing from the pie?
6. Much of the problem lies hidden under the crust in the ingredients. What ingredients made up the problem?
7. We know the pie is alright because the ingredients are alright. Maybe the problem is in how the pie is baked, for example.

These questions, along with visualizing a pie on a blackboard, can help to relax and refocus family members so that they are willing to disclose their issues. The metaphor provides an opportunity to obtain a clearer picture of the family. Interventions are seen in metaphorical context and can be presented to the client(s) so that resistance is minimized.

References

Duhl, B. *From the inside out and other metaphors.* New York: Brunner/Mazel, 1983.

Rule, W. R. Family therapy and the pie metaphor. *Journal of Marital and Family Therapy*, 1983, *9*, 101–103.

9.2 GENOGRAM ANALYSIS

Families transmit values, role expectancies, and general attitudes from generation to generation in the form of family legacies. The struggle of countless preceding generations are evident in the structure of the nuclear families. A chain of destiny is present in every generative relationship. Marriage is the interlocking of two major family legacies. The seeds of divorce may be planted into a marriage by incompatible legacies, cultures, and religion.

A genogram is a convenient tool to help in identifying the legacies that are transmitted by the multigenerational transmission system. Although family themes, rules, secrets, and dysfunctions are transmitted over countless generations, it is usually sufficient to construct a three-generational genogram to provide the clinical understandings needed in therapy.

Wachtel (1982) has described a number of clinical applications for the genogram. It can be used as a technique for joining, as a tool to reduce anger in family interaction, as a methodology for uncovering emotions, and as a source of clues to discover solutions to the family dysfunction.

Family members who come for therapy are often emotionally distant in their relationship with one another. Consequently the therapist may be viewed as an intruder by one or more of the family members, who resent the intrusion. The genogram can be helpful in such situations because the focus of attention is removed from the present conflict to more neutral historical issues. Rather than moving rapidly into the problem area, rapport can be built with the family while gaining information about the themes, values, and beliefs underlying the family dynamics.

Some couples come into therapy with open hostility, each attacking and recounting the previous wrongs of the spouse. Until the conflict can be reduced, constructive therapy cannot commence. The genogram is a method by which the family of origin can be brought into the sessions, and thus temporarily reduce the focus on the spouses. The therapist, "by commenting on family patterns, by reframing, by using positive connotations, and by speculating on the effect of the family history on the individual and his or her current relationships, can help the couple to see their problems from a new angle" (Wachtel, 1982, p. 337).

Getting in touch with emotions is rigidly opposed by some clients. Alternatively, providing factual data about one's family is seen as less threatening. The therapist can respond to the factual information with "emotional" language, modeling and drawing the client into a recognition of his or her emotions.

When interactions in the family of origin are being described, comments are often made by family members indicating how difficult situations might have been handled in more constructive ways. Similarities may exist between the difficulties in the family of origin and in the family being seen for therapy. The suggested solution drawn from the family of origin may be applicable to the situation at hand and be acceptable to the family members making the observation (Wachtel, 1982).

Procedure

The first step in developing a genogram is to obtain general factual data as outlined at the end of this exercise. Next family members are asked to list adjectives describing the family members. Open-ended questions can be used to broaden the description of specific adjectives. When there is uncertainty about particular family members, it is appropriate to ask what they have heard about specific people. The general conception of what is believed about persons (or relationships) is of importance. Persons in the family of origin may be viewed differently by specific family members coming for therapy.

It is appropriate for the therapist to comment on patterns and assumptions that are relevant to the family as the information surfaces. Since this is a lengthy process, it can be used as an activity occupying only a portion of several sequential sessions.

The genogram should not be started until the family difficulties (presenting problems) have been discussed and understood. There may be immediate difficulties that require the therapist's attention (Wachtel, 1982).

Information to Identify on the Genogram

The following information should be identified in the genogram.

1. Family members
2. Present ages
3. Dates of birth
4. Sibling positions
5. Places of birth, current domicile (indicates migration and disbursal)
6. Dates of marriages
7. Dates of divorces/separations
8. Legacies (names, occupations, behaviors)
9. Dates of death (indicates longevity and losses)

10. Causes of death (tragedies and ill-nesses)

11. Occupations (indicates values, life-styles, talents, interests, and socioeconomic levels)

Subjective Information to Identify on the Genogram

Family roles to be identified occupied include, for example: scapegoat, caretaker, rebel, martyr, rogue, baby, princess/prince, perfectionist, mediator, authority, roué, blamer. The family roles give character to the genogram and may be elicited through questioning the members as to which word comes to mind when they think about a certain person in the family.

Structural Information to Identify on the Genogram

The following structural information should be identified in the genogram

1. Organizational patterns such as power structure, boundaries, triangles, alliances /coalitions, enmeshment/disengagement.

2. Communication patterns.

Reference

Wachtel, E. F. The family psyche over three generations: The genogram revisited. *Journal of Marital and Family Therapy*, 1982, *8*, 335–343.

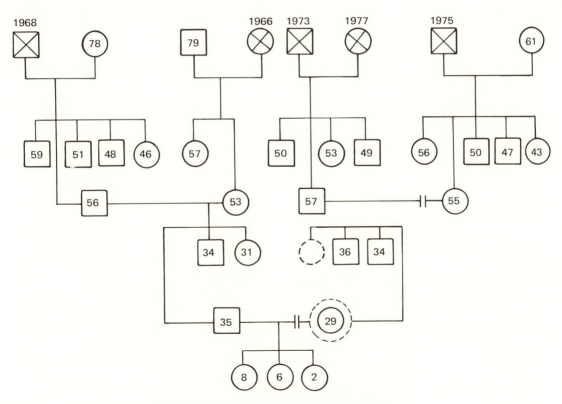

Figure 9.2.1. Example of a multigenerational genogram without descriptive data

9.3 THE FAMILY FLOOR PLAN

The family floor plan (Coppersmith, 1980) is a technique used in the training of therapists and for the purpose of family assessment and intervention. Insight can be gained into patterns of family interaction and structure by analyzing the family of origin or the present family. By use of the family floor-plan exercise, information can be obtained to understand such dynamics as family rules, roles, and myths.

Procedure for Constructing a Family Floor Plan

Each participant is provided with a large sheet of paper, colored pencils, and pens. Participants are asked to draw a floor plan of the house in which they lived as a child (if more than one house was lived in, the person is asked to choose the one that was most memorable). As the drawing begins, the therapist makes the following statements and raises questions. These exercises have been proposed by Copersmith (1980).

Instructions

1. As you draw note the mood of each room for you.

2. Let yourself recall the smells, sounds, colors, and the people in this house.

3. Was there a particular room where people gathered?

4. When extended family visited, where did they go?

5. Were there rooms you could not enter?

6. Did you have a special place in this house?

7. Let yourself be aware of how issues of closeness and distance, privacy or the lack of privacy, were experienced in this house.

8. What was the place of this house in the neighborhood in which it stood? Did it fit or not?

9. Let yourself recall a typical event that occurred in this house; let yourself hear typical words that were spoken by family members.

The responses given are viewed as typical of the family dynamics. Context, affect, and expression of the family are remembered as the participant moves through the experience.

If the exercise is completed during a training session, the trainees are asked to form dyads and talk to one another about their "home," describing events that are remembered. When this has been completed, the group comes together and processes what has been learned from the experience. Allow approximately 60 to 90 minutes for the exercise.

Use with Clients During Therapy

1. During a family session, have the parents draw the floor plan of the house of their own families of origin. The children's role is that of observer. Structurally the children and parents form separate subsystems, with children taking the role of learner. The family can gain a new sense of historicity, which gives depth and stability to it. The exercise is also helpful in discovering expectations rooted in the family of origin.

2. Children can perform the task while the parents watch. The therapist draws attention to the children's view of family interaction and boundary issues.

3. In a family or marital session, each family member draws a floor plan of his or her present home. The questions listed earlier are modified to fit the situation. The goal of the exercise is to discover such dynamics as rules, alliances, boundaries, stresses, and supports. Where the family members are disengaged, the exercise helps to involve all persons in a common task. The dynamics of enmeshment and differentiation can be readily observed in the family interaction. The task then becomes a valuable assessment tool for the therapist.

Reference

Coppersmith, E. The family floor plan: A tool for training, assessment, and intervention in family therapy. *Journal of Marital and Family Therapy*, 1980, *15*, 141–144.

9.4 THE FAMILY MAP

The family map is a way of illustrating family systems. It provides a visual aid for the discussion of family systems and such related concepts as membership, subsystems and their boundaries, flow of information and activity, alignment, and hierarchy. It also provides a way of "seeing" how these concepts "look" in a particular family system. The family map "freezes" a family system at a given point in time, and thus allows for reflective analysis of the system's characteristics (Wedemeyer & Grotevant, 1982).

If used in therapy, the family map will help family members clarify their individual perceptions of the family system. Comparison of family maps drawn by various members of the same family can provide a basis for discussion. In fact the process of discussing family maps alone can be an effective means of eliciting family interaction and teamwork in problem solving. Moreover, making family maps can be just plain fun, and introduces added variety into the therapy process.

Wedemeyer and Grotevant (1982) give some directions for making a family a map:

1. Decide what family you will picture (family of origin or procreation). If you have more than one family for some reason, you may do both.

2. Trace and cut out circles on a plain piece of paper, making enough for yourself and each person or set of persons or things you want to include. There are no restrictions on whom you include or how you symbolize them (parents, siblings, neighbors, pets, your father's golf game—whoever or whatever has a significant effect on the family). If you wish, you may vary size, shape, or color of the units to express yourself more fully.

3. Label each circle. A single circle may have one name, or more than one if you see those people/things as a unit.

4. Arrange the circles on the colored paper provided so they express the relationships you feel in your family. When you feel comfortable with the total arrangement, firmly glue them in place.

5. Draw any boundary or connecting lines you feel complete the picture.

6. Attach a page explaining what you have done. Explain who the components are (age, sex, relationship to you, why included), why you arranged them as you did, and the meaning of any connecting or boundary lines and of any special use of size, shape, or color.

7. Finally, list any people you left out whom you might logically have included and explain why you left them out.

Reference

Wedemeyer, N. V., & Grotevant, H. D. Mapping the family system: A technique for teaching family systems theory concepts. *Family Relations*, 1982, *31*, 185–193.

9.5 COMMUNICATION EXERCISES

Series 1

This series of exercises is adapted from Mease and Hollinbeck (1971). They are based on four dysfunctional communication patterns and can be used as training exercises in dyads. They are:

1. I'm valuable—You are not. ("I'm valuable" has the power.)

2. I'm not valuable—you are valuable. ("I'm not valuable" has the power.)

3. I'm more valuable than you are—I'm more valuable than you are. (Power struggle.)

4. I'm less valuable than you are—I'm less valuable than you are. (Power struggle.)

First Exercise

Pair off. Each pick a role in pattern 1. Dialogue for three minutes on the subject of meeting a deadline. Stop and process. Switch roles; continue for three more minutes. Stop and process. Go on to patterns 2, 3, and 4 in the same manner.

Second Exercise

The purpose of this exercise is to practice leveling communication in order to break through dysfunctional communication patterns. Mease and Hollinbeck (1971) give suggestions to help in this exercise.

1. Recognize which of the four patterns you are in.

2. Use the DESI or DEE responses (see section on "The Process of Communication" in this handbook) to block the dysfunctional pattern.

3. Use DESI or DEE until each person is free from the dysfunctional pattern.

4. Talk directly about the process of the relationship, dealing with feelings and content of the interaction.

Series 2

These exercises are adapted from the writings of Virginia Satir (1972) and are based on the communication roles (blamer, placator, computer, and mascot) that she identified. The

exercises may be used for training purposes as well as in group therapy or family therapy sessions. The following example demonstrates this exercise. It may be adapted according to the size and nature of the group as well as the amount of time that is available.

Forming Groups

Introduce the material on roles in the section on "The Process of Communication" in this handbook. Divide people into groups of two. Have each person try to develop a physical representation or stance (Satir provides a pictoral example of each role) that is representative of each role. Go through each role one at a time. Hold the position for two minutes. Then talk to each other about how the positions felt. Did the physical stance give any insight into the role it represented?

First Exercise

Request each person in the dyad to pick a role. As one of a pair, tell the other person which role you are taking. Role play for two minutes on the topic of deciding where to go to eat a meal. Stop at the end of two minutes. Take a deep breath. Close your eyes. Get in touch with how you feel physically and emotionally. Then talk with your partner about the role play. How did you feel about your role, toward the other person, and so on? Change roles and repeat the exercise until each person has performed every role.

Second Exercise

Join with another dyad to form a group of four. Each person picks a communication role but does not tell the others what it is. Role play either a family making a decision about when they are going to see their grandparents, or an office group deciding on holiday schedules. If the family role play is done, choose who will play the various family roles (mother, father, children). Dialogue using the stereotypic communication roles for five minutes. Then stop. Close your eyes. Take a deep breath. Get in touch with how you felt physically and emotionally about yourself and toward the other members of the group. Then discuss with the members of each group what the role play was like. Talk about which roles conflict with or complement other roles. Change roles and repeat the exercise as many times as desired. Process how these roles connect with your own family or office communication styles, and so forth.

Third Exercise

Repeat exercise 2 but have people change roles in midstream when they begin to feel uncomfortable. Go on for 15 minutes. Stop and talk about this among the group members.

Fourth Exercise

Again repeat exercise 2 but have one person who was not verbally chosen beforehand begin to respond with the leveling response. At the end of five minutes, stop and process. Talk about how the person who was leveling felt and how the leveling response affected the rest of the group.

References

Mease, W., & Hollinbeck, R. *Family communication systems*. Minneapolis: Human Synergistics, 1971.

Satir, V. *Peoplemaking*. Palo Alto, Calif.: Science and Behavior Books, 1972.

9.6 SCULPTING

The Role of Sculpting

Sculpting may be viewed as the creation of visual and spatial metaphors constructed as a living tableau. The sculpture consists of people who are arranged to embody the essential features of their interrelationship. In a sculpture the internal view or script of relational patterns becomes externalized in an active, physical, and spatial metaphor. This process helps the client(s) develop insights into the pattern and structure of their interpersonal relationships. Possibilities for structural and behavioral change can grow out of this kind of experience. Sculpting helps the clients distance themselves from the emotional ties of the family or other systems they are sculpting. During this process they see and physically experience the current patterns of relationship as well as discover new ways of being in a relationship (Constantine, 1978).

Sculpting may be used with individuals, couples, families, extended families and therapy or training groups.

Components of Sculpting

There are, according to Constantine (1978), three components in every sculpting event.

1. *Developing the connection or mapping the physical and metaphorical space*. This process involves tracking the connection between the external, physical space and the sculptor's internal personal metaphor. Connections can be established, for example, regarding closeness/distance in the physical space and the emotional closeness/distance in the relationships by having the participants move about in the physical space expressing their feelings regarding closeness/distance.

2. *Sculpting*. Sculpting is the process of actually forming physical/spatial sculpts of the

relationships. The sculptor is directly involved in the process—moving people about, placing people in the appropriate representations of the relationships as he or she sees them, and placing himself or herself in the sculpt. The therapist typically will act as a monitor or coach in the process. Even the most carefully scripted sculpts change as the sculptor gains new awareness from actually going through the experience as he or she taps into unconscious memories or processes. It is important not to rush the sculpting process so that all the information and experience possible will come out. Closing too soon can block this.

3. *Debriefing or processing*. This process serves as the bridge connecting the image to the here and now. Everyone involved—sculptor, therapist, participants, observers (if there are any)—has different perceptions of the sculpting experience and needs. These experiences need to be processed so that new insights are developed.

Categories of Sculpting

Constantine (1978) cites three major categories of sculpting: (1) simple spatializations; (2) boundary sculptures; (3) family (or other system) sculptures. The following exercises are examples of the kinds of sculpting that can be done.

Simple Spatializations

1. *Linear sculpting* can be conducted in a room on a figurative line between two points. The end points define the extremes of the set being sculpted. Some examples of end points would be intellectual/emotional, thoughtful/spontaneous, aggressive/passive, always/never. Signs at either end representing poles are helpful in defining the space. Ask the participants to walk up and down the line. As they do so, ask them to be aware of their perceptions at the various points along the line.

Have them stop at whatever point along the line seems right to them. Have the participants process the experience while they are still standing in their chosen spots. Ask processing questions such as: How did you end up where you did? Were you surprised? What were you feeling/thinking as you went through the exercise? To what degree were you conscious of how and where others were placing themselves along the line? Who were you aware of? Why? To what degree were you influenced by them? Last, you can repeat the exercise using a different set (Constantine, 1978).

2. *Matrix/Sculpting* is the addition of a second dimension to a linear sculpture. This is very effective in exploring further implications of the original set (linear sculpt) while still using the same space. An example might be to develop a sculpt for a set dealing with aggressive/passive tendencies and then sculpt the frequency or seriousness of the aggression.

While standing in their chosen spots, have people turn 90 degrees and place themselves along the matrix of frequency very often/seldom while staying parallel to their original spots on the linear sculpt. Then process the experience.

3. *Polar sculpting* involves using an object as a center or reference in the room and placing oneself in relation to the object in regard to closeness or distance from the object. Three examples follow.

a. An object (coat, chair, whatever) representing the image of the "heart" of the family is placed in the center of the room. Family members are asked to walk about the room exploring the space in relation to the "heart" or "core" of the family. They are then asked to place themselves in relation to the center. This is processed for each person. The sculpture may be further defined by having family members move in relation to each other until the distances are representative of how things really are in the family. Again, process the exercise with everyone present.

b. *Value sculpting* deals with such concepts as "alcoholism" or "open marriage" and the degree of acceptance/rejection, comfort/discomfort that is generated by the value-laden or affect-laden concepts. A concept is written on cardboard (or the like) and is placed in the center of the room. Participants walk around the room and finally place themselves in relation to the concept. The metaphorical set represents the degree of acceptance and/or comfort regarding the concept or the degree of rejection/discomfort regarding the concept. Then the exercise for everyone present is processed and insights are revealed.

c. This is another example of value sculpting. Place two chairs in the center of the room representing "family of origin." Participants walk around the room and place themselves at whatever distance they wish from the center of the room. This represents how *like* or *unlike* their present family is from their family of origin. Another way of organizing the exercise would be to define how similar or dissimilar the participants would expect their new family situation in relation to their family of origin.

Boundary Sculpture

Boundary sculpting represent an individual's own personal space in relation to others. Areas that are imaged are: how close others may come, how they may enter, who may enter and leave, how many may enter and leave, from which direction(s) may others enter and leave, at what speed may others enter or leave, how two or more individuals' spaces interrelate. Sculpturing sets are particularly helpful with people who are in conflict because the sculpting helps get underneath much of the verbal jousting or masking that goes on (Duhl, 1983).

Bunny Duhl (1983), one of the developers of sculpting, describes the situation that gave rise to the origin of boundary sculpting. Two people, a man and a woman, in a training class were constantly bickering with each other. In exasperation the training team developed a sculpture that became known as *boundary* sculpture in order to try to get at the underlying areas of conflict. The team asked the man to pick out a representation of his own personal territory. He chose a 9- by 12-foot rug. He was asked if there were any boundaries. He replied that it was an open space, but he would sit in a chair in the back corner, thus defining a space within a space. As the woman entered his space, he was upset because she came close to him much too fast. As she came in again more slowly, he asked her to stop a short way onto the rug, thus delineating a second boundary. The man was asked to demonstrate the most appropriate manner in which to approach him. His manner was very slow, halting every few steps, always one step at a time. The woman was asked to participate in the same exercise. Her boundaries were wide open. She moved quickly into spaces and moved out again. Both persons' histories were explored along this line and showed clearly how they had developed their respective boundary systems. As their metaphors were joined, the nature of the conflict became evident without ever dealing with the content of their bickering. Both began to realize that neither was "wrong," but that their fighting stemmed from their boundary preferences and personal styles. They learned that they did not have to be understood by the other in order to be alright as a person.

Family or System Sculpture

Family or system sculpting involves doing a sculpt of one's family or other grouping. It may be done with the actual family members or with people in a training or therapy group representing the system to be sculpted. This sculpt is particularly useful for looking at structural issues in the family and can easily lead to insights and interventions.

Usually one member of the family or group will be the sculptor. There are numerous ways to do the sculpting. One is to pick a particular time in the sculptor's life. Then the sculptor chooses the cast that will explore the physical space. Next work is done in defining and describing the boundaries of the family. Then the sculptor begins to bring people into the sculpture one at a time, exploring that person's interactions with the sculptor and members already added. Following this the sculptor assembles the family, and positions members in relation to each other. The sculptor adds body movements and facial expressions, and develops a stop action of a typical family interaction sequence. Next the entire sequence is repeated several times. This is important, though it seems silly, but much additional information may come out. Last there is an extensive processing by all participants involved in the exercise. The therapist or others can ask how this sculpture can be modified and/or offer suggestions. If this sculpture is being done with an actual family, all members need the opportunity to be sculptors (Constantine, 1978).

There are many variations of this basic theme, such as going through a whole family life cycle, doing multigenerational sculptures, doing family or origin work, or doing an office system.

Finally, there are several types of sculptures, known as minisculptures (Constantine, 1978), which, as the name suggests, may be done in less time than the normal sculpture. Minisculptures generally omit the steps of exploring the physical space and repeating the sequence three times. Examples of minisculpture follow.

Dimensionalized Sculpture

This focuses on a particular limited aspect of the relationship such as emotional closeness/distance and power. Closeness/distance are represented by spatial closeness and distance, while power is represented by height. The higher up, the more powerful is the individual.

Object Sculpture

The family or group sits in a circle with a styrofoam cup in the middle. Each person is told to get in touch with how he or she feels about his or her family (be it present family, family of origin, or other system). The person is to express, physically and nonverbally, how he or she feels about the family. The cup either can

be placed in the center for any person to pick up, or it can be passed around the circle. After all have expressed themselves on the cup, each person explains what he or she did and why. This simple exercise seems to help groups open up in a nonthreatening way. A second round with the cup would be to express what each person would like his or her family to be.

Typological Sculpture

This uses various previously structured relational styles, such as Virginia Satir's four communication roles, in creating sculptures. The therapist may build a sculpture around these given roles, assigning different family members to whatever roles fit them. Constantine (1978) cautions that this form may lay too many of the therapist's assumptions on the client.

Conclusions

Sculpting can be a rich and creative means of enacting the structure and process of the family. It takes creativity and flexibility to go with the movement that people present and to adjust to new scenarios rapidly. Sculpting can be a useful tool to assist the therapist in providing such flexibility.

References

Constantine, L. Family sculpture and relationship mapping techniques. *Journal of Marriage and Family Counseling*, 1978, *12*, 13–23.
Duhl, B. *From the inside out and other metaphors*. New York: Brunner/Mazel, 1983.

CHAPTER **10**

INSTRUMENTATION

10.1 STRUCTURAL–STRATEGIC FAMILY ASSESSMENT SCALE

The Structural–Strategic Family Assessment Scale consists of two parts. Part 1 is optional and includes demographic, medical, and familial questions useful for obtaining identifying data. Part 2 consists of eight subscales with Likert-type items to which the therapist responds on a five-point scale ranging from dys-functional functioning to effective functioning. Each of the subscales identifies an important dimension of family dynamics and is part of the multidimensional family assessment model. The eight subscales of the Structural–Strategic Family Assessment Scale are as follows:

Scale   *Dimensions*

1   Family Development Stages—The degree to which the tasks appropriate to the stage of development are performed.

2   Family Life Context—An analysis of the sources of support and stress in the family's ecology; that is, networks, culture, ethnicity, religion.

3   Family Structure—An evaluation of the family's organization, roles, and boundaries.

4   Family Flexibility—A study of the family's capacity for elaboration and restructuring as revealed by its potential for reorganization. An ability to respond to new information and make necessary structural changes.

5   Family System Resonance—An analysis of the family's sensitivity to the needs of individual members.

6   Family Communication Process—A study of the syntax, semantics, and pragmatics of communication in the family.

7   Marital System Dynamic—An examination of marital satisfaction, balances, reciprocity, complementarity, cohesion, and commitment.

8   Individual Dynamics and Pathology—An analysis of individual dysfunction, individual pathology, and disruption of individual developmental process.

Table 10.2.1
Summary of Assessment Dimensions

Dimension	*Key Concepts*
Family Developmental Stages	Each stage must be resolved if adaptive growth is to continue. Stage 1: Premarriage—dating and making choice and commitment to one person. Stage 2: Marriage—ending primary gratification with parents and redirecting energies into marriage. Stage 3: Birth of first child and childbearing require solidification of marriage and establishment of parental roles. Stage 4: Involves individuation of each member. Stage 5: Departure of children and reworking of parental roles. Stage 6: Integration of loss, acceptance of social, economic, and physical changes in old age. *Patterns of family functioning* Optimal: Each stage is resolved adequately. Dysfunctional: Family members are stuck at various stages and function inappropriately at current stage.
Family Life Context	Factors in the ecological environment that sustain, enhance, or impair the operations of the family. Addresses transcontextual parameters of child rearing. Relations between home and ecological and cultural settings. *Patterns of family functioning* Optimal: Nurturant supportive ecological environment. Dysfunctional: Conflicted interconnections between home and ecological structures and alienating environment.
Family Structure	The links that connect one part of the whole to the other parts forms the basis of family structure. "Codes" describe the nature of the interconnections between parts, structure, and performance. *Patterns of family functioning* Optimal: Structure is well defined, elaborated, flexible, and cohesive. Dysfunctional: Structure has pathological triangles and alliances, and power struggles, and lacks cohesiveness and differentiation.
Family Flexibility	Describes the boundary system of individual parts and the whole. Boundary functioning is determined by system rules that regulate the exchange of information between systems and within system itself. *Patterns of family functioning* Optimal: Adequate exchange of information between systems and within systems. Dysfunctional: Rules governing information exchange are either rigid or nondiscriminatory.

Family Resonance   This is the measure of sensitivity the system has to the needs of its members. Includes expression of affect, level of tolerance of different beliefs, openness and fluidity of system, good problem-solving skills.
Patterns of family functioning
    Optimal: Empathic involvement of members, openness and fluidity of system, good problem-solving ability.
    Dysfunctional: Symbiotic, narcissistic, and absence of involvement; cannot identify problem or develop behavioral alternatives.

Communication Processes   Identify pattern of communication:
    Clear and direct
    Clear and indirect
    Masked and direct
    Masked and indirect
    Incongruent
Patterns of family functioning
    Optimal: Clear, direct, and congruent.
    Dysfunctional: Masked, indirect, and incongruent.

Marital System   Parents chief architects of system.
Patterns of family functioning
    Optimal: High degree of vitality, commitment and satisfaction, nurturance, support, and sexual gratification.
    Dysfunctional: Marital relations not addressed and accountability not maintained.

Individual Issues   Identification of individual pathology, depression, acting out behaviors, delinquency, and so forth. Examination of intrapsychic functioning of individual members.
Patterns of family functioning
    Optimal: No individual pathology.
    Dysfunctional: Serious scapegoating and individual pathology.

Structural Strategic Family Assessment Scale

PART I. Identifying data

1. Names of family members, age, sex, and other persons inside and outside home who are significant participants.

   _____

   _____

   _____

2. Living arrangements (apartment, home, etc.)

   _____

3. Number of years married? _____

4. Occupations and incomes

   _____

5. Education: Mother _____   Father _____

                 Child A _____   Child B _____

                 Child C _____   Child D _____

6. Special features: previous marriage, separations, pregnancies, illnesses, deaths, etc.

   _____

   _____

7. Presenting complaints

   _____

   _____

8. Family conflicts and impairment of family functions

   _____

   _____

9. Family attitudes toward problem and toward intervention

   _____

   _____

10. Previous interventions

    _____

    _____

PART II. Scales

SCALE 1: FAMILY DEVELOPMENTAL STAGES

Stages completed (please check where problems emerge)

One   Premarital _____

Two   Early marriage _____

Three   Child-bearing years _____

Four   Children in school _____

Five   Reduction in family size _____

Six   Dyadic independence reestablished _____

Seven   Advanced age _____

Performance of stage-critical family development tasks

```
|_____|_____|  _____
1                        3                        5
Inadequate               Adequate                 Very well
```

Total score _____
(5)

SCALE 2: FAMILY LIFE CONTEXT

1.   Networking (psychosocial support system)

Score

```
|_____|_____|  _____
1                        3                        5
Impoverished             10 to 12                 Social intactness
less than four to five   people                   20 or more people
people in network        in network               in network
```

2.   Community involvement

```
|_____|_____|  _____
1                        3                        5
Social insularity                                 Integration
and alienation                                    and mutuality
```

Total score _____
(10)

SCALE 3. FAMILY STRUCTURE

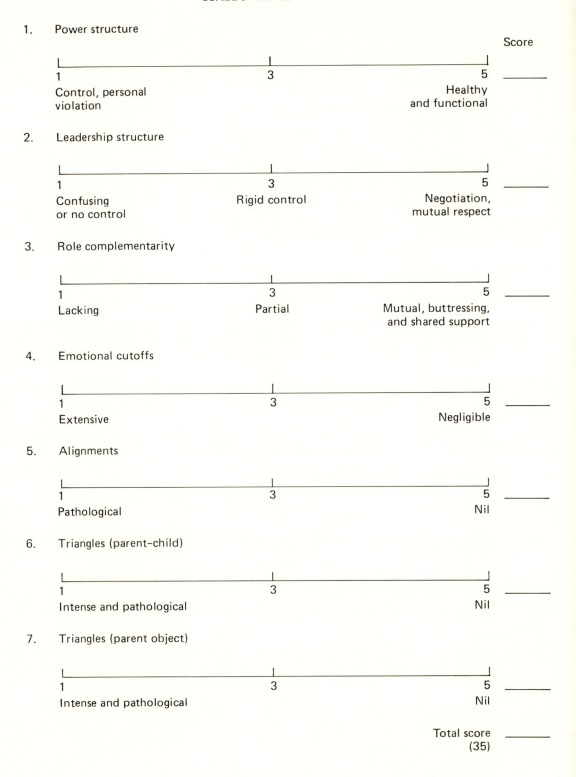

1.   Power structure

                                                                          Score

     1   3   5   _____
     Control, personal   Healthy
     violation   and functional

2.   Leadership structure

     1   3   5   _____
     Confusing   Rigid control   Negotiation,
     or no control   mutual respect

3.   Role complementarity

     1   3   5   _____
     Lacking   Partial   Mutual, buttressing,
                                                                    and shared support

4.   Emotional cutoffs

     1   3   5   _____
     Extensive   Negligible

5.   Alignments

     1   3   5   _____
     Pathological   Nil

6.   Triangles (parent–child)

     1   3   5   _____
     Intense and pathological   Nil

7.   Triangles (parent object)

     1   3   5   _____
     Intense and pathological   Nil

                                                    Total score   _____
                                                         (35)

SCALE 4. FAMILY FLEXIBILITY

1.   Boundaries (spouse system)

Score

1	3	5
Rigid		Permeable	_____

2.   Boundaries (sibling subsystem)

1	3	5
Rigid		Permeable	_____

3.   Rules

1	3	5
Rigid		Flexible	_____

4.   Rules

1	3	5
Arbitrary and inconsistent		Sensitively enforced and consistent	_____

5.   Goal-directed negotiation and problem solving

1	3	5
Extremely inefficient		Efficient	_____

6.   Role flexibility

1	3	5
Rigid		Flexible	_____

Total score   _____
(30)

SCALE 5. FAMILY RESONANCE

1.   Enmeshment

                                                                    Score

   |_____|_____|
   1   3   5   _____
   Fused   Autonomous,
                                                differentiated

2.   Disengagement

   |_____|_____|
   1   3   5   _____
   Distant   Autonomous,
                                                differentiated

3.   Role fulfillment (parents–spouses)

   |_____|_____|
   1   3   5   _____
   Inadequate role   Satisfying
   fulfillment

4.   Role fulfillment (sibling)

   |_____|_____|
   1   3   5   _____
   Inadequate role   Satisfying
   fulfillment

5.   Role clarity

   |_____|_____|
   1   3   5   _____
   Blurred   Clear

6.   Tolerance of differing beliefs

   |_____|_____|
   1   3   5   _____
   Dogmatic   Acceptance

7.   Affect (expression)

   |_____|_____|
   1   3   5   _____
   Anger/frustration   Affection, warmth,
                                                empathy

                                         Total score   _____
                                              (35)

SCALE 6. COMMUNICATIONS

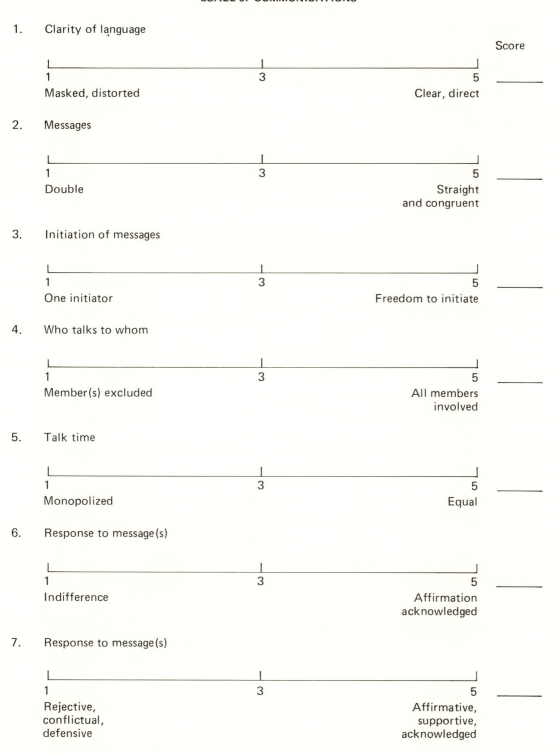

1. Clarity of language

    Score

    1   3   5   _____
    Masked, distorted   Clear, direct

2. Messages

    1   3   5   _____
    Double   Straight
    and congruent

3. Initiation of messages

    1   3   5   _____
    One initiator   Freedom to initiate

4. Who talks to whom

    1   3   5   _____
    Member(s) excluded   All members
    involved

5. Talk time

    1   3   5   _____
    Monopolized   Equal

6. Response to message(s)

    1   3   5   _____
    Indifference   Affirmation
    acknowledged

7. Response to message(s)

    1   3   5   _____
    Rejective,   Affirmative,
    conflictual,   supportive,
    defensive   acknowledged

SCALE 6. COMMUNICATIONS (Continued)

8. Patterns and sequences

1 3 5	_____
Blaming Reconciliating	

9. Patterns and sequences

    1   3   5   _____
    Distancing   Warm and empathic

10. Patterns and sequences

    1   3   5   _____
    Placating   Honest and open

11. Patterns and sequences

    1   3   5   _____
    Distracting   Leveling

12. Patterns and sequences

    1   3   5   _____
    Competing   Warm and
                             agreeable

13. Patterns and sequences

    1   3   5   _____
    Attention getting   Acceptance and
                             tolerance

14. Invasiveness (degree to which members speak for one another
    or make "mind" reading statements)

    1   3   5   _____
    Many invasions   No evidence
                             of invasiveness

                                Total communications
                                            score   _____
                                            (70)

SCALE 7. MARITAL SYSTEM FUNCTIONING

1. Levels of marital involvement and expression of affection

Score

```
L_____|_____J
1                        3                        5      _____
Empty shell marriage                    Vital, alive marriage
```

2. Marital commitment (degree to which self is identified with
   the marital relationship)

```
L_____|_____J
1                        3                        5      _____
Low                                              High
```

3. Long-term oscillating balances (bank account of exchanges)

```
L_____|_____J
1                        3                        5      _____
High-level inequities                 Suitable fairness
```

4. Barter system trade-offs (contingency contracting)

```
L_____|_____J
1                        3                        5      _____
Ineffective                              Effective
```

5. Marital external "push" forces

```
L_____|_____J
1                        3                        5      _____
Low or high                              Realistic
```

6. Marital external "pull" forces

```
L_____|_____J
1                        3                        5      _____
High or low                              Realistic
```

7. Marital congruity

   a. Dyadic consensus (concordance in spouses'
      perceptions of relationship)

```
L_____|_____J
1                        3                        5      _____
Low level                              High level
```

Total score   _____
(35)

SCALE 8. INDIVIDUAL ISSUES AND PATHOLOGY

1. Depression

Score

|⎯⎯⎯⎯⎯⎯⎯⎯⎯⎯⎯⎯⎯⎯⎯|⎯⎯⎯⎯⎯⎯⎯⎯⎯⎯⎯⎯⎯⎯⎯| ⎯⎯⎯⎯⎯
1   3   5

Depression, hopelessness   Joy

2. Anxiety

|⎯⎯⎯⎯⎯⎯⎯⎯⎯⎯⎯⎯⎯⎯⎯|⎯⎯⎯⎯⎯⎯⎯⎯⎯⎯⎯⎯⎯⎯⎯| ⎯⎯⎯⎯⎯
1   3   5

Highly anxious   Contentment

3. Aggression

|⎯⎯⎯⎯⎯⎯⎯⎯⎯⎯⎯⎯⎯⎯⎯|⎯⎯⎯⎯⎯⎯⎯⎯⎯⎯⎯⎯⎯⎯⎯| ⎯⎯⎯⎯⎯
1   3   5

Hostility   Affection, acceptance, warmth

Total score   ⎯⎯⎯⎯⎯
(15)

SUMMARY FAMILY SCORES

Subtests

1. Family development process (5)   ⎯⎯⎯⎯⎯

2. Family life context (10)   ⎯⎯⎯⎯⎯

3. Family structure (35)   ⎯⎯⎯⎯⎯

4. Family flexibility (30)   ⎯⎯⎯⎯⎯

5. Family resonance (35)   ⎯⎯⎯⎯⎯

6. Communications (70)   ⎯⎯⎯⎯⎯

7. Marital system (35)   ⎯⎯⎯⎯⎯

8. Individual issues (15)   ⎯⎯⎯⎯⎯

Total score   ⎯⎯⎯⎯⎯
((240 possible)

10.2 THERAPY SKILLS INVENTORY

Introduction

There are a number of ways in which this inventory can be utilized by trainers. The inventory may be administered as an introductory exercise in a seminar or workshop. Results of the inventory will provide the trainer with an understanding of the range of skills of the learner. Low scores can also serve as an objective measure that the trainer may use to caution persons who have a minimal resource of therapeutic skills against attempting to work beyond their ability.

The broad range of skills presented can be used as a guide to further training. The categorizing of skills according to theoretical positions provides a framework for the development of a student skills' profile.

Skills Inventory Rating

The trainee inventory of skills consists of 32 items with a five-part scale.

Rate yourself from 1 to 5 in each skill listed. Use the following criteria to establish your rating.

1. Have not worked with this skill (or skills) at all.

2. Introductory level of skill (or skills); do not feel that competent or comfortable with skill as yet.

3. Some familiarity with; would feel competent and comfortable using this skill (or skills) some of the time.

4. Very familiar with; feel very competent and comfortable using this skill (or skills) with a wide range of clients in a variety of situations, while working with a team behind a one-way mirror.

5. Very familiar with; feel very competent and comfortable using this skill (or skills) with a wide range of skills in a variety of situations, while working alone.

SKILLS INVENTORY RATING SCALE

I: Basic interviewing skills

1. Active listening	1	2	3	4	5
2. Attending	1	2	3	4	5
3. Establishing rapport	1	2	3	4	5
4. Paraphrasing	1	2	3	4	5
5. Empathy	1	2	3	4	5
6. Reflecting	1	2	3	4	5
7. Summarizing	1	2	3	4	5
8. Self-disclosing	1	2	3	4	5
9. Client exploration	1	2	3	4	5
10. Confrontation	1	2	3	4	5
11. Interpreting test data	1	2	3	4	5
12. Information giving	1	2	3	4	5

II.   Learning theory skills

1. Contingency management	1	2	3	4	5
2. Desensitization	1	2	3	4	5
3. Reinforcement	1	2	3	4	5
4. Shaping	1	2	3	4	5
5. Cognitive modification	1	2	3	4	5
6. Communications skills training	1	2	3	4	5
7. Conflict resolution skills training	1	2	3	4	5
8. Sexual dysfunction training	1	2	3	4	5
9. Social modeling skills training	1	2	3	4	5
10. Charting behaviors	1	2	3	4	5

III.   Adlerian therapy skills

1. Interpreting	1	2	3	4	5
2. Hypothesizing	1	2	3	4	5
3. Life-style analysis	1	2	3	4	5
4. Family constellation analysis	1	2	3	4	5
5. "Spitting in the soup"	1	2	3	4	5
6. Parent education	1	2	3	4	5

IV.   Other psychodynamic skills

1. Regression	1	2	3	4	5
2. Uncovering	1	2	3	4	5
3. Association method	1	2	3	4	5
4. Use of metaphor	1	2	3	4	5
5. Hypnosis	1	2	3	4	5
6. Egosyntonic technique	1	2	3	4	5

V.   Gestalt therapy skills

1. Present centeredness	1	2	3	4	5
2. Awareness	1	2	3	4	5
a. Body structure	1	2	3	4	5
b. Movement	1	2	3	4	5
c. Body processes	1	2	3	4	5
d. Sensations	1	2	3	4	5
e. Voice	1	2	3	4	5
3. Two-chair technique	1	2	3	4	5
(intrapsychic conflict)	1	2	3	4	5
4. Personalizing pronouns	1	2	3	4	5
5. Changing verbs	1	2	3	4	5
a. Changing "can't" to "won't"	1	2	3	4	5
b. Changing "have to" to "choose to"	1	2	3	4	5

6. Changing sentences	1	2	3	4	5
a. "But" to "and"	1	2	3	4	5
b. Questions to statements	1	2	3	4	5
c. How, what, instead of why?	1	2	3	4	5
7. Listening to self	1	2	3	4	5
8. Fantasy approaches	1	2	3	4	5
a. Identification	1	2	3	4	5
b. Projection	1	2	3	4	5
9. Responsibility training	1	2	3	4	5
a. I give you the power	1	2	3	4	5
b. Creating feelings	1	2	3	4	5
10. Bipolarities	1	2	3	4	5
a. Topdog/underdog	1	2	3	4	5
b. Ambivalences	1	2	3	4	5
c. Opposites	1	2	3	4	5

VI. Experiential family techniques

1. Sculpting	1	2	3	4	5
2. Family-map analysis	1	2	3	4	5
3. Chair technique	1	2	3	4	5
4. Role reversal	1	2	3	4	5
5. Genogram analysis	1	2	3	4	5
6. Interpreting games	1	2	3	4	5
7. Psychodrama	1	2	3	4	5

VII. Structural techniques

1. Joining the family	1	2	3	4	5
2. Shifting hierarchies	1	2	3	4	5
3. Restructuring	1	2	3	4	5
4. Enactment	1	2	3	4	5
5. Changing world view	1	2	3	4	5
6. Enacting new transactions	1	2	3	4	5
7. Relabeling	1	2	3	4	5
8. Changing seating	1	2	3	4	5
9. Side-taking	1	2	3	4	5
10. Reversing roles	1	2	3	4	5
11. Feeding back observations of transactions	1	2	3	4	5
12. Detriangulation	1	2	3	4	5

VIII. Strategic therapy skills

1. One-up/one-down	1	2	3	4	5
2. Double binding	1	2	3	4	5
3. Prescription	1	2	3	4	5
4. Double prescription	1	2	3	4	5
5. Use of metaphor	1	2	3	4	5
6. Positive connotation	1	2	3	4	5
7. Problem redefinition	1	2	3	4	5
8. Directives	1	2	3	4	5
9. Symptom exaggeration	1	2	3	4	5
10. Paradoxical strategies	1	2	3	4	5
11. Pretending	1	2	3	4	5
12. Balancing power	1	2	3	4	5
13. Shifting hierarchies and sequences	1	2	3	4	5
14. Shifting alliances	1	2	3	4	5
15. First- and second-order change	1	2	3	4	5

Trainer Profile of Skills

	Maximum	Beginning	Midterm	Final
Basic skills	60			
Learning theory	50			
Adlerian	30			
Psychodynamic	30			
Gestalt	105			
Experiential	35			
Structural	60			
Strategic	80			
Total	455			

10.3 FAMILY GENOGRAM SYMBOLS

A genogram is a structural diagram of a family's generational relationship system. It uses the following symbols to illustrate these relationships. These are laid out in detail in Figure 10.1 following.

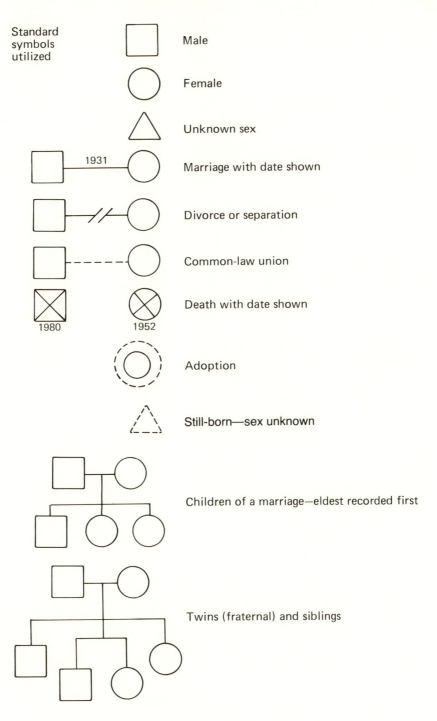

Figure 10.1-Family genogram symbols

CHAPTER 11

ADDITIONAL RESOURCES

11.1 JOURNALS IN FAMILY THERAPY

Staying abreast of current knowledge in any field of expertise can be a difficult task. One of the methods that is used in many disciplines is to subscribe to journals in the chosen field of study. The advantage of journals is that they (1) deal with a wide variety of topics within a given field; (2) focus on specific issues succinctly; (3) take a relatively short time to produce and, therefore, the material is usually current; (4) usually contain lengthy bibliographies for each topic, providing a resource for further in-depth study.

1. *Family Coordinator* (until 1979) and then became *Family Relations* (published quarterly)
   National Council on Family Relations
   1219 University Avenue S.E.,
   Minneapolis, MN 55414

2. *Family Process* (published quarterly)
   The Nathan W. Ackerman Family Institute
   149 East 78th Street
   New York, NY 10021

3. *Journal of Family Counseling* (until 1977) when it became *International Journal of Family Counseling* (published twice per year)
   Transaction Inc.
   Rutgers University
   New Brunswick, NJ 08903

4. *Journal of Family Issues* (published quarterly)
   Sage Publications Inc.
   275 South Beverly Drive
   Beverly Hills, CA 90212

5. *Journal of Marriage and the Family* (published quarterly)
   National Council on Family Relations
   1219 University Avenue S.E.
   Minneapolis, MN 55414

6. *Journal of Marriage and Family Counseling* (until 1978) then *Journal of Marriage and Family Therapy* (published quarterly)
   AAMFT Journal Business Office
   924 West Ninth Street
   Upland, CA 91786

Bibliography

Ackerman, N. W. (1958). *The psychodynamics of family life*. New York: Basic Books.

Ackerman, N. W. (1966). Family psychotherapy today: Some areas of controversy. *Comprehensive Psychiatry, 30*, 375–388.

Alexander, J. F. (1973). Defensive and supportive communications in normal and deviant families. *Journal of Consulting and Clinical Psychology, 10*, 223–231.

Alexander, J. F., & Barton, C. (1976). Behavioral systems therapy with delinquent families. In D. H. L. Olson (Ed.), *Treating relationships*. Lake Mills, Iowa: Graphic.

Alexander, J., Barton, C., Schiavo, R. S., & Parsons, B. V. (1976). Systems-behavioral intervention with families of delinquents: Therapist characteristics, family behavior and outcome. *Journal of Consulting and Clinical Psychology, 44*, 656–664.

Alexander, J. F., & Parsons, B. V. (1973). Short-term behavioral intervention with delinquent families: Impact on family process and recidivism. *Journal of Abnormal Psychology, 81*, 219–255.

Allred, G. H., & Kersey, F. L. (1977). The AIAC. A design for systematically analyzing marriage and family counselling: A progress report. *Journal of Marriage and Family Counselling, 3*, 17–25.

Andolfi, M. (1980). Prescribing the families' own dysfunctional rules as a therapeutic strategy. *Journal of Marital and Family Therapy, 6*, 29–36.

Andolfi, M., Menghl, P., Nicoló, A., & Saccu, C. (1980). Interaction in rigid systems: A model of intervention in families with a schizophrenic member. In M. Andolfi & I. Zwerling (Eds.), *Dimensions of family therapy*. New York: Guilford Press.

Ansbacher, H. L., & Ansbacher, R. R. (1956). *The individual psychology of Alfred Adler*. New York: Basic Books.

Aponte, H. J. (1974). Organizing treatment around the family's problems and their structural bases. *Psychiatric Quarterly, 48*, 8–12.

Aponte, H. J. (1976). Family–school interview. *Family Process, 15*, 303–310.

Aponte, H. J. (1976). Underorganization in the poor family. In P. J. Guerin (Ed.), *Family therapy: Theory and practice*. New York: Gardner Press.

Aponte, H. J. (1979). Diagnosis in family therapy. In C. B. Germain (Ed.), *Social work practice*. New York: Columbia University Press.

Aponte, H. J. (1980). Family therapy and the community. In M. Gibbs, J. R. Lachenmeyer, & J. Sigel (Eds.), *Community psychology: Theoretical and empirical approaches*. New York: Gardner Press.

Aponte, H. J., & Van Deusen, J. M. (1981). In A. L. Gurman & P. D. Kniskern (Eds.), *Handbook of family therapy*. New York: Brunner/Mazel.

Averswald, E. H. (1968). Interdisciplinary versus ecological approach. *Family Process, 7*, 202–215.

Averswald, E. H. (1971). Family change and the ecological perspective. *Family Process, 10*(3), 263–280.

Augsburger, D. (1976, June). *Anger management training*. Symposium at meeting of the Christian Association for Psychological Studies of the Western Association of Christians for Psychological Studies, Santa Barbara, Calif.

Bates, R. F. (1950). *Interaction process analysis*. Cambridge, Mass.: Addison-Wesley Press.

Bach, G. P., & Wyden, P. (1969). *The intimate enemy: How to fight fair in love and marriage*. New York: Morrow.

Baker, L., & Barcai, A. (1970). Psychosomatic aspects of diabetes mellitus. In O. W. Hill (Ed.), *Modern trends in psychosomatic medicine* (vol. 2). London: Butterworths.

Baker, L., Minuchin, S., Milman, L., Liebman, R., & Todd, T. (1975). Psychosomatic aspects of juvenile diabetes mellitus: A progress report. In *Modern problems in pediatrics* (vol. 12). Basel: Karger.

Baker, I., Minuchin, S., & Rosman, B. (1974). The use of beta-adrenergic blockade in the treatment of psychosomatic aspects of juvenile diabetes mellitus. In A. Snart (Ed.), *Advances in beta-adrenergic blocking therapy* (vol. 5). Princeton, N.J.: Excerpta Medica.

Bandler, R., & Grinder, J. (1975). *The structure of magic*. Cupertino, Calif.: Meta Publications.

Bandler, R., Grindler, J., & Satir, V. (1976). *Changing with families*. Palo Alto, Calif.: Science and Behavior Books.

Barker, P. (1981). Paradoxical techniques in psychotherapy. In D. Freeman & B. Trule (Eds.), *Treating families with special needs*. Ottawa: Alberta Association of Social Workers.

Bateson, G. (1958). Cultural problems posed by a study of schizophrenic processes. In A. Auerback (Ed.), *Schizophrenia: An integrated approach*. New York: Ronald Press.

Bateson, G. (1958). *Naven* (2nd ed.). Stanford, Calif.: Stanford University Press.

Bateson, G. (1972). *Steps to an ecology of mind*. New York: Ballantine Books.

Bateson, G. (1978). Discussion of ideas which handicap therapists. In M. M. Berger (Ed.), *Beyond the double bind*. New York: Brunner/Mazel.

Bateson, G. (1979). *Mind and nature.* New York: Dutton.

Bateson, G., Jackson, D., Haley, J., & Weakland, J. (1963). Note on the double bind. *Family Process, 2,* 154–161.

Bateson, G., Jackson, D. D., Haley, J., & Weakland, J. (1956). Toward a theory of schizophrenia. *Behavioral Science, 1,* 251–264.

Bateson, G., & Reusch, I. (1951). *Communications: The social matrix of society.* New York: W. W. Norton.

Beavers, W. R. (1977), *Psychotherapy and growth: A family systems perspective.* New York: Brunner/Mazel.

Beels, C. C., & Ferber, A. (1969). A family therapy: A view. *Family Process, 8,* 280–318.

Beels, C. C., & Ferber, A. (1972). What family therapists do. In A. Ferber, M. Mendelson, & A. Napier (Eds.), *The book of family therapy.* New York: Science House.

Bell, J. E. (1961). *Family group therapy* (Monograph No. 64). U.S. Department of Health, Education and Welfare.

Bell, J. E. (1975). *Family therapy.* New York: Jason Aronson.

Bell, N. W. (1969). Terms of a comprehensive theory of family psychopathology relationships. In G. H. Zuk & I. Borzormenyi-Nagy (Eds.), *Family therapy and disturbed families.* Palo Alto, Calif.: Science and Behavior Books.

Benjamin, L. S. (1974). Structural analysis of social behavior. *Psychological Review, 81,* 392–425.

Benjamin, L. S. (1977). Structural analysis of a family in therapy. *Journal of Consulting and Clinical Psychology, 45,* 391–406.

Benjamin, I. S. (1979). Structural analysis of differentiation failure. *Psychiatry, 42,* 1–23.

Berenson, D. (1976). Alcohol and the family system. In P. J. Guerin (Ed.), *Family therapy: Theory and Practice.* New York: Gardner Press.

Berenson, D. (1976). Family approach to alcoholism. *Psychiatric Opinion, 13,* 33–38.

Berenson, D. (1979). The therapist's relationship with couples with an alcoholic member. In E. Kaufman & P. Kaufmann (Eds.), *The family therapy of drug and alcohol abuse.* New York: Gardner Press.

Berger, A. (1965). A test of the double bind: Hypothesis of schizophrenia. *Family Process, 4,* 198–205.

Berger, H., Honig, P., & Liebman, R. (1977). Recurrent abdominal pain: Gaining control of the symptom. *American Journal of Disorders of Childhood, 131,* 1340–1344.

Berger, M. M. (Ed.) (1978). *Beyond the double bind: Communication and family systems, theories, and techniques with schizophrenics.* New York: Brunner/Mazel.

Bergin, A. (1971). The evaluation of therapeutic outcomes. In A. Bergin & S. Garfield (Eds.), *Handbook of psychotherapy and behavior change: An empirical analysis.* New York: John Wiley & Sons.

Bergin, A., & Garfield, S. (Eds.) (1971). *Handbook of psychotherapy and behavior change: An empirical analysis.* New York: John Wiley & Sons.

Berne, E. (1964). *Games people play.* New York: Grove Press.

Bertalanffy, L. von (1950). An outline of general systems theory. *British Journal of the Philosophy of Science, 1,* 134–165.

Bertalanffy, L. von (1968). *General systems theory.* New York: George Braziller.

Betof, N. (1977). *The effects of a forty-week family therapy training program on the organization and trainees.* Unpublished dissertation, Temple University, Salt Lake City, Utah.

Beukenkamp, C. (1971). *Fortunate strangers.* North Hollywood, Calif.: Newcastle.

Birchler, C. B., & Spinks, S. (1980). Behavioral systems marital and family therapy: Integration and clinical application. *American Journal of Family Therapy, 8,* 6–28.

Birdwhistell, R. (1970). *Kinesics and context: Essays on body motion communication.* Philadelphia: University of Pennsylvania Press.

Bloch, D. A. (1973). Techniques of family therapy: A conceptual frame. In D. A. Bloch (Ed.), *Techniques of family psychotherapy: A primer.* New York: Grune & Stratton.

Bloch, D. A. (1977, June). (Review of Rabkin's Strategic Therapy). *Behavioral science book service* (pamphlet).

Bodin, A. M. (1965). *Family interaction, coalition, disagreement, and compromise in problem, normal, and synthetic family triads.* Unpublished doctoral dissertation, State University of New York at Buffalo.

Bodin, A. M. (1968). Conjoint family assessment: An evolving field. In P. McReynolds (Ed.), *Advances in psychological assessment* (vol. 1). Palo Alto, Calif.: Science and Behavior Books.

Bodin, A. M. (1968). Conjoint family therapy. In W. E. Rinacke (Ed.), *Readings in general psychology.* New York: American Book Co.

Bodin, A. M. (1969). Family interaction: A social-clinical study of synthetic, normal, and problem family triads. In W. D. Winter & A. J. Ferreira (Eds.), *Research in family interaction.* Palo Alto, Calif.: Science and Behavior Books.

Bodin, A. M. (1969). Family therapy training literature: A brief guide. *Family Process, 8,* 272–279.

Bodin, A. M. (1971). Training in conjoint family therapy. In *Project summaries of experiments in mental health training*. Chevy Chase, Md.: National Institute of Mental Health, U.S. Department of Health, Education and Welfare.

Bodin, A. M. (in preparation). Family violence. In D. Everstine & L. Everstine (Eds.), *Violent interaction*.

Bodin, A. M. (1977). Videotape applications in training family therapists. In P. Watzlawick & J. H. Weakland (Eds.), *The interactional view*. New York: W. W. Norton.

Boszormenyi-Nagy, I., & Spark, G. M. (1973). *Invisible loyalties*. New York: Harper & Row.

Bowen, M. (1968). Alcoholism as viewed through family systems theory and family psychotherapy. *Annuals New York Academy of Science, 233*.

Bowen, M. (1966). The use of family theory in clinical practice. *Comprehensive Psychiatry, 7*, 345–374.

Bowen, M. (1975). Family therapy after 20 years. In J. Dyrus & C. Freedman (Eds.), *American handbook of psychiatry* (vol. 5). New York: Basic Books.

Bowen, M. (1976). Theory in the practice of psychotherapy. In P. J. Gverin, Jr. (Ed.), *Family therapy*. New York: Gardner Press.

Bowen, M. (1978). *Family therapy in clinical practice*. New York: Jason Aronson.

Broderick, C. B., & Schrader, S. S. (1981). The history of professional marriage and family therapy. In A. Gurman & D. Kniskern (Eds.), *Handbook of family therapy*. New York: Brunner/Mazel.

Buckley, W. (1968). *Modern systems research for the behavioral scientist: A sourcebook*. Chicago: Aldine.

Bugental, D., Love, L., Kaswan, J., & April, C. (1971). Verbal–nonverbal conflict in parental messages to normal and disturbed children. *Journal of Abnormal Psychology, 77*, 6–10.

Campbell, D., & Stanley, J. (1963). *Experimental and quasi-experimental designs for research*. Chicago: Rand McNally.

Caracena, P. F., & Vicory, J. R. (1969). Correlates of phenomenological and judged empathy. *Journal of Counseling Psychology, 16*, 510–515.

Cagoya, L., Presser, B., & Sigal, J. J. (1974). *Family therapist intervention scale—I*. Unpublished manuscript, Institute of Community and Family Psychiatry, Jewish General Hospital, Montreal.

Cleghorn, J., & Levin, S. (1973). Training family therapists by setting instructional objectives. *American Journal of Orthopsychiatry, 43*, 439–446.

Cohen, J. (1960). A coefficient of agreement for nominal scales. *Educational and Psychological Measurement, 20*, 37–46.

Constantine, L. (1978). Family sculpture and relationship mapping techniques. *Journal of Marriage and Family Counseling, 27*, 13–23.

Constantine, L.L. (1984.) Dysfunction and failure in open family systems. *Journal of marital and family therapy*, 10, 1-17.

Coppersmith, E. (1980). The family floor plan: A tool for training, assessment, and intervention in family therapy. *Journal of Marital and Family Therapy, 32*, 141–144.

Corey, G. (1982). *Theory and practice of counselling and psychotherapy*. Monterey: Brooks/Cole.

Davis, P., Stern, D., & Van Deusen, J. (1977). Enmeshment–disengagement in the alcoholic family. In F. Seixas (Ed.), *Alcoholism: Clinical and experimental research*. New York: Grune & Stratton.

De Chenne, T. K. (1973). Experiential facilitation in conjoint marriage counseling. *Psychotherapy: Theory, Research and Practice, 10*, 212–214.

Dewey, E. (1971). Family atmosphere. In A. Nikelly (Ed.), *Techniques for behavior change*. Chicago: Charles C. Thomas.

DiLoreto, A. O. (1971). *Comparative psychotherapy: An experimental analysis*. Chicago: Aldine-Atherton.

Dittes, T. E. (1959). Previous studies bearing on content analysis of psychotherapy. In T. Dollar & F. Auld (Eds.), *Scoring human motives: A manual*. New Haven, Conn.: Yale University Press.

Dittman, A. T. (1972). *Interpersonal messages for emotion*. New York: Springer.

Doane, J. (1978). Family interaction and communication deviance in disturbed and normal families: A review of research. *Family Process, 17*, 357–376.

Dollard, J., & Auld, F. (1959). *Scoring human motives: A manual*. New Haven, Conn.: Yale University Press.

Dowling, E. (1979). Co-therapy: A clinical researcher's view. In S. Walrond-Skinner (Ed.), *Family and marital therapy*. London: Routledge & Kegan Paul.

Dreikurs, R. (1959). *Adlerian family counseling: A manual for counseling centers*. Eugene, Oreg.: University of Oregon Press.

Dreikurs, R. (1967). *Psychodynamics, psychotherapy and counselling*. Chicago: Alfred Adler Institute.

Duhl, B. (1983). *From the inside out and other metaphors*. New York: Brunner/Mazel.

Duncan, S., Jr., & Fiske, D. W. (1977). *Face-to-face interaction: Research, methods and theory*. Hillsdale, N.J.: Lawrence Erlbaum.

Duval, E. M. (1977). *Marriage and family development* (5th ed.). New York: J. C. Lipincott.

Egan, G. (1982). *The skilled helper* (2nd ed.). Belmont, Calif.: Brooks/Cole.

Ekman, P., Friesen, W. V., & Ellsworth, P. (1972). *Emotion in the human face: Guidelines for research and an integration of findings.* New York: Pergamon Press.

Elbert, S., Rosman, B., Minuchin, S., & Guerney, B. (1964). A method for the clinical study of family interaction. *American Journal of Orthopsychiatry, 34,* 885–894.

Epstein, N. B., & Bishop, D. S. (1973). Position-paper—Family therapy: State of the art—1973. *Canadian Psychiatric Association Journal, 18,* 175–183.

Epstein, N. B. & Bishop, D. S. (1981). Problem-centered systems therapy of the family. in A. S. Gurman & D. K. Kniskern (Eds.) *Handbook of Family Therapy* New York, Brunner/Mazel.

Epstein, N. B., Bishop, D. S., & Levin, S. (1978). The McMaster Model of family functioning. *Journal of Marriage and Family Counseling, 4,* 19–31.

Erikson, E. H. (1959). *Identity and the life cycle.* New York: International Universities Press.

Erickson, M. H. (1954). Indirect hypnotic therapy of a bedwetting couple. *Journal of Clinical and Experimental Hypnosis, 2,* 171–174.

Erickson, M. H. (1962). The identification of a secure reality. *Family Process, 1,* 294–303.

Erickson, M. H., & Rossi, E. L. (1979). *Hypnotherapy: An exploratory casebook.* New York: Irvington.

Everstine, D. S., Bodin, A. M., & Everstine, L. (1977). Emergency psychology: A mobile service for police crisis calls. *Family Process, 16,* 281–292.

Farrelly, F., & Brandsma, J. (1974). *Provocative therapy.* Fort Collins, Col.: Shields.

Ferber, A., Mendelsohn, M., & Napier, A. (1972). *The book of family therapy.* New York: Science House.

Ferreira, A. J. (1960). The "double bind" and delinquent behavior. *Archives of General Psychiatry, 3,* 359–367.

Ferreira, A. J. (1963). Family myth and homeostasis. *Archives of General Psychiatry, 9,* 457–463.

Ferreira, A. J., & Winter, W. D. (1965). Family interaction and decision-making. *Archives of General Psychiatry, 13,* 214–223.

Ferreira, A. J., & Winter, W. D. (1966). Stability of interactional variables in family decision-making. *Archives of General Psychiatry, 14,* 352–355.

Fisch, R. (1956). Resistance to changes in the psychiatric community. *Archives of General Psychiatry, 13,* 359–366.

Fisch, R., Watzlawick, P., Weakland, J., & Bodin, A. (1973). On unbecoming family therapists. In A. Ferber, M. Mendelsohn, & A. Napier (Eds.), *The book of family therapy.* Boston: Houghton Mifflin.

Fisch, R., Weakland, J., & Segal, L. (1963). *The tactics of change.* San Francisco: Jossey-Bass.

Flemenhaft, K., & Carter, R. (1974). Family therapy training: A statewide program for mental health centers. *Hospital and Community Psychiatry, 25,* 789–791.

Flemenhaft, K., & Carter, R. (1977). Family therapy training: Program and outcome. *Family Process, 16,* 211–218.

Ford, F. R., & Herrick, J. (1974). Family rules—Family life styles. *American Journal of Orthopsychiatry, 44,* 61–69.

Foucault, M. (1965). *Madness and civilization.* New York: Pantheon Books.

Framo, J. (Ed.) (1972). *Family interaction: A dialogue between family researchers and family therapists.* New York: Springer.

Framo, J. (1976). Family of origin as a therapeutic resource for adults in marital and family therapy: You can and should go home again. *Family Process, 15,* 193ff.

Framo, J. (1975). Personal reflections of a family therapist. *Journal of Marriage and Family Counseling, 21,* 15–28.

Frank, J. (1973). *Persuasion and healing: A comparative study of psychotherapy* (rev. ed.). Baltimore: Johns Hopkins University Press.

Frankl, V. E. (1960). Paradoxical intention. *American Journal of Psychotherapy, 14,* 520–535.

Freeman, M. (1978). Brief therapy and crisis aid explored. *American Psychological Association Monitor,* Sept./Oct., 6–7.

Freud, S. (1954). *The origins of psychoanalysis: Letters to William Fliess.* New York: Basic Books.

Freud, S. (1964). An outline of psycho-analysis. In S. Freud, *Complete psychological works* (standard ed.) (vol. 23). London: Hogarth.

Friesen, J. D. (1982). *Structural-Strategic Family Assessment Scale handbook.* Unpublished document, University of British Columbia, Vancouver.

Fry, W. F., Jr. (1962). The marital context of an anxiety syndrome. *Family Process, 1,* 245–252.

Fry, W. (1963). *Sweet madness: A study of humor.* Palo Alto, Calif.: Pacific Books.

Gardner, H. (1972). *The quest for mind: Piaget, Levi-Straus and the structuralist movement.* New York: Random House.

Garfield, S. L., & Bergin, A. F. (1971). Therapeutic conditions and outcome. *Journal of Abnormal Psychology, 77,* 108–114.

Garfinkel, P., & Garner, D. (1982). *Anorexia nervosa: A multidimensional perspective.* New York: Brunner/Mazel.

Garrigan, J. J., & Bambrick, A. F. (1975). Short-term family therapy with emotionally disturbed children. *Journal of Marriage and*

Family Counseling, 1, 379–385.

Garrigan, J. J., & Bambrick, A. (1977). Family therapy for disturbed children: Some experimental results in special education. *Journal of Marriage and Family Counseling, 3*, 83–93.

Garrigan, J. J., & Bambrick, A. F. (1977). Introducing novice therapists to "go-between" techniques of family therapy. *Family Process, 16*, 237–246.

Garrigan, J. J., & Bambrick, A. F. (1979). New findings in research on go-between process. *International Journal of Family Therapy, 1*, 76–85.

Gibb, J. R. (1961). Defensive communications. *Journal of Communications, 3*, 141–148.

Glass, G. V., & Smith, M. L. (1976). *Meta-analysis of psychotherapy outcome studies*. Paper presented at the Society for Psychotherapy Research, San Diego, Calif.

Golden, R. (1974). *A validation study of the family assessment battery*. Unpublished doctoral dissertation, Georgia State University.

Goldenberg, H., & Goldenberg, I. (1980). *Family therapy: An overview*. Monterray, Calif.: Brooks/Cole.

Goldenberg, I., & Goldenberg, H. (1981). Family systems and the school counselor. *The School Counselor, 28*, 165–177.

Gordon, T. (1970). *P.E.T.: Parent effectiveness training*. New York: Peter Wyden.

Goren, S. (1979). A systems approach to emotional disorders of children. *Nursing Clinics of North America, 14*, 462–465.

Gottman, J. (1978). *Couples Interaction Scoring System (CISS): Coding manual*. Unpublished manuscript, Department of Psychology, University of Illinois, Champaign.

Gottman, J., & Bakeman, R. (1979). The sequential analysis of observational data. In M. Lamb, S. Soumi, & G. Stephenson (Eds.), *Social interaction analysis*. Madison: University of Wisconsin Press.

Gottman, J. M., & Markman, H. J. (1978). Experimental designs of psychotherapy research. In S. I. Garfield & A. E. Bergin (Eds.), *Handbook of psychotherapy and behavior change: An empirical analysis*. New York: John Wiley & Sons, pp. 23–62.

Gottman, J., Markman, H., & Notarius, C. (1977). The topography of marital conflict: A sequential analysis of verbal and non-verbal behavior. *Journal of Marriage and Family, 39*, 461–477.

Greenberg, G. S. (1974). *Conjoint family therapy: An entree to a new behavior therapy*. D.S.W. dissertation, Tulane University, New Orleans, La.

Greenberg, G. S. (1977). The family interactional perspective: A study and examination of the

tem. Unpublished manuscript, University of Oregon, Eugene.

Howells, J. G. (Ed.) (1971). *Theory and practice of family psychiatry*. New York: Brunner/Mazel.

Jackson, D. D. (1953). Psychotherapy for schizophrenia. *Scientific American, 188*, 58–63.

Jackson, D. D. (1957). The question of family homeostasis. *Psychiatric Quarterly Supplement, 37*, 79–90.

Jackson, D. D. (1959). Family interaction, family homeostasis. and some implications for conjoint family psychotherapy. In J. Masserman (Ed.), *Individual and family dynamics*. New York: Grune & Stratton.

Jackson, D. D. (1959). Managing of acting out in a borderline personality. In A. Burton (Ed.), work of Don D. Jackson. *Family Process, 16*, 385–412.

Greenberg, G. S. (1980). Problem focused brief family interactional psychotherapy. In L. R. Wolberg & M. L. Aronson (Eds.), *Group and family therapy*. New York: Brunner/Mazel.

Guerin, P. J. (1976). Family therapy: The first 25 years. In P. J. Guerin (Ed.), *Family therapy: Theory and practice*. New York: Gardner Press.

Gurman, A. S. (1973). Marital therapy: Emerging trends in research and practice. *Family Process, 12*, 45–54.

Gurman, A. S. (1977). The patient's perception of the therapeutic relationship. In A. S. Gurman & A. M. Razin (Eds.), *Effective psychotherapy: A handbook of research*. New York: Pergamon Press.

Gurman, A. S. (1978). Contemporary marital therapy: A critique and comparative analysis of psychoanalytic, behavioral and systems theory approaches. In T. J. Paolino & B. S. McCrady (Eds.), *Marriage and marital therapy*. New York: Brunner/Mazel.

Gurman, A. S., & Kniskern, D. P. (1978). Deterioration in marital and family therapy: Empirical, conceptual and clinical issues. *Family Process, 17*, 3–20.

Gurman, A. S., & Kniskern, D. P. (1978). Research on marital and family therapy: Progress, perspective and prospect. In S. L. Garfield & A. E. Bergin (Eds.), *Handbook of psychotherapy and behavior change: An empirical analysis* (2nd ed.). New York: John Wiley & Sons.

Gurman, A., & Kniskern, D. (1981). *Handbook of family therapy*. New York: Brunner/Mazel.

Gurman, A. S., & Razin, A. M. (Eds.) (1977). *Effective psychotherapy: A handbook of research*. New York: Pergamon Press.

Guttman, H. A., Spector, R. M., Sigal, J. J., Epstein, N. B., & Rakoff, V. (1972). Coding of affective expression in conjoint family therapy. *American Journal of Psychotherapy, 26*,

185–194.

Haley, J. (1955). Paradoxes in play, fantasy and psychotherapy. *Psychiatric Research Reports, 2*, 52–58.

Haley, J. (1958). An interactional explanation of hypnosis. *The American Journal of Clinical Hypnosis, 1*(2), 41–57. Reprinted in D. D. Jackson (Ed.), *Human communication: Vol. 2. Therapy, communication, and change.* Palo Alto, Calif.: Science and Behavior Books, 1968.

Haley, J. (1959). Family of the schizophrenic: A model system. *American Journal of Nervous and Mental Disorders, 129*, 357–374.

Haley, J. (1959). Interactional description of schizophrenia. *Psychiatry, 4*, 321–332.

Haley, J. (1960). Observation of the family of the schizophrenic. *American Journal of Orthopsychiatry, 30*, 460–467.

Haley, J. (1962). Family experiments: A new type of experimentation. *Family Process, 1*, 265–293.

Haley, J. (1962). Whither family therapy? *Family Process, 1*, 69–100.

Haley, J. (1963). Marriage therapy. *Archives of General Psychiatry, 8*, 213–234.

Haley, J. (1963). *Strategies of psychotherapy.* New York: Grune & Stratton.

Haley, J. (Ed.) (1967). *Advanced techniques of hypnosis and therapy: The selected papers of Milton H. Erickson, M.D.* New York: Grune & Stratton.

Haley, J. (1969). Editor's farewell. *Family Process, 8*, 149–158.

Haley, J. (1969). *Power tactics of Jesus Christ and other essays.* New York: Grossman.

Haley, J. (1970). Approaches to family therapy. *International Journal of Psychiatry, 9*, 233–242.

Haley, J. (1971). Family therapy: A radical change. In J. Haley (Ed.), *Changing families.* New York: Grune & Stratton.

Haley, J. (1971). *Family therapy and family research: An annotated bibliography.* New York: Grune & Stratton.

Haley, J. (1971). Review of the family therapy field. In J. Haley (Ed.), *Changing families.* New York: Grune & Stratton.

Haley, J. (1972). Beginning and experienced family therapists. In A. Ferber, M. Mendelsohn, & A. Napier (Eds.), *The book of family therapy.* New York: Science House.

Haley, J. (1972). We became family therapists. In A. Ferber, M. Mendelsohn, & A. Napier (Eds.), *The book of family therapy.* Boston: Houghton Mifflin.

Haley, J. (1972). We're in family therapy. In A. Ferber, M. Mendelsohn, & A Napier (Eds.), *The book of family therapy.* New York: Science House, pp. 113–122.

Haley, J. (1973). Strategic therapy when a child is presented as the problem. *The Journal of the American Academy of Child Psychiatry, 12*, 641–659.

Haley, J. (1973). *Uncommon therapy.* New York: W. W. Norton.

Haley, J. (1975). Why a mental health clinic should avoid family therapy. *Journal of Marriage and Family Counseling, 1*, 3–13.

Haley, J. (1976). *Problem solving therapy.* San Francisco: Jossey-Bass.

Haley, J. (1979). Ideas that handicap therapy with young people. *International Journal of Family Therapy, 1*, 29–45.

Haley, J. (1980). *Leaving home: The therapy of disturbed young people.* New York: McGraw-Hill.

Haley, J., & Hoffman, L. (1967). *Techniques of family therapy.* New York: Basic Books.

Hare-Mustin, R. (1975). Treatment of temper tantrums by a paradoxical intervention. *Family Process, 14*, 481–485.

Hare-Mustin, R. (1976). Paradoxical tasks in family therapy: Who can resist? *Psychotherapy: Theory, Research and Practice, 13*, 128–130.

Heckel, R. V. (1972). Predicting role flexibility in group therapy by means of a screening scale. *Journal of Clinical Psychology, 28*, 570–573.

Heckel, R. V. (1975). A comparison of process data from family therapy and group therapy. *Journal of Community Psychology, 3*, 254–257.

Heinrichs, D. (1976, June). *Psychoanalytic approach to anger management training.* Symposium at meeting of the Christian Association for Psychological Studies and the Western Association of Christians for Psychological Studies, Santa Barbara, Calif.

Held, B. (1982). Entering a mental health system: A Strategic–Systemic approach. *Journal of Strategic and Systemic Therapies, 3*, 40–49.

Herr, J. J., & Weakland, J. H. (1979). *Counseling elders and their families: Practical techniques for applied gerontology.* New York: Springer.

Hertel, R. K. (1972). Application of stochastic process analysis to the study of psychotherapeutic processes. *Psychological Bulletin, 77*, 421–430.

Hoffman, L. (1971). Deviation-amplifying processes in normal groups. In J. Haley (Ed.), *Changing families.* New York: Grune & Stratton.

Hoffman, L. (1976). Breaking the homeostatic cycle. In P. Guerin (Ed.), *Family therapy: Theory and practice.* New York: Gardner Press.

Hollinbeck, R., & Mease, W. (1971). *Family communication systems.* Minneapolis, Minn.: Human Synergistics.

Hollis, F. (1967). Coding and application of a typology of casework treatment. *Social Casework, 48*, 489–497.

Hollis, F. (1967). Explorations in the development of a typology of casework treatment. *Social Casework, 48*, 335–341.

Hollis, F. (1968). Continuance and discontinuance in marital counseling and some observations on joint interviews. *Social Casework, 49*, 167–174.

Hollis, F. (1968). Profile of early interviews in marital counseling. *Social Casework, 49*, 35–43.

Honig, P., Liebman, B., Malone, C., Koch, C., & Kaplan, S. (1976). Pediatric–psychiatric liaison as a model for teaching pediatric residents. *Journal of Medical Education, 51*, 929–934.

Hops, H., Wills, T. A., Patterson, G. R., & Weiss, R. L. (1971). *Marital interaction coding sys-Case studies in counseling and psychotherapy*. New York: Prentice-Hall.

Jackson, D. D. (1960). *The etiology of schizophrenia*. New York: Basic Books.

Jackson, D. D. (1962). Interactional psychotherapy. In M. I. Stein (Ed.), *Contemporary psychotherapies*. Glencoe, Ill.: Free Press.

Jackson, D. D. (1963). A suggestion for the technical handling of paranoid patients. *Psychiatry, 26*, 306–307.

Jackson, D. D. (1964). *Myths of madness*. New York: Macmillan.

Jackson, D. D. (1965). Family rules: The marital *quid pro quo. Archives of General Psychiatry, 12*, 589–591.

Jackson, D. D. (1965). Study of the family. *Family Process, 4*, 1–20.

Jackson, D. D. (Ed.) (1968). *Communication, family, and marriage*. Palo Alto, Calif.: Science and Behavior Books.

Jackson, D. D. (Ed.) (1968). *Human communication: Vol. 1. Communication, family, and marriage*. Palo Alto, Calif.: Science and Behavior Books.

Jackson, D. D. (Ed.) (1968). *Human communication: Vol. 2. Therapy, communication, and change*. Palo Alto, Calif.: Science and Behavior Books.

Jackson, D. D., & Haley, J. (1963). Transference revisited. *The Journal of Nervous and Mental Disease, 137*, 363–371.

Jackson, D. D., Riskin, J., & Satir, V. M. (1961). A method of analysis of a family interview. *Archives of General Psychiatry, 5*, 321–339.

Jackson, D. D., & Satir, V. M. (1968). A review of psychiatric developments in family diagnosis and family therapy. In D. Jackson (Ed.), *Therapy communication and change*. Science and Behavior Books.

Jackson, D. D., & Yalom, I. (1966). Family research on the problem of ulcerative colitis. *Archives of General Psychiatry, 15*, 410–418.

Jacob, T. (1975). Family interaction in disturbed and normal families: A methodological and substantive review. *Psychological Bulletin, 82*, 33–65.

Jacobson, N. S. (1978). A review of the research on the effectiveness of marital therapy. In T. J. Paolino & B. S. McCrady (Eds.), *Marriage and marital therapy*. New York: Brunner/Mazel.

Jesse, E., & L'Abate, L. (1980). The use of paradox with children in an inpatient treatment setting. *Family Process, 19*, 59–64.

Kaplan, H. S. (1979). *Dosorders of sexual desire*. New York: Brunner/Mazel.

Kaplan, S., Rosman, B., Liebman, R., & Honig, P. (1977). The log as a behavioral measure in a program to train pediatric residents in child psychiatry. *Special Interest Group/Health Profession Education Bulletin*.

Kaufman, E., & Kaufman, P. (1979). From a psychodynamic orientation to a structural family therapy approach in the treatment of drug dependency. In E. Kaufman & P. Kaufman (Eds.), *The family therapy of drug and alcohol abuse*. New York: Gardner Press.

Keeney, B. P. (1979). Ecosystemic epistemology: An alternate paradigm for diagnosis. *Family Process, 18*, 117–129.

Kersey, F. I. (1976). *An exploratory factorial validity study of Allred's interaction analysis for counselors*. Unpublished master's thesis, Brigham Young University, Salt Lake City, Utah.

Kiesler, D. J. (1973). *The process of psychotherapy: Empirical foundations and systems of analysis*. Chicago: Aldine.

Kiesler, D. J., Mathieu, P. L., & Klein, M. H. (1970). A summary of the issues and conclusions. In C. R. Rogers, E. T. Gendlin, D. J. Kiesler, & C. B. Truax (Eds.), *The therapeutic relationship and its impact: A study of psychotherapy with schizophrenics*. Madison, Wis.: Psychiatric Institute, Bureau of Audio Visual Instruction.

Klein, N. C., Alexander, J. F., & Parsons, B. V. (1977). Impact of family systems intervention on recidivism and sibling delinquency: A model of primary prevention and program evaluation. *Journal of Consulting and Clinical Psychology, 45*, 469–474.

Klein, M. H., & Gurman, A. S. (1980). Ritual and reality: Some clinical implications of experimental designs for behavior therapy of depression. In L. Rehm (Ed.), *Behavior therapy for depression*. New York: Academic Press.

Kniskern, D. P., & Gurman, A. S. (1980). Advances and prospects for family therapy research. In J. P. Vincent (Ed.), *Advances in family intervention, assessment and theory* (vol. 2).

Greenwich, Conn.: JAI Press.

Kniskern, D. P., & Gurman, A. S. (1980). Future directions for family therapy research. In D. A. Bagarozzi (Ed.), *New perspectives in family therapy*. New York: Human Sciences Press.

Kniskern, D. P., & Gurman, A. S. (1980). Research on training in marriage and family therapy: Status, issues and directions. In I. Zwerling & M. Andolfi (Eds.), *Dimensions of family therapy*. New York: Guilford.

Kuhn, T. S. (1970). *The structure of scientific revolutions* (2nd ed.). Chicago: University of Chicago Press.

L'Abate, L. (1975). A positive approach to marital and family intervention. In L. R. Wolberg & M. L. Aronson (Eds.), *Group therapy: 1975*. New York: Stratton Intercontinental Medical Book Co.

L'Abate, L. (1977). Intimacy is sharing hurt feelings: A reply to David Mace. *Journal of Marriage and Family Counseling, 23*, 13–16.

L'Abate, L., & Weeks, G. (1978). A bibliography of paradoxical methods in psychotherapy of family systems. *Family Process, 17*, 95–98.

Laing, R. D. (1965). Mystification, confusion, and conflict. In I. Boszormenyi-Nagy & J. L. Framo (Eds.), *Intensive family therapy: Theoretical and practical aspects*. New York: Harper & Row.

Lane, M. (1970). *Introduction to structuralism*. New York: Basic Books.

Langsley, D. G., Fairbairn, R. H., & DeYoung, C. D. (1968). Adolescence and family crises. *Canadian Psychiatric Association Journal, 13*, 125–133.

Langsley, D. G., & Kaplan, D. M. (1968). *The treatment of families in crisis*. New York: Grune & Stratton.

Langsley, D. G., Machotka, P., & Flomenhaft, K. (1971). Avoiding mental hospital admission: A follow-up study. *American Journal of Psychiatry, 127*, 1391–1394.

Langsley, D., Pittman, F., Machotka, P., & Flomenhaft, K. (1968). Family crisis therapy: Results and implications. *Family Process, 7*, 145–158.

Leary, T. (1957). *Interpersonal diagnosis of personality*. New York: Ronald Press.

Lederer, W. J., & Jackson, D. D. (1968). *The mirages of marriage*. New York: W. W. Norton.

Lewis, M., & Rosenblum, L. H. (Eds.) (1974). *The effect of the infant on its caregiver*. New York: John Wiley & Sons.

Liddle, H. A. (1982). Family therapy training: Current issues, future trends. *International Journal of Family Therapy, 4*, 2ff.

Liddle, H. A. (1982). On the problems of eclecticism: A call for epistemologic clarification and human-scale theories. *Family Process, 21*, 243–250.

Liebman, R., Honig, P., & Berger, H. (1976). An integrated treatment program for psychogenic pain. *Family Process, 15*, 397–405.

Liebman, R., Minuchin, S., & Baker, L. (1974). An integrated treatment program for Anorexia Nervosa. *American Journal of Psychiatry, 131*, 432–436.

Luborsky, L., Singer, B., & Luborsky, L. (1975). Comparative studies of psychotherapies. *Archives of General Psychiatry, 32*, 995–108.

Luthman, S., & Kirschenbaum, N. (1974). *The dynamic family*. Palo Alto: Science and Behavior Books.

Mace, D. R. (1976). Marital intimacy and the deadly love-anger cycle. *Journal of Marriage and Family Counseling, 21*, 131–137.

MacFadden, C. (1977). *The serial*. New York: Knopf Publishing Co.

MacGregor, R., Ritchie, A., Serrano, A., Schuster, F., McDonald, F., & Goolishian, H. (1964). *Multiple impact therapy with families*. New York: McGraw-Hill.

Madanes, C. (1980). Protection, paradox and pretending. *Family Process, 19*, 73–85.

Madanes, C. (1982). *Strategic family therapy*. Washington: Jossey-Bass.

Madanes, C., & Haley, J. (1977). Dimensions of family therapy. *Journal of Nervous and Mental Disease, 165*, 88–98.

Mahler, M. (1968). *On human symbiosis and the vicissitudes of individuation* (Vol. 2). New York: International Universities Press.

Maliver, B. (1973). *The encounter game*. New York: Stein and Day.

Mandel, H. P., Weizmann, F., Millan, B., Greenhow, J., & Speirs, D. (1975). Reaching emotionally disturbed children: Judo principles in remedial education. *American Journal of Orthopsychiatry, 45*, 867–874.

Marlowe, K. (1983). After the affair. *CATEF Newsletter, 3*.

Maruyama, M. (1983). The second cybernetics: Deviation amplifying mutual causative processes. *American Scientist, 51*, 164–179.

Masters, W. H., & Johnson, V. E. (1970). *Human sexual inadequacy*. Boston: Little, Brown.

Mayerovitch, J. (1972). *A reliability study of a new system for coding family therapists' verbalizations*. Unpublished master's thesis, Western Michigan University, Kalamazoo.

Mease, W., & Hollinbeck, R. (1971). *Family communication systems*. Minneapolis, Minn.: Human Synergistics.

Meehl, P. E. (1977). *Psychodiagnosis: Selected papers*. New York: W. W. Norton.

Meissner, W. W. (1970). Thinking about the family—Psychiatric aspects. *Family Process, 15*,

131–170.

Miller, J. G. (1965). Living systems—Basic concepts. *Behavioral Science, 10*, 193–411.

Minuchin, S. (1974). *Families and family therapy.* Cambridge, Mass.: Harvard University Press.

Minuchin, S., Baker, L., Rosman, B., Liebman, R., Milman, L., & Todd, T. (1975). A conceptual model of psychosomatic illness in children. *Archives of General Psychiatry, 32*, 1031–1038.

Minuchin, S., & Fishman, H. C. (1981). *Family therapy techniques.* Cambridge, Mass.: Harvard University Press.

Minuchin, S., Montalvo, B., Guerney, B., Rosman, B., & Schumer, F. (1967). *Families of the slums.* New York: Basic Books.

Minuchin, S., Rosman, B., & Baker, L. (1978). *Psychosomatic families: Anorexia nervosa in context.* Cambridge, Mass.: Harvard University Press.

Mishler, E., & Waxler, N. (1968). *Interaction in families.* New York: John Wiley & Sons.

Mishler, E. G., & Waxler, N. (1970). *Family processes and schizophrenia.* New York: Jason Aronson.

Mishler, E. G., & Waxler, N. (1975). Family interaction processes and schizophrenia: A review of current theories. In E. Mishler & N. Waxler (Eds.), *Family processes and schizophrenia.* New York: Jason Aronson.

Mishler, E., & Waxler, N. (1975). The sequential patterning of interaction in normal and schizophrenic families. *Family Process, 14*, 17–50.

Mitchell, K. M., Bozarth, J. D., & Krauft, C. C. (1977). A reappraisal of the therapeutic effectiveness of accurate empathy, non-possessive warmth and genuineness. In A. S. Gurman & A M. Razin (Eds.), *Effective psychotherapy: A handbook of research.* New York: Pergamon Press.

Modow, L. (1977). Do you have any of these symptoms of repressed anger? *New Woman.* (Fort Lauderdale, Fla.).

Montalvo, B. (1973). Aspects of live supervision. *Family Process, 12*, 343–359.

Morris, G. O., & Wynne, I. C. (1965). Schizophrenic offspring and aparental styles of communication: A predictive study using excerpts of family therapy recordings. *Psychiatry, 28*, 19–44.

Mozdzierz, G., & Lottman, T. (1978). Games married couples play. Unpublished Manuscript, Vancouver.

MRI (1979, June). *Newsletter of the Mental Research Institute, 1*, 3–4.

O'Hanlon, W. (1982). Strategic pattern intervention. *Journal of Strategic and Systemic Therapies, 4*, 26–33.

Olson, D. H. L. (1972). Empirically unbinding the

double bind: Review of research and conceptual formulations. *Family Process, 11*, 69–94.

Olson, D. H. L. (Ed.) (1976). *Treating relationships.* Lake Mills, Iowa: Graphic.

O'Mahoney, M. T. (1978). *The marital therapy session report.* Unpublished manuscript, Institute of Psychiatry, Northwestern Memorial Hospital, Chicago.

Omer, H. (1982). The macrodynamics of Ericksonian therapy. *Journal of Strategic and Systemic Therapies, 5*, 34–44.

Orlinsky, D. E., & Howard, K. I. (1975). *Varieties of psychotherapeutic experience: Multivariate analysis of patients' and therapists' report.* New York: Teachers College Press.

Orlinsky, D. E., & Howard, K. I. (1978). The relation of process to outcome in psychotherapy. In S. L. Garfield & A. E. Bergin (Eds.), *Handbook of psychotherapy and behavior change: An empirical analysis* (2nd ed.). New York: John Wiley & Sons.

Palazzoli-Selvini, M. (1970). The families of patients with anorexia nervosa. In E. J. Anthony & C. Koupernik (Eds.), *The child and his family.* New York: John Wiley & Sons.

Palazzoli-Selvini, M. (1978). *Self-starvation: From individual to family therapy in the treatment of anorexia nervosa.* New York: Jason Aronson.

Palazzoli-Selvini, M., Boscolo, L., Cecchin, G. F., & Prata, G. (1974). The treatment of children through brief therapy of their parents. *Family Process, 13*, 429–442.

Palazzoli-Selvini, M., Boscolo, L., Cecchin, G. F., & Prata, G. (1977). Family rituals: A powerful tool in family therapy. *Family Process, 16*, 445–453.

Palazzoli-Selvini, M., Boscolo, L., Cecchin, G., & Prata, G. (1978). *Paradox and counterparadox: A new model in the therapy of the family in schizophrenic transaction.* New York: Jason Aronson.

Palazzoli-Selvini, M., Boscolo, L., Cecchin, G., & Prata, G. (1978). Ritualized prescription in family therapy: Odd days and even days. *Journal of Marriage and Family Counseling, 4*, 3–9.

Palazzoli-Selvini, M., Boscolo, L., Cecchin, G., & Prata, G. (1980). Hypothesizing — circularity —neutrality: Three guidelines for the conductor of the session. *Family Process, 19*, 3–12.

Palazzoli-Selvini, M., Boscolo, L., Cecchin, G., & Prata, G. (1980). Problem of the referring person. *Journal of Marital and Family Therapy, 6*, 3–9.

Palombo, S. R., Merrifield, J., Weigert, W., Morris, G. O., & Wynne, L. C. (1967). Recognition of parents of schizophrenics from excerpts of family therapy interviews. *Psychiatry, 30*, 405–412.

Paolino, T. J., & McCrady, B. S. (Eds.) (1978). *Marriage and marital therapy: Psychoanalytic, behavioral, and systems theory perspectives.* New York: Brunner/Mazel.

Papp, P. (1979). Paradoxical strategies and countertransference. *American Journal of Family Therapy, 7*, 11–12.

Papp, P. (1980). The Greek chorus and other techniques of paradoxical therapy. *Family Process, 19*, 45–57.

Papp, P. (1981). Paradoxes. In S. Minuchin & H. C. Fishman (Eds.), *Family therapy techniques.* Cambridge, Mass.: Harvard University Press.

Parsons, B. V. (1972). *Family therapy training manual.* Unpublished manuscript, University of Utah, Salt Lake City.

Parsons, B. V., & Alexander, J. F. (1973). Short-term family intervention: A therapy outcome study. *Journal of Consulting and Clinical Psychology, 41*, 195–201.

Patterson, G. R. (1971). *Families: Applications of social learning to family life.* Research Press Co.

Patterson, G. R. (1976). The aggressive child: Victim and architect of a coercive system. In E. J. Mash, L. A. Hamerlynck, & I. C. Handy (Eds.), *Behavior modification and families.* New York: Brunner/Mazel, pp. 267–316.

Patterson, G. R., Cobb, J. A., & Ray, R. (1972). A social-engineering technology for retraining the families of aggressive boys. In H. Adams & I. Unikel (Eds.), *Georgia Symposium in experimental clinical psychology* (vol. 11). Springfield, Ill.: Charles C. Thomas.

Patterson, G. R., Ray, R. S., Shaw, D. A., & Cobb, J. A. (1969). *Manual for coding of family interactions.* Unpublished manuscript, Oregon Research Institute and University of Oregon, Eugene.

Piaget, J. (1970). *Structuralism.* New York: Basic Books.

Pinsof, W. M. (1976). *Truax's Accurate Empathy Scale: A critical review of the research.* Unpublished manuscript, Center for Family Studies, Department of Psychiatry, Northwestern University Medical School, Chicago.

Pinsof, W. M. (1979). The Family Therapist Behavior scale (FTBS): Development and evaluation of a coding system. *Family Process, 18*(4), 451–461.

Pinsof, W. M. (1979). *The Family Therapist Coding System (FTCS) coding manual.* Chicago: Center for Family Studies, Department of Psychiatry, Northwestern University Medical School.

Pittman, F. S., Flomenhaft, K., DeYoung, C., Kaplan, D., & Langsley, D. G. (1966). Techniques of family crisis therapy. In J. Masserman (Ed.), *Current psychiatric therapies.* New York: Grune & Stratton.

Pittman, F. S., Langsley, D. G., Flomenhaft, K., DeYoung, C., Machotka, P., & Kaplan, D. M. (1971). Therapy techniques of the family treatment unit. In J. Haley (Ed.), *Changing families.* New York: Grune & Stratton.

Postner, R. S., Guttman, H., Sigal, J., Epstein, N. B., & Rakoff, V. (1971). Process and outcome in conjoint family therapy. *Family Process, 10*, 451–474.

Presser, B. G., Sigal, J. J., Mayerovitch, J., & Chagova, I. (1974). *Individual differences in family therapists' style: A coding system and some results.* Paper at annual meeting of the Canadian Psychological Association, Windsor, Ontario.

Rabkin, R. (1977). *Strategic psychotherapy.* New York: Basic Books.

Rado, S. (1958). From the metaphysical ego in the bio-cultural action-self. *Journal of Psychology, 46*, 279–290.

Rank, M. R., & Le Croy, C. W. (1983). Toward a multiple perspective in family theory and practice: The case of social exchange theory, symbolic interactionism, and conflict theory. *Family Relations, 32*, 441–448.

Rapoport, R. (1965). Normal crises, family structure and mental health. In H. J. Parad (Ed.), *Crisis intervention.* New York: FSAA.

Rappoport, J., & Chinsky, M. J. (1972). Accurate empathy: Confusion of a construct. *Psychological Bulletin, 77*, 400–401.

Raskin, D. E., & Klein, Z. E. (1976). Losing a symptom through keeping it: A review of paradoxical treatment techniques and rationale. *Archives of General Psychiatry, 33*, 548–555.

Raush, H. L. (1965). Interaction sequences. *Journal of Personality and Social Psychology, 2*, 487–499.

Raush, H. L. (1972). Process and change: A markov model for interaction. *Family Process, 2*, 275–298.

Reid, J. B. (1970). Reliability assessment of observation data: A possible methodological problem. *Child Development, 41*, 1143–1150.

Rhodes, S. L. (1977). A developmental approach to the life cycle of the family. *Social Casework, 58*, 301–311.

Rice, D. G., Fey, W. F., & Kepees, J. G. (1972). Therapist experience and style in co-therapy. *Family Process, 11*, 1–12.

Rice, D. G., Gurman, A. S., & Razin, A. M. (1974). Therapist sex, style and theoretical orientation. *Journal of Nervous and Mental Disease, 159*, 413–421.

Rice, D. G., Razin, A. M., & Gurman, A. S. (1976).

Spouses as co-therapists: Variables and implications for patient–therapist matching. *Journal of Marriage and Family Counseling, 2*, 55–62.

Rice, L. N. (1965). Therapist's style of participation and case outcome. *Journal of Consulting Psychology, 29*, 150–160.

Riskin, J. (1976). ''Non-labelled'' family interaction: Preliminary report on a prospective study. *Family Process, 15*, 433–439.

Riskin, J., & Faunce, E. E. (1968). *Family interaction scales scoring manual.* Unpublished manuscript, Mental Research Institute, Palo Alto, Calif.

Riskin, J., & Faunce, E. E. (1970). Family interaction scales. I: Theoretical framework and method. *Archives of General Psychiatry, 22*, 504–512.

Riskin, J., & Faunce, E. E. (1970). Family interaction scales. III: Discussion of methodology and substantive findings. *Archives of General Psychiatry, 22*, 527–537.

Riskin, J., & Faunce, E. E. (1972). An evaluative review of family interaction research. *Family Process, 11*, 365–456.

Riskin, J., & McCorkle, M. E. (1979). ''Nontherapy'' family research and change in families: A brief clinical research communication. *Family Process, 18*, 161–162.

Ritzer, G. (1974). Indigenous non-professionals in community mental health: Boon or boondoggle? In P. Roman & H. Trice (Eds.), *The sociology of psychotherapy.* New York: Jason Aronson.

Robinson, L. R. (1975). Basic concepts in family treatment: A differential comparison with individual treatment. *American Journal of Psychiatry, 132*, 1045–1048.

Rogers, C. R. (1951). *Client-centered therapy.* Boston: Houghton Mifflin.

Rogers, C. R. (1957). The necessary and sufficient conditions of therapeutic personality change. *Journal of Consulting Psychology, 21*, 95–103.

Rogers, C. R., Grendlin, E. T., Kiesler, D. J., & Truax, C. B. (1967). *The therapeutic relationship and its impact: A study of psychotherapy with schizophrenics.* Madison: University of Wisconsin Press.

Rohrbaugh, M., Terner, H., Press, S., White, L., Raskin, P., & Pickering, M. R. (1977). *Paradoxical strategies in psychotherapy.* Symposium at meeting of the American Psychological Association, San Francisco.

Rosen, J. N. (1953). *Direct analysis.* New York: Grune & Stratton.

Rosen, R. D. (1977). *Psychobabble: Fast talk and quick cure in the era of feeling.* New York: Atheneum.

Rosenberg, J. B., & Lindblad, M. B. (1978). Behavior therapy in a family context: Elective mutism. *Family Process, 17*, 77–82.

Rosman, B., Minuchin, S., & Liebman, R. (1975). Family lunch session: An introduction to family therapy in anorexia nervosa. *American Journal of Orthopsychiatry, 45*, 847–853.

Rule, W. R. (1983). Family therapy and the pie metaphor. *Journal of Marital and Family Therapy, 9*, 101–103.

Sackett, G. P. (1977). A taxonomy of observational techniques and a theory of measurement. In G. P. Sackett & H. C. Haywood (Eds.), *Observing behavior: Data collection and analysis methods.* Baltimore: University Park Press.

Sackett, G. P., & Haywood, H. C. (Eds.) (1977). *Observing behavior: Data collection and analysis methods.* Baltimore: University Park Press.

Sager, C. J., & Kaplan, H. S. (1972). *Progress in group and family therapy.* New York: Brunner/Mazel.

Salzberg, H. C. (1962). Effects of silence and redirection on verbal responses in group psychotherapy. *Psychological Reports, 11*, 455–461.

Sanders, J. P. (1974). *A study in counselor evaluation scale validation: An exploratory examination of naive counselors' scores on Allred's interaction analysis for counselors with selected scores on the Strong Vocation Interest Blank.* Unpublished master's thesis, Brigham Young University, Salt Lake City, Utah.

Satir, V. (1965). The family as a treatment unit. *Confina Psychiatrica, 8*, 37–42.

Satir, V. (1967). *Conjoint family therapy* (rev. ed.). Palo Alto, Calif.: Science and Behavior Books.

Satir, V. (1972). *People making.* Palo Alto, Calif.: Science and Behavior Books.

Schachter, S., & Singer, J. E. (1962). Cognitive, social, and physiological determinants of emotional state. *Psychological Review, 69*, 379–399.

Schaefer, E. S. (1965). A configurational analysis of children's reports of parent behavior. *Journal of Consulting Psychology, 29*, 552–557.

Scheflen, A. E. (1966). Natural history method in psychotherapy: Communicational research. In L. A. Gottschalk & A. H. Auberbach (Eds.), *Methods of research in psychotherapy.* New York: Appleton-Century-Crofts.

Scheflen, A. E. (1973). *Communicational structure: Analysis of a psychotherapy transaction.* Bloomington and London: Indiana University Press.

Scherz, F. (1971). Maturational crises and parent–child interaction. *Social Casework, 52*, 362–369.

Schuham, A. I. (1967). The double bind hypothesis

a decade later. *Psychological Bulletin, 68*, 409–410.

Shapiro, R. (1974). Therapist attitudes and premature termination in family and individual therapy. *Journal of Nervous and Mental Disease, 159*, 101–107.

Shapiro, R., & Budman, S. (1973). Defection, termination, and continuation in family and individual therapy. *Family Process, 12*, 55–67.

Sigal, J. J., Guttman, H. A., Chagoya, L., & Lasry, J. C. (1973). Predictability of family therapists' behavior. *Canadian Psychiatric Association Journal, 18*, 199–202.

Sigal, J. J., Lasry, J. C., Guttman, H., Chagoya, L., & Pilon, R. (1977). Some stable characteristics of family therapists' interventions in real and simulated therapy sessions. *Journal of Consulting and Clinical Psychology, 45*, 23–26.

Sigal, J. J., Presser, B. G., Woodward, C. W., Santa-Barbara, J., Epstein, N. B., & Levin, S. (1979). *Therapists' interventions in a simulated family as predictors of outcome in family therapy.* Unpublished manuscript, Institute of Community and Family Psychiatry, Jewish General Hospital, Montreal.

Singer, M. T., & Wynne, L. C. (1965). Thought disorder and family relations of schizophrenics. IV: Results and implications. *Archives of General Psychiatry, 12*, 201–212.

Singer, M. T., & Wynne, L. (1966). Communication styles in parents of normals, neurotics and schizophrenics: Some findings using a new Rorschach scoring manual. In I. Cohen (Ed.), *Family structure, dynamics and therapy.* Washington, D.C.: Psychiatric Research Reports of the American Psychiatric Association (No. 20).

Skynner, A. C. (1981). An open-systems, group analytic approach to family therapy. In A. Gurman & D. Kniskern (Eds.), *Handbook of family therapy.* New York: Brunner/Mazel.

Sloane, R. B., Staples, F. R., Cristol, A. H., Yorkston, N. J., & Whipple, K. (1975). *Psychotherapy versus behavior therapy.* Cambridge, Mass.: Harvard University Press.

Sluzki, C. E. (1978). Marital therapy from a systems theory perspective. In T. J. Paolino & B. S. McCrady (Eds.), *Marriage and marital therapy: Psychoanalytic, behavioral and systems theory perspectives.* New York: Brunner/Mazel.

Sluzki, C. E., & Beavin, J. (1965). Symmetry and complementarity: An operational definition and a typology of dyads. *Acta Psiguiatrica y Psicologica de America Latina, 11*, 321–330.

Sluzki, C. E., & Ransom, D. C. (Eds.) (1976). *Double bind: The foundation of the communicational approach to the family.* New York: Grune & Stratton.

Sluzki, C. E., & Veron, E. (1971). The double bind as universal pathogenic situation. *Family Process, 10*(4), 397–410.

Sojit, C. M. (1971). The double bind hypothesis and the parents of schizophrenics. *Family Process, 10*, 53–74.

Solomon, M. A. (1973). A developmental, conceptual premise for family therapy. *Family Process, 12*, 179–196.

Solyom, L., Garza-Perez, J., Ledwidge, B. L., & Solyom, C. (1972). Paradoxical intention in the treatment of obsessive thoughts: A pilot study. *Comprehensive Psychiatry, 13*, 291–297.

Soper, P. H., & L'Abate, I. (1977). Paradox as a therapeutic technique: A review. *International Journal of Family Counseling, 5*, 10–21.

Sorrells, J. M., & Ford, F. R. (1969). Toward an integrated theory of families and family therapy. *Psychotherapy: Theory, research and practice, 6*, 150–160.

Speek, R., & Attneave, C. (1973). *Family networks.* New York: Vintage Books.

Speer, D. C. (1970). Family systems: Morphostasis and morphogenesis, or "is homeostasis enough?" *Family Process, 9*, 259–278.

Stanton, M. D. (1977). The addict as savior: Heroin death and the family. *Family Process, 16*, 191–197.

Stanton, M. D. (1978). Some outcome results and aspects of structural family therapy with drug addicts. In D. Smith, S. Anderson, M. Buxton, T. Chung, N. Gottlieb, & W. Harvey (Eds.), *A multicultural view of drug abuse: Selected proceedings of the National Drug Abuse Conference—1977.* Cambridge, Mass.: Sehenkman.

Stanton, M. D. (1980). Family therapy: Systems approaches. In G. P. Sholevar, R. M. Benson, & B. J. Blinder (Eds.), *Emotional disorders in children and adolescents: Medical and psychological approaches in treatment.* Jamaica, N.Y.: S.P. Medical and Scientific Books.

Stanton, M. D. (1980). Marital therapy from a Structural/Strategic viewpoint. In P. Sholevar (Ed.), *Marriage is a family affair.* New York: Spectrum.

Stanton, M. D. (1980). Who should get credit for change which occurs in therapy? In A. S. Gurman (Ed.), *Questions and answers in the practice of family therapy.* New York: Brunner/Mazel.

Stanton, M. D. (1981). An integrated Structural/Strategic approach to family therapy. *Journal of Marital and Family Therapy*, Oct., 427–439.

Stanton, M. D. (1981). Strategic approaches to family therapy. In A. S. Gurman & D. P. Kniskern (Eds.), *Handbook of family therapy*. New York: Brunner/Mazel.

Stanton, M. D., & Todd, T. C. (1979). Structural family therapy with drug addicts. In E. Kaufman & P. Kaufmann (Eds.), *The family therapy of drug and alcohol abuse*. New York: Gardner Press.

Stanton, M. D., & Todd, T. (1980). A critique of the Wells and Dezen review of the results of nonbehavioral family therapy. *Family Process, 19*, 169–176.

Stanton, M. D., & Todd, T. (1980). Engaging resistant families in treatment. II: Some principles gained in recruiting addict families. *Family Process, 19*, 145–150.

Stanton, M. D., Todd, T. C., & associates (1981). *The family therapy of drug addiction*. New York: Guilford Press.

Stanton, M. D., Todd, T. C., Heard, D. B., Kirschner, S., Kleiman, J. I., Mowatt, D. T., Riley, P., Scott, S. M., & Van Deusen, J. M. (1978). Heroin addiction as a family phenomenon: A new conceptual model. *American Journal of Drug and Alcohol Abuse, 5*, 125–150.

Stanton, M. D., Todd, T., Steier, F., Van Deusen, J., Marder, L., Rosoff, R., Seaman, S., & Skibinski, E. (1979). *Family characteristics and family therapy of heroin addicts: Final report, 1974–1978*. Philadelphia: Philadelphia Child Guidance Clinic.

Steinbeck, L. (1977). *Nest-leaving: Family systems of runaway adolescents*. Doctoral dissertation, California School of Professional Psychology at San Francisco.

Straus, M. (1969). *Family measurement techniques: Abstracts of published instruments, 1935–1965*. Minneapolis: University of Minnesota Press.

Strodtbeck, F. (1951). Husband and wife interaction over revealed differences. *American Sociological Review, 16*, 468–473.

Stuart, R. B. (1980). *Helping couples change*. New York: Guilford Press.

Sullaway, M., & Christensen, A. (1983). Assessment of dysfunctional interaction patterns in couples. *Journal of Marriage and the Family, 45*, 653–659.

Tarris, J. Anger Management. Unpublished manuscript, Vancouver B.C., 1982.

Teisman, M. W. (1979). Jealousy: Systematic, problem-solving therapy with couples. *Family Process, 18*, 151–160.

Tomm, K. (1980). Towards a cybernetic systems approach to family therapy at the University of Calgary. In D. S. Freeman (Ed.), *Perspectives on family therapy*. Vancouver: Butterworths.

Tomm, K. M., & Wright, L. M. (1979). Training in family therapy: Perceptual, conceptual and executive skills. *Family Process, 18*, 227–250.

Tripp, R. M. (1975). *An exploratory study of Allred's interaction analysis for counselors: The relationship of naive counselors' scores on the AIAC to their scores on selected scales of the MMPI*. Unpublished master's thesis, Brigham Young University, Salt Lake City, Utah.

Truax, C. B. (1961). A scale for the measurement of accurate empathy. *Psychiatric Institute Bulletin, 1*(12), 20–30.

Truax, C. B., & Carkhuff, R. R. (1967). *Toward effective counseling and psychotherapy: Training and practice*. Chicago: Aldine.

Tucker, S. J., & Pinsof, W. M. (1979). *The evaluation of family therapy training*. Chicago: Center for Family Studies, Northwestern University Medical School.

Turk, J. L., & Bell, N. W. (1972). Measuring power in families. *Journal of Marriage and the Family, 34*, 215–222.

Van Deusen, J., Stanton, M. D., Scott, S., & Todd, T. (1980). Engaging resistant families in treatment, I: Getting the drug addict to recruit his family members. *International Journal of the Addictions, 15*, 126–135.

Vogel, E. F., & Bell, N. W. (1960). The emotionally disturbed child as the family scapegoat. In N. W. Bell & E. F. Vogel (Eds.), *A modern introduction to the family*. Glencoe, Ill.: Free Press.

Wachtel, E. F. (1982). The family psyche over three generations: The genogram revisited. *Journal of Marital and Family Therapy, 8*, 335–343.

Walrond-Skinner, S. (Ed.) (1979). *Family and marital therapy*. London: Routledge & Kegan Paul.

Watson, W. (1975). *An exploratory study of Allred's interaction analysis for counselors: The relationship of selected AIAC ratio scores to Truax accurate empathy scale scores*. Unpublished master's thesis, Brigham Young University, Salt Lake City, Utah.

Watzlawick, P. (1955). Brief communications, paradoxical predictions. *Psychiatry, 28*, 358–373.

Watzlawick, P. (1963). A review of the double bind theory. *Family Process, 2*, 132–153.

Watzlawick, P. (1964). *An anthology of human communication: Text and tape*. Palo Alto, Calif.: Science and Behavior Books.

Watzlawick, P. (1966). A structured family interview. *Family Process, 5*, 256–271.

Watzlawick, P. (1973). The Utopia syndrome. *Swiss Review of World Affairs, 22*, 19–22. Also in P. Watzlawick & J. H. Weakland (Eds.), *The interactional view: Studies of the Mental Research Institute, Palo Alto, 1965–1974*. New York: W. W. Norton, 1977.

Watzlawick, P. (1976). *How real is real?* New York: Random House.

Watzlawick, P. (1978). *The language of change: Elements of therapeutic communication*. New York: Basic Books.

Watzlawick, P., Beavin, J. H., & Jackson, D. D. (1967). *Pragmatics of human communication: A study of interactional patterns, pathologics, and paradoxes*. New York: W. W. Norton.

Watzlawick, P., Beavin, J. H., Sikorski, I., & Mecia, B. (1970). Protection and scapegoating in pathological families. *Family Process, 9*, 27–39.

Watzlawick, P., & Coyne, J. C. (1980). Depression following stroke: Brief, problem-focused treatment. *Family Process, 19*, 13–18.

Watzlawick, P., & Weakland, J. H. (1977). *The interactional view: Studies of the Mental Research Institute, Palo Alto, 1965–1974*. New York: W. W. Norton.

Watzlawick, P., Weakland, J., & Fisch, R. (1974). *Change: Principles of problem formation and problem resolution*. New York: W. W. Norton.

Weakland, J. H. (1960). The double bind hypothesis of schizophrenia and three party interaction. In D. D. Jackson (Ed.), *The etiology of schizophrenia*. New York: Basic Books.

Weakland, J. H. (1976). Communication theory and clinical change. In P. J. Guerin (Ed.), *Family therapy: Theory and Practice*. New York: Gardner Press.

Weakland, J., Fisch, R., Watzlawick, P., & Bodin, A. M. (1974). Brief therapy: Focused problem resolution. *Family Process, 13*, 141–168.

Weblin, J. E. (1962). Psychogenesis and asthma: An appraisal with a view to family research. *British Journal of Medical Psychology, 36*, 211–225.

Wedemeyer, N. V., & Grotevant, H. D. (1982). Mapping the family system: A technique for teaching family systems theory concepts. *Family Relations, 31*, 185–193.

Weeks, G. R., & L'Abate, L. (1979). A compilation of paradoxical methods. *American Journal of Family Therapy, 7*, 61–76.

Weiss, R. L. (1979). Strategic behavioral marital therapy. In J. P. Vincent (Ed.), *Advances in family intervention: Assessment and theory: Vol. 1*. Greenwich, Conn.: JAI Press.

Wells, R., & Dezen, A. (1978). The results of family therapy revisited: The nonbehavioral methods. *Family Process, 17*, 251–274.

Wells, R. A., Dilkes, T. C., & Trivelli, N. (1972). The results of family therapy: A critical review of the literature. *Family Process, 11*, 189–208.

Wen-Shung, T., & McDermott, J. (1979). Triaxial family classification. *Journal of the American Academy of Child Psychiatry, 18*(1), 22–43.

Whitehead, A. N., & Russell, B. (1910–1913). *Principia mathematica* (vols. 1–3). Cambridge, England: Cambridge University Press.

Wiener, N. (1947). Time, communication, and the nervous system. In R. W. Miner (Ed.), *Technological mechanisms* (vol. 50 of the *Annals of the New York Academy of Sciences*), New York.

Wiener, N. (1950). *The human use of human beings: Cybernetics and society*. Boston: Houghton Mifflin.

Wiener, N. (1961). *Cybernetics* (2nd ed.). Cambridge, Mass.: M.I.T. Press.

Wilder-Mott, C. (1979). The Palo Alto group: Difficulties and directions of the interactional view for human communication research. *Human Communication Research, 5*, 171–186.

Wilson, G. T., & Evans, I. (1971). The patient–therapist relationship in behavior therapy. In A. S. Gurman & A. M. Razin (Eds.), *Effective psychotherapy: A handbook of research*. New York: Pergamon Press.

Winder, P. H. (1968). Vicious and virtuous circles: The role of deviation amplifying feedback in the origin and perpetuation of behavior. *Psychiatry, 31*(4), 309–324.

Winter, L. R. (1971). The qualified pronoun count as a measure of change in family psychotherapy. *Family Process, 10*, 243–248.

Winter, W. D., & Ferreira, A. J. (Eds.) (1959). *Research in family interaction*. Palo Alto, Calif.: Science and Behavior Books.

Wynne, L. (1972). Communication disorders and the quest for relatedness in families of schizophrenics. In C. J. Sager & H. S. Kaplan (Eds.), *Progress in group and family therapy*. New York: Brunner/Mazel.

Zeigler-Driscoll, G. (1977). Family research study at Eagleville Hospital and Rehabilitation Center. *Family Process, 16*, 175–190.

Zeigler-Driscoll, G. (1979). The similarities in families of drug dependents and alcoholics. In E. Kaufman & P. Kaufman (Eds.), *The family therapy of drug and alcohol abuse*. New York: Gardner Press.

Zuk, G. H. (1966). The go-between process in family therapy. *Family Process, 5*, 162–178.

Zuk, G. H. (1971). *Family therapy: A triadic based approach*. New York: Behavioral Publications.

Zuk, G. (1975). Engagement and termination as critical incidents in therapy. In G. Zuk (Ed.), *Process and practice in family therapy*. Haverford, Pa.: Psychiatry and Behavioral Science Books.

Zuk, G. H. (1975). *Process and practice in family therapy*. Haverford, Pa.: Psychiatry and Behavioral Science Books.

Zuk, G. H. (1976). Family therapy: Clinical hodgepodge or clinical science? *Journal of Marriage and Family Counseling, 2*, 299–303.

Zuk, G. H. (1978). Value conflict in today's family. *Marriage and Family Living, 60*, 18–20.

Zuk, G. H., Boszormenyi-Nagy, I., & Heiman, E. (1963). Some dynamics of laughter during family therapy. *Family Process, 2*, 302–314. Reprinted in G. H. Zuk (Ed.), *Family therapy: A triadic based approach*. New York: Behavioral Publications, 1971.

Zuk, G. H., & Rubinstein, D. (1965). A review of concepts in the study and treatment of families of schizophrenics. In I. Boszormenyi-Nagy & J. L. Framo (Eds.), *Intensive family therapy*. New York: Harper & Row.

SUBJECT INDEX